Praise for

THE 10 GREATEST GIFTS WE GIVE EACH OTHER

"A joyful, heartfelt, laugh-out-loud love story that ranks up there with any Hollywood romantic comedy. A thoroughly entertaining read."

—STEVE LuKANIC, screenwriter of *For Richer or Poorer*, producer/director, *13 Families*

"Reading *The 10 Greatest Gifts We Give Each Other* is like watching a Hallmark channel movie on the TV in your mind."

—ROB OWEN, TV writer/critic, *Pittsburgh Post-Gazette*

"*The 10 Greatest Gifts We Give Each Other* is raw, honest, humorous ... The priorities of this couple will have you feel that your faith in humanity has been restored!"

—*San Francisco Book Review*

"This promising debut ... is an unexpectedly fun, delightful read ... With a sharp eye for detail and vivid prose, Barbara Lynn-Vannoy is at once revealing, fun, serious, and wise."

—DIANE DONOVAN, senior reviewer of *Midwest Book Review*

"My husband and I guffawed and wept our way through this book. It is aspirational, real, and very funny."

—KAREN T⋯ ⋯r of

Canyon Vo⋯ ⋯*yon*

con

The
10 Greatest Gifts We Give Each Other

A MEMOIR ON THE
MAGIC OF MARRIAGE VOWS

Barbara Lynn-Vannoy

ADMONT
PRESS

ISBN (paperback): 978-1-7333952-1-2
ISBN (Kindle): 978-1-7333952-2-9
ISBN (EPUB): 978-1-7333952-3-6
ISBN (Audiobook): 978-1-7333952-6-7

Book design and production: www.DominiDragoone.com
Editorial: Sandra Wendel, Write On, Inc
Cover photo: Castle © Zelfit/iStock, music © Barbara Lynn-Vannoy
All other photos from the author's personal collection.

Published by
Admont Press
P.O. Box 245
Morrison, Colorado 80465

For Steve

The question is not "Will you find your wings?"
It's "What are you going to wear
with all those magnificent feathers?"
—LEIGH STANLEY

Contents

Part III

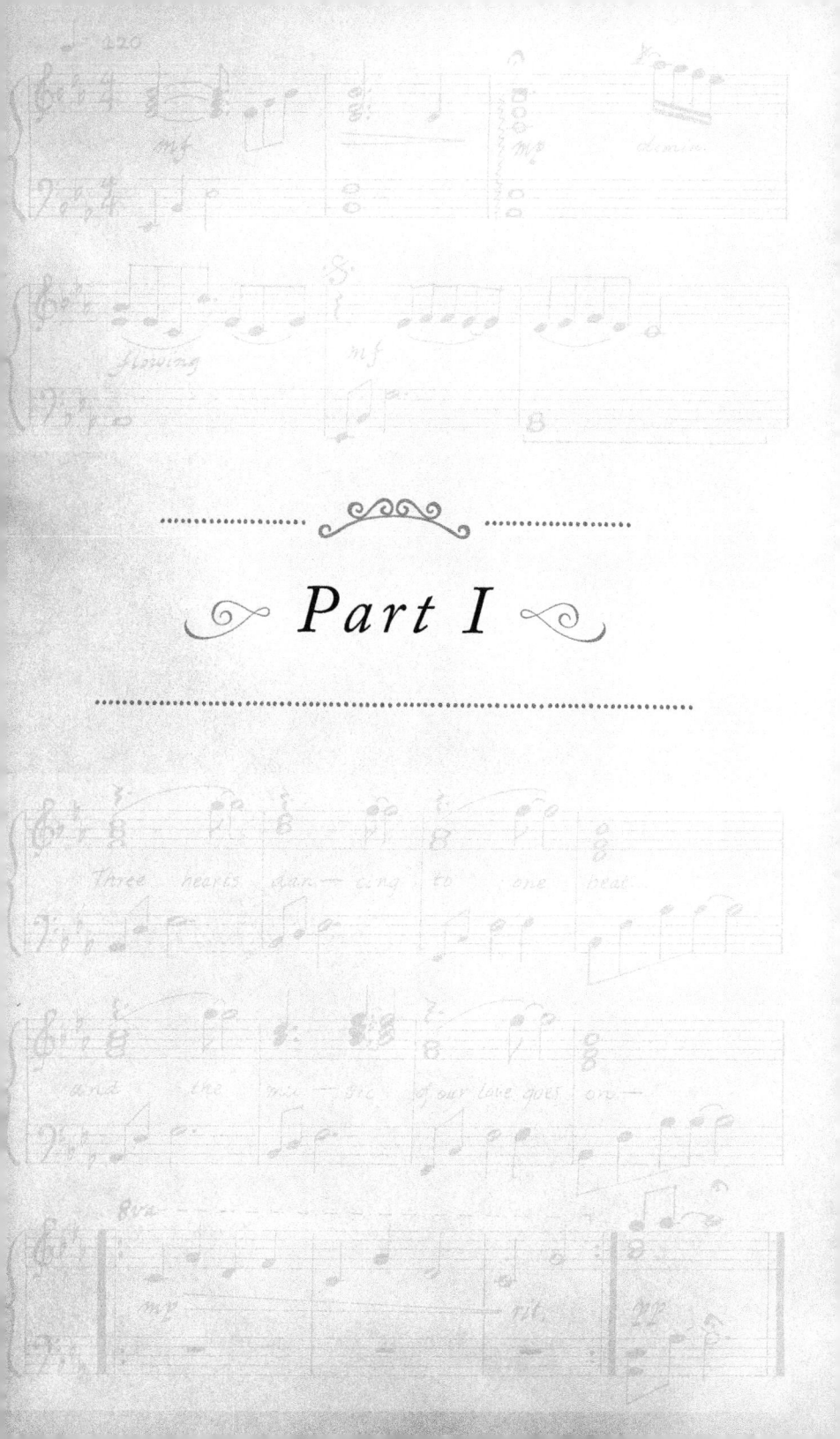

Part I

1

Serendipity Smiles

"NEVER DO THIS FOR A MAN!" I YELLED OVER MY SHOULDER to my thirteen-year-old daughter, Katie. I sprinted faster toward our house to save me time. *Why did I give myself only an hour?* I'd just stuffed two leashes into Katie's hands—one leash leading to an eighty-pound puppy, and the other to a twelve-pound bichon frise. I felt a pang of guilt. *Was I a bad mom?* I halted and whirled around to check. Yep. The bichon, Honey, and the lab, Cooper, had lassoed Katie by her ankles on the greenbelt's path. And the look on Katie's face? Bewildered. Frantic. Perturbed. *Are you my mother?*

My soul answered yes. Choosing to race toward a man began my marriage journey.

Steve had called me during our dog walk and asked if I could meet him—for the first time—for a hike. My response was honest, unexpected, but reasonable for a woman who hadn't dated in twelve years: "But I haven't bathed in three days."

For reasons unknown, Steve persisted. "I'd love it if you took a shower and came over. When can you be here?"

Thirty minutes later, I pulled out of my driveway. I pressed the radio on as I drove to his house. I couldn't believe it.

Serendipity had pulled up a chair, held my face in its hands, and whispered, "Don't miss this." Andrea Bocelli and Celine Dion's rendition of "The Prayer" filled my SUV. Of the thousands of songs tooling around inside my head, this one happened to strike a life-changing chord a month earlier.

The song had made a cameo appearance during my first-grade Christmas party. A group of unusually chummy moms encircled my desk—so chummy, in fact, that for the first time in my career, I shed my teaching armor and became a mere mortal. As I opened my loot of Christmas gifts, these women watched in earnestness, hoping their child's gift would become legendary. My students sat in circles playing a listening game about passing an object either to the left or right. The room moms thought it was a great game; I knew better. I knew it was nothing less than six-year-old torture. Twister mind torture.

I turned left myself, toward the quiet town of Morrison, away from my suburban house bordering a beltway carrying 100,000 cars per day. Steve lived in Willow Springs, an exclusive community cushioned from the hum of suburbia. The twenty-minute drive gave me time to rehearse my story of how he popped into my life:

At my teacher's desk, I had ripped open a gift wrapped in metallic red paper and turned it right side up. Andrea Bocelli and Celine Dion's sepia faces graced a CD cover that featured their glorious duet, "The Prayer." To this day, I believe the song was recorded in a heavenly studio in some secret chamber. It's the only song that brings tears to my eyes, no matter how many times I've heard it.

I touched the CD cover, sighed, and, looking to the heavens, uttered the words that would change my life: "If I ever get married again, I want this song sung at my wedding."

I wanted it sung because even though I was a singer, it was out of my octave league.

Our Junior Achievement parent volunteer, Gail, leaned close to me, touched my arm, and asked loudly, "Are you dating anyone?"

All the moms shifted their stares back from their confused children to their red pepper–faced teacher.

"Oh, no. I just meant that if I—"

Gail spoke, fortune teller-like. "I know someone," she whispered. She grinned at her own ingenuity and repeated, "I know someone."

"Who? Who?" chorused my Dixie Chick moms.

Gail announced her candidate. "His name's Steve, a friend of my fiancé, and he would love someone like you."

"Okay, ladies," I said, rising from my desk, rescuing my baffled students. "Let's get the food ready."

The moms guffawed, enjoying my embarrassment. But I wasn't interested and had tuned out Gail's advertisement. *How could a teacher get involved in a relationship through one of her own students? How unprofessional.*

But Gail persisted. In January, she began haunting me, first on bus duty, then on a field trip. A week later, she wildly waved her arms as I ushered my class into an awards assembly. On Groundhog Day, she showed up again, arriving early to stand with her daughter at the front of my class as I assumed my morning duty. I couldn't avoid her now. She raised her eyebrows and gave me a hopeful thumbs-up.

"So, Ms. Lynn, what are your thoughts about Steve?" she asked.

This stalker had to stop. I already had twenty-six of them, in training, who followed me around in two lines all day, every day. I feigned interest in Gail. Besides high standards, I had manners. "Tell you what, Gail, why don't you email me Steve's information and when the school year's done, I'll think about it."

"It's a start," she said, heaving a reluctant but triumphant battle sigh. "Oh, let me guess, you've got cold feet, right?"

"For sure," I lied. I had no cold feet. She, on the other hand, had OCD.

"Do you want his phone number too?"

"Women call men now?" I asked, surprised. I hadn't dated since 1995. Dating was avant-garde to me, like dry-erase boards.

Gail must have noticed my bulging eyes. "Well, some women don't like giving their phone numbers out. I'll send everything to you."

Thank God I could cross her off my list. The school bell rang. I faced my kids. Switching gears, I touched Darci's nose and grinned.

"Good morning, everybody! Sam! Nice haircut." I grazed his buzzed head. "Mind if I get one like it so we can be twins?"

Sam was most often mute, so his body wiggled in response. I strolled down the rest of my line, a sergeant reviewing a platoon. One girl in the middle stomped on a classmate's feet.

"Ashley! Stop it! End of the line." My voice narrowed. "Now. You know why." I spotted Peter's head bobbing for attention. "Peter, I got your mom's message and my answer is yes. And what holiday is today?"

"Groundhog's Day!" screamed the children.

I loved my job.

"Did any of you see Punxsutawney Phil on the news this morning?"

Glee turned to blank looks, except for one overachiever.

"I did! He saw his shadow and that means we have six more weeks of winter," said my future weathercaster.

"We're going to make groundhogs today. C'mon."

My minions followed me into our classroom, a nod to my childhood first-grade room forty years earlier, its trimmings nostalgically pure. Red and white paper chains—600 links glued together with sticky, stubby fingers—draped the walls, offsetting the cacophony of color, shapes, patterns, and other sensory overloads that defined my world. A number line skirted the front wall, with vowel and spelling charts posted low, munchkin-height high. Lusciously illustrated picture books topped every cabinet like framed family photos, and student work adorned bulletin boards inside polka-dotted borders. A green alphabet strip hemmed the chalkboard.

I opened my computer screen and pulled up the attendance folder. A notification icon appeared—an email from Gail.

Already?

I groaned, but I opened and scanned it.

Then I sat down and read it slowly. Twice.

In one nanosecond, I threw my professionalism out the window.

That night after dinner, Steve's number appeared on my caller ID. I ran upstairs for privacy and picked up the phone. I tried to sound normal. Confident. Not giddy, but grown-up: not me.

"Hello?" I asked, summoning my femininity from the dead.

"Hello, Barb? This is Steve Vannoy."

His voice was grown-up, silky, pure, confident. Its echo nestled into my core, and my heart hammered all the giddiness out of my body. "Hi, Steve," I answered, my voice and soul entwined. "How is your evening going?"

"Busy! I'm not home long."

2

Exhaling Single Parenting

I PULLED INTO STEVE'S DRIVEWAY TWENTY MINUTES later and slowed to a stop, gawking. Steve obviously lived in a different echelon than I. Curiously, a Sesame Street melody popped into my head: *One of these things is not like the others.*

His house reminded me of *The Addams Family* mansion, a gabled monolith, set apart from surrounding homes on top of a foothill ridge, which offered a commanding view of Denver. Nearby houses—palaces, really—begged for apologies due to their sheer size, sporting waterfalls and coiffured lawns. Not Steve's. Au naturel was the theme: dried mountain grasses and wildflower stems littered his property, with turn-of-the-century farm equipment rusted out, scattered everywhere.

This was the home of a globe-trotting entrepreneur? I double-checked the address. I was at the right house, so I turned off the engine. Breathing in all the air my lungs could hold, I laid out a prayer on the mantle of oxygen: *God, work with me here. I liked his voice on the phone a week ago. Let Steve be even better in person. Let me look pretty to him. Just let me be me. Calm me down, calm me down.*

I opened my eyes and exhaled twelve years of single parenting. Fixing my hair one last time, I checked my lip liner and tasted cherry gloss; I was prepared for a hike. I walked up his circle driveway, equivalent to half a block in my neighborhood. As I stepped up hand-carved flagstone steps, a murder of crows perched in the cottonwood tree next to the porch eyed my approach. I maneuvered around them and reached the front door. Near the doorbell were three CDs, nailed randomly on the cedar siding. I squinted and read one of their labels: *John Denver's Greatest Hits.*

Finally, some normalcy. Something in common. I liked John Denver's music.

I rang the doorbell and waited for this mystery man. Keys jingled, the door swung open, and I saw a pair of glasses.

People wearing glasses catch my attention; glasses frame the sparkle of souls.

Inside the frames were hazel eyes—like mine—on a tall, black-haired man with a face as refreshing as a sparrow's song in May. Steve's face matched the photo on his company's website: chiseled chin, confident gaze, midfifties. Ready to hike, he sported convertible pants and a blue North Face shirt, a brand I couldn't afford.

I smiled.

"You shower fast," he said. "I didn't think you'd get here in an hour. Any trouble finding the house?"

I loved the casualness, so I added to it. "Oh no, not at all." I relaxed, as much as I could, since I hadn't dated a man since Bill Clinton was president. "It's great to finally meet you. Phone calls only go so far."

"You're right. With my travel schedule, it's a miracle we finally meet at all. Here." He unlocked the screen door. "C'mon in."

I walked through what would become a threshold of kindness disguised as a door. He ushered me into a dark foyer. Extending his hand with awkward formality, he nodded. "Hello, Barb, I'm Steve."

We were two courting peacocks minus feathers or instinct. No problem. My blond hair took control. I offered my hand.

I responded, "Hi, Barb, I'm Steve."

Amused, he asked, "Date often?"

I recovered quickly. "No, Barb, I clearly don't."

He gestured into the darkness. "I'll show you around a bit before we hike."

We walked through the foyer and turned toward a soft light in the great room, and an out-of-body experience consumed me. The foyer was the tunnel and the soft light was the light at the end of *the* tunnel. Hand-carved oak bookshelves, two stories tall, lined the length of the great room's wall, cradling hundreds—no, at least a thousand—books inside. Backdropping the room was a stone fireplace, set diagonally, pushing the books in my direction. I had met my match, another bibliomaniac, and Steve's bibliomania was the fine print I wanted to know. I needed to touch the books and stay near their loveliness.

"May I?" I asked, leaning into the shelves.

"Of course," he answered, stepping behind me.

The book spines, some smooth, others weathered, stood ready for my inspection: Louis L'Amour, Thai culture, Hemingway, business and entrepreneurial titles, and rows of vintage antiques. Tipping one book toward me, I brushed its tainted cover and sniffed its musty aroma; the aroma carried me back to the comforting scents and sounds of childhood, to my childhood first-grade classroom and its dank cloakroom, the crackling of new primers opening—that crisp staccato in the air!—breathing in the binding glue, inhaling new worlds. I touched more titles on meditation, world history, all the books cultured people should read when they grow up, which for me would require resurrection.

I remembered Steve was present. "Steve, I've never seen anything like this," I whispered. "It's astonishing." And I got lost again, longing to climb inside the bookshelf and hide, like I did as a six-year-old in the Sioux Falls library, when its lights flickered five minutes before closing. I had stuffed myself inside the nearest metal shelf I could find, like a chick in an egg ready to hatch, and held my breath, praying the librarian would overlook me, setting me free to explore my universe of books overnight.

She spotted me on the bottom shelf, wedged between the F and G volumes of World Book.

Presently, I eyed Steve's stacks, then met his gaze. "Read much?" I asked.

"All of them." His eyes grew quizzical. "It's odd, Barb. With as much conversation as we've had on the phone, we've never talked about what we like to read. What would I find on your shelves?"

"Besides your *New York Times* best seller for parents like me?"

He grinned.

I felt like a moron, like I was the only woman who had ever said that to him. But I did answer his question. With gusto.

"Children's picture books," I said. And I sensed the rush coming on, like riding in the front car of a roller coaster that's cresting the first hill. The clicking had stopped and the free-falling began.

"But only those with the highest quality illustrations," I said, refining my taste, "illustrations that set you free and make the world go away and the ones that make you laugh out loud and then you chuckle a couple hours later and people ask, 'What's so funny?' so you have to tell them. Illustrators like James Stevenson and Rosemary Wells…and the books by Nancy Tillman and Jan Brett, you know, the ones that stretch your heart wide so kids fit inside it."

The roller coaster jerked in a new direction.

"And I have all the Newbery books. Do you know about 'em? They're the best children's authors whose words—" I groveled for meaning, the coaster's chain clicking again. "—whose words transport you. Like Roald Dahl and Louis Sachar. I've read the Wayside School series at least a dozen times to my kids at—"

"Of course, a first-grade teacher would love picture books and chap—"

"—and David Wimmer," I finished. Momentum carried me higher and my eyes widened. "You. Would. Love. It. He illustrated *All the Places to Love*. It's about growing up in farm country. I'll show it to you, being a Nebraska farm boy and all. You'd like it."

The ride screeched to an end. I sighed. But I was a woman and couldn't leave empty space in the air. "I know you'd love it."

Steve signaled a time-out. "I would love to see that farm book, Barb."

Over his shoulder, I noticed a decorated twelve-foot Christmas tree, still lit. Odd. It was February 12. The day belonged to Abe Lincoln, not Jesus.

"Oh, that," he said. "I've been traveling in Europe a lot since the beginning of the year." He rubbed his forehead. "Haven't had a chance to take it down yet. I've been waiting for my daughters, Ali and Emmy—they're back at college, I told you—to come over and help me with it. But I'm in Thailand next week." He perked up. "Which is why I called you today. So how about that hike now? I'll show you the rest of the house when we get back."

We crossed his street and stepped into a foothills wilderness. Steve's front yard (or whatever it was) opened into miles of trails. We headed toward some red rock formations jutting up from the hillside.

But it wasn't a hike.

Good Lord, it was a launch.

I panted, fueling my sputtering lungs as Steve pranced up the rocky side, Big Billy Goat Gruff-like. And I correctly suspected that he could easily carry on conversations while climbing at a forty-five-degree angle.

"So now that you're here," Steve began, untangling the scrub oak branches hanging over the trail, "I have to ask. Gail said it took her over a month to convince you to meet me. She said something about you not wanting to use a student to meet a guy. What happened?"

"Well," I gasped, "Gail was relentless and, finally...to get her off my back...I asked for your information. But I guess that backfired, huh?"

"Depends on what you mean by backfiring."

I sucked in more air. "It means that, in the one paragraph email she sent me, I decided to throw out my moral conviction and talk to you that night."

He didn't miss a step and strode on faster, unaffected. "Must've been quite an email. Wait here, let me go ahead around that switchback and check if the trail's too icy."

I gladly stopped and watched him hike ahead. Gail's email convinced me I could trust this man with children. Given that my first marriage had failed, I had decided to keep things simple and put Katie first. Actually, I was quite busy, with three full-time jobs: raising Katie, educating students, and fixing me. I was the ugly Christmas sweater turned inside out, snagged with resentment and pilly balls of grief and judgment.

Eight years of therapy finally birthed the ultimate freedom—forgiveness toward life's unfairness, toward my former husband, toward myself, for making ignorant choices that gifted Katie with a broken home. What's more, for twelve years, especially in the 1990s, I watched too many young single moms deposit their kids on back burners and cavort from one boyfriend's place to another.

The ensuing drama played out over and over in my classroom through batty behavior and distractions, followed by an inevitable conference the teary-eyed parents would request. They'd want me to know what was going on at home, as if I didn't know already. Kids talked, or I asked them, if they begin withdrawing or randomly tripping friends. But Gail's email on Groundhog Day got my attention:

Ms. Lynn, his name is Steve Vannoy. He is a New York Times best-selling author of The 10 Greatest Gifts I Give My Children. *He started his own leadership company about 15 years ago and travels all over the world with it. He had a modeling agency back in the 1980s. You may have heard of it. His two daughters, Ali and Emmy, are in college. He loves adventure and especially hiking. He grew up in Nebraska. He's been divorced forever, maybe twenty years. I think you two would be perfect for each other. Think about it.*

"Trail's clear!" Steve called. "Come on up, I'll wait here."

I yelled back cheerfully. "Coming!" Barely. I slogged ahead, looking for something interesting to distract the climb's challenge—colorful rocks, streaks in the red bluffs. Would I share what I read about his life in the papers?

I had immediately recognized the name Steve Vannoy in Gail's email. He appeared in Denver haut monde pages, a well-respected, self-made success story. Small world. I even helped one of his models make the cheerleading squad in my high school. When Steve's business crashed and bankruptcy followed, the *Denver Post* wrote disparaging articles, front-page news. But more germane to me, however, was his book. Strapped for cash and advice after my divorce, I began checking out parenting books from the library. *The 10 Greatest Gifts* was one of them. I read it and deemed his thoughts worthy of my cash, with a special place on a small bookshelf next to my bed. (You can understand someone's life by the books in their home. You can understand someone's soul by the books on their nightstand.) I had highlighted and scribbled notes on my copy. His wisdom gave me confidence that a man might be trusted not only with my heart but with a child's, like Katie's. She deserved the highest expression of love and respect from men too. And Steve's background gave me hope.

I saw Steve's hiking boots and looked up, grinning. He realized my rocket fuel was low. He offered his kind hand; I took it. First date and we held hands. He held it a bit longer, probably checking for a pulse.

"Gail said you were beautiful, and she was right."

I nodded and smiled thank-you since the altitude change had rendered me incoherent.

Halfway up the foothill, I glanced to the right. A strangely familiar formation of red rock loomed: a slender obelisk rising twenty-five feet, symmetrically erect with ridged edges, curved into a rounded tip. My eyes widened.

It looked like a penis.

I pretended I didn't see it. I lowered my head and kept lugging. Steve stopped ahead of me, touched my arm, and pointed at that rock formation, his voice unflappable. News anchor steady.

"Look, Barb, there's Penis Rock."

"Oh?" I looked up, feigning innocence. "Ohhhhh. I see." My face matched Steve's. Expressionless.

We studied Penis Rock together in silence.

Steve continued climbing. I, on the other hand, continued staring at Penis Rock. I'd been divorced for over a decade.

We scaled one of the highest points in Morrison, Colorado, and took in spectacular views of Denver and Mount Lindo's Cross. It's the largest lit cross in the States, an American nod to Rio's El Cristo. At night, the cross watches over the city, a local lifeguard. During the day, it's where my dad and I would drive when he needed a panoramic view, as opposed to the tunnel vision his pancreatic cancer offered.

But today, somehow, the cross had new meaning.

We returned to a spotless house—thanks to a housekeeper—and continued the tour. Steve led me into the sunroom, although sunroom is a misnomer: It was Noah's sister ship for plants. Hundreds of plants adorned this three-story cedar atrium, 50 feet long by 20 feet wide (that's 33 cubits by 13 cubits). English ivy danced between purple-pink orchids. A thirty-year-old cactus towered over kalanchoe buds. Philodendrons cascaded down two stories, spilling into succulents and roses that cozied up into southern windows. The room breathed life, and being in it made me feel more alive too.

"How long does this take to water?" I asked, recalling the poinsettia pleading for its last rights on my kitchen windowsill.

"Everyone asks that." I found out quickly enough. I would soon become the bona fide sunroom pool boy when he traveled— half his life.

We moseyed into the kitchen adjacent to the sunroom.

"How do you concentrate on cooking with a view like this?" I asked, looking out the five kitchen windows, over lakes and fairways and bluffs.

He brushed away invisible dust on the countertops. "I don't cook, I do restaurant leftovers."

I did too. It's called dinner when your child plays soccer and basketball and softball.

The walk-in pantry was roughly the size of my own kitchen and had one or two anomalies, like a pup tent and a pair of black rubber boots with broken buckles. It also didn't have a lick of food in it, having morphed into a man cave. Sleeping bags, camping lanterns, toolboxes, and a 1960s silver coffee pot littered the floor.

"The last place I want to show you is my library." He paused. "I don't bring anyone up to see it."

I wondered if there was a dead body up there or something. But then I remembered the books when I first entered his house. "What are all those books in your great room?"

"My overflow."

Because we hadn't climbed enough that day, Steve led me up the library's staircase, giving a few moments for uninterrupted thoughts to stampede across my brain. *This house is huge, like 6,000 square feet maybe? This man has it all together. I don't belong here.* Steve stopped and apologized for a black dot on one step. "Pardon that dead fly."

Oh, please. Let's be ridiculous. My mind raced, imagining

what I'd have to apologize for at my house, according to his standards. I won't bore you with all of them. Well, maybe a few. In the interest of time, let's narrow it down to my bedroom. More precisely, my queen bed, surface area only. At any time one might find gnawed dog bones, an occasional house-trained rabbit, a crusted paper plate of spaghetti, ungraded spelling tests, or overdue library books.

Back to the dead fly problem.

I stepped into Steve's library and discovered that one can visit heaven twice. I was Belle and he became my Beast. I searched for Mrs. Potts, a yellow dress, Chip—anything to complete the scene. More vaulted walls of books lined library #2, resplendent with leather chaise lounges, Tiffany floor lamps, and airy sky-lights casting warm glows on a walkout deck offering sweeping views of the Rocky Mountains, Red Rocks Amphitheatre, and Denver's skyline.

I laughed out loud. *What was I doing here? It was absurd. What was a middle-aged, middle-class, suburban teacher doing in the middle of all this?*

His library furnishings crowded out my thoughts. A time capsule of photos and mementos lined the shelves' crannies. It was grown-up show-and-tell time. I sat at Steve's rolltop desk, traced its hand-carved rosewood swirls, and made myself com-fortable. He obviously brought me up to the library for a reason. "Tell me what all these things are," I said, relaxing.

People are most generous when their gift is attention.

He pointed to a vintage placard titled Little Stevie and the Emperors. "That's my first band."

Steve's interior world was appearing, so I figured my snake-skin could start shedding too. "So you're little Stevie there—the other two are older. Were they wussy or something?"

"No, this one is my older brother, John."

I inserted my size ten foot into my mouth.

He continued. "I clearly had the talent, can't you tell from the picture? And my biceps? Impressive."

"For a four-year-old, maybe, but how old were you in the picture, maybe twelve? And tell me the truth about that red shirt you're wearing. A hand-me-down from John, right?"

"You must be the youngest too."

"Yep, two older brothers. I got the turtlenecks with stretched-out arms."

He picked up a sepia eight-by-ten photo with faces echoed inside his own. "These are my parents, Ma and Papa—John, but he went by Warren, and Helen, on their fiftieth."

And we traveled down his memory road, the one that made all the difference. "Here's the first edition cover of *The 10 Greatest Gifts* before Simon and Schuster picked it up." He stepped in front of another frame. "Here I am at my Nestlé session in Geneva." At the end of the bookshelf stood a Frosted Flakes box with Steve's face on it. "Kellogg's put my face on the box after a session," he said, rattling it. "Great people. This is getting embarrassing."

"Keep going," I insisted. His show-and-tell topped every classroom presentation I had ever sat through, and his articulation was far better than the toothless, sometimes speech-impaired versions I translated. Three oversized posters, prints of leggy, ravishing women, summoned my insecurity.

I licked my lips, checking for gloss. Twenty-five years ago, I wished I could be one of his models when I was in high school. Steve owned the largest agency between New York and Los Angeles. He hobnobbed with Eileen Ford from the Ford Modeling Agency in New York and movie producers in California.

Vannoy Talent Agency—the reason for his greatest rise and notorious crash. The whole city knew.

I shuffled my feet and stared at them, knowing Steve once owned a thriving modeling agency and was now the CEO of a global company. We lived in different strata, like Apollo and the plebs. My stratum was a common one, and his, one I couldn't fathom. And I didn't understand something else either.

I glanced up, and my voice softened, "Steve, why don't you bring anyone up here? This room is who you are."

Silence. "I don't know." And I think he meant it, but he tried unraveling his confusion. "I don't bring anyone up here because it's my personal stuff."

"Then why me?"

He studied me for the longest time. "I know you're safe. It feels good having you here."

Layers of protection peeled away. *Was I reading him right? Were we beginning to see who the other was?*

It was the best reason for living.

"I like being here, Steve."

He offered his hand once again. "Would you like to dance?"

"Huh?"

"Can I dance with you?"

I shrugged and became thirty years younger. "Sure."

Behind me, I heard a CD cover snap and a remote click. Steve stepped in front of me and drew me toward him while Josh Groban's voice filled the library with "Jesu, Joy of Man's Desiring." The song hijacked me back to a moment on wedding days, when a bazillion other brides like me walked down the aisle to its tune.

Really, God? This isn't funny.

I pulled back and looked up at Steve, trying to comprehend what was going on. I gazed into this man's eyes, trying to stay present, trying to comprehend who he was—who I was—who I was becoming. He pulled me close again, shoulder to shoulder, my body rigid.

Neither of us could dance, so instead we hung on each other like junior high drapes and spun a few circles. But the beauty of Josh's voice soaked inside me, overshadowing the melody, and I relaxed into his tenor voice. I understood nothing but accepted everything and began to understand that Josh's voice could be the bridge from my broken past to my surreal present. The song ended.

"One more dance," Steve whispered in my ear.

And when the next track started, my heart hollowed. Josh and Charlotte Church began singing "The Prayer." Tears pricked my eyes.

Josh crooned, and Charlotte trilled in gibberish Latin, complementing the mush inside my head.

Good one, God. Actually, this is funny. I think my entire body smiled.

Steve picked up the shift in me as his cue to lean in and kiss me, cupping my cheek in his hand.

"No, no, wait," I said smoothly. "Not until the end."

After twelve years, I closed my eyes, wanting to capture every nuance spilling forth from the song, the pull of crescendos, the fermata's hold, the voices, higher than heaven.

And as Josh's and Charlotte's voices gave way, we acquiesced into the divine expression of their voices and kissed long into the silence after the song.

The song was a refreshing remake and, conveniently, the last track of the CD.

Steve spoke first and broke the perfectly awkward spell. "So," he began, looking at his books on the shelves as if they would somehow jump off and offer the right words for him to snatch and use, "just so you know, there's one place on the house tour you can't see. There's a secret room behind one of these bookshelves."

"Of course, there is, Steve. I'd expect nothing less from you."

I don't remember anything after that. It was a blur. I was falling in love. Falling in love is a bit like stepping on the glimmers of light spinning inside a kaleidoscope. Nothing is in focus, orientation is needless. It's about being in the light, being on the move, and being beautiful all at once.

Oh. I do remember both of us leaving his house, though.

Steve's limo driver picked him up.

Steve went to Thailand.

I went to Costco.

3

Shades of Red

....

"MOM! IT'S SIX FIFTY. YOU HAVE TO GET UP AND GO TO WORK."
Katie stood at my bedroom door, arms akimbo, dressed for school. While in my womb, she transfused every punctual and tidy DNA strand flowing through my veins. She also inherited my teacher look. I felt it now.

"Five more minutes," I mumbled. I could get ready in thirty minutes, twenty-five if I pulled my hair back. And if Katie offered to let the dogs out...

"I'll take Honey and Cooper out and get them fed," she said. She smiled and hugged me first. "Happy Valentine's Day, Mom. Cooper, let's go outside."

I heard Cooper's gangly body trouncing down the stairs, a train on roller skates. Honey peeked her matted head from under the covers and plopped on my chest, our morning ritual, always the reason for my extra five-minute delay.

"Mommy loves Honey," I said to her every morning of her life.

I thought of Steve. I hadn't heard from him and resigned myself to celebrating Valentine's Day alone again. What were the chances of us anyway? He was an adventurer, a rich, globe-trotting entrepreneur with a house that contributed to urban sprawl. I was a homebody, a frugal soccer mom who graded papers during practice. I lived in a house I built using garage sale money.

I dropped Katie off at her school and headed to my own. I always went to school, never to work. There's a difference. To me, work is a chore; following my passion is not. And in over twenty years of teaching, I've never sat down and figured out exactly how much money I made in one week. Besides, learning to divide by forty is superfluous for a first-grade teacher.

Whenever people ask me what grade I teach, I brace myself. When they hear I teach first grade, they invariably picture my kids like a litter of puppies in a pet store window, cute and nearly brainless. Let me tell you. My kids are brilliant. Never underestimate children. I don't teach to their minds. Or their hearts. I teach to their spirits, and not one child has failed me. Ever. I mind-boggle them by reminding them they are made from the remnants of star-dusted constellations.

When I tell them this, their eyes sparkle to prove it.

Today wouldn't be too academic, a rarity at Bear Creek Elementary. The better part of the morning would be spent watching students arrange their valentine boxes in ABC order. Poor Jake, Jack, and Justin. And Jessica. Then, just before lunch, the real melee would start when twenty-six children would deliver over six hundred cards without maiming each other.

The school bell rang. I surveyed my classroom. Sixty sharpened pencils short-circuited any excuses for loafers. The calendar had a red heart where the number fourteen should be. I straightened my desks into five perfect rows. I'd tied a "No Homework Coupon" to my valentines for my students. All was ready. Almost. I slid one adult chair to the back of the room, isolating it.

I kept it empty for Jesus, a reminder to be nice to children.

My class followed me into our classroom, serpentine-like, and their voices lit the room. "Hi, Ms. Lynn," said my student Candace as I pulled up my attendance on the computer. She pointed at my head and squealed, "Hey, you forgot to do your hair!"

No, Candace, I didn't forget.

I couldn't resist. I can never resist. "Hey, Candace, I forgot to put your 100 percent spelling test in my gradebook."

Candace looked puzzled, borderline obtuse. Candace had not aced inferential thinking yet.

Red and white shirts, skirts, and socks passed me by. So did cupcakes, cinnamon dots, cherry sours, red cookies, heart cookies, red licorice, hot tamales, and cinnamon bears—tools for our math lesson today. We would categorize them. Measure them. Introduce the concept of spheres. Model division by two. Who got the remainders? Hello! The kids would eat the rest. Ears and eyes brought the learning in, but taste buds brought the learning to mastery.

Every morning, my students' first rule required them to make beelines for their own desks before mine. But on holidays, this rule never worked:

"When do we pass out valentines?"

"Is it time to pass out valentines?"

"I need to go to the bafroom."

The sycophant was next.

"*I love you*, Ms. Lynn, but I forgot my valentines at home. Can you call my mom?"

"My hamster died last night."

"When do we open valentines?"

"Hey. I like your hair."

My desk phone rang. *Thank you, God.* It was Gaylene, the principal's secretary.

"Barb? I have a call for you from a Steve Vannoy. Do you want it?"

I got a sugar rush to my heart. "Yes, put him through, thanks."

The phone beeped. "Hello, this is Ms. Lynn," I said, shooing the kids in a different direction, like a marching band director does.

"Ms. Lynn, I just wanted to wish you a Happy Valentine's Day," Steve said.

Gutsy move. What does this mean? Are we valentines? He sounded too formal, but I loved it. "Well, thank you. Are you in Thailand?"

My student Chelsea tapped my shoulder. "Can I go to the bathroom?"

I noticed Chelsea's crossed legs, but Steve's voice trumped them. "Yes, go anywhere you want, Chelsea. Sorry, Steve, what did you say?"

"Bangkok. I'm in Bangkok." Pause. "Okay. That's all I wanted to say. My session's on a break."

It felt like he had done his duty, like a boy scout helping an old lady cross the street.

Silence. "Um, bye?" I asked.

Another wet drape moment.

"Yes. You have a good day."

I could tell he was going to hang up, and I had to get it out.

Scrunching every syllable together, I said quickly, "AndHappyValentine'sDaytoyou!"

He hung up.

I felt a valentine tingle, the first in fourteen years. I blissfully sat as my kids geared up for the day, swiping fingers in frosting, turning in homework. I loved my life. I loved my kids. I loved my daughter and dogs. I loved—

The phone rang again. My heart raced. This time it was Sue, our enrollment secretary.

"I didn't get your attendance," she said.

"Sorry, Sue, I got sidetracked." I saw one empty desk. "The only absent student is Chelsea Brainard."

"Chelsea's here in the office," Sue replied. "She said you told her she could go anywhere she wanted, so she came up here for a tooth fairy box."

Oh. "How unprofessional of me," I replied. "We're all here, Sue."

"Sort of," Sue replied.

I entered my attendance online to make everyone official and noticed an email notification from Steve. I clicked on it: *Barb, I'd love to celebrate your birthday with you next Sunday. Can I take you snowshoeing in Keystone?*

I jumped up and squealed. My kids didn't respond. They're used to having a teacher who acted unprofessionally.

"BARB, OUR FIRST-GRADE TEAM IS ALWAYS THE LAST TO leave school every day, but here we are again," my friend Diane said the next Friday afternoon, a half hour after the last school bell rang. We thumbed through book orders at the Red Rocks Grill. "Geez, girl," she continued, "the buses haven't even finished their routes yet and you split. Let me guess. Steve, right?"

"He wants to take me snowshoeing on my birthday. I need to find warm boots tonight."

"Girl, you hate the cold."

"Yeah."

"Explain how, in two weeks, you go from not needing a man, being perfectly happy with your life for way too long to…giving a guy your entire birthday? On a mountain? Seriously, fill me in."

That was easy. "First off, it just so happens that Steve has a national track record in parenting—five hundred thousand readers long—who already scouted him out for me and Katie," I explained. "Second, I've never respected a man so quickly before—he's authentic, he's got a huge passion to serve. And he's Lutheran, " I continued, "and travels around the world, which makes him very interesting. Isn't that enough?"

"Not to mention he's rich," said Diane.

I thought about that truth for a minute. "I did mention that, didn't I?" I admitted. "You're right." With more conviction, I added, "I don't have to worry about supporting him financially, you're right. But he doesn't act rich. He's from Nebraska." I circled my top choice in the Scholastic order. Round and round.

"Uh huh," said Diane.

"I'm proud of myself that I figured out how to give Katie a good home. And I feel it's time to get out of my comfort zone, and he feels safe to do that."

"So what does it feel like? Now?" Diane asked, leaning in. "I mean, Mike and I have been married for twenty-one years. At some point all women wonder what it'd be like…if they got divorced or their husband dies. And you've lived it."

"I had no choice. I survived, I guess. My skin's thicker now. But most of the time I still feel like I need to be a man and a woman at the same time for Katie. But now I just want to feel like a woman again. Soft, you know?"

Diane smiled. "Be sure you buy a pair of wool socks with your boots."

MY FORTY-FOURTH birthday felt like the Iditarod. Steve and I rented snowshoes and journeyed into a 10,000-foot valley next to Keystone for a romantic picnic. A born adventurer, Steve intended to reach Nome by four o'clock, but we managed only four miles up the frozen river. The wind sliced through our layers, blustered my cheeks, and froze my eyelashes shut. Steve guided me behind a Charlie Brown tree to break the tempests and occasional whiteout conditions. He threw down a twin sheet for warmth and comfort.

I'm not lying about the tree, the tempests, the whiteouts, or the twin sheet for warmth and comfort.

The scene reminded me of an Eskimo documentary film my fifth-grade teacher required us to watch. The Eskimos battle fierce weather in pursuit of caribou. Once the caribou are hunted down, youngsters rush up so the hunter can gouge the caribou eyes and the kiddos can pop the delicacies into their mouths.

"Close your eyes and open your mouth, Barb. I have some surprises, delicacies," Steve shouted.

"They are closed," I yelled over the wind, reminding him. And trusting the caribou had long migrated, I opened my mouth. I tasted chocolate-covered strawberries. And hot chocolate. And ham. Finally, a tuna salad sandwich.

Who fed this man as a child?

But soon I smelled a rose he had pulled out of his backpack. And Steve's magnanimous acts began: "Happy birthday, birthday girl," he whispered, pulling a trash bag from the pack. Wrapped presents spilled out, each with its own card. "Open one now and one each day for nine more days," he instructed.

I opened one, a pair of plastic hands that clapped—to celebrate me. "They're to let you know I'm thinking of you when I'm in Japan." The other gifts included a candle ("to remind you of your glow"), a blowfish squirt toy ("a trusty way to get a student's attention back"), and a stress ball ("I'm thinking you need it").

"I know you have this thing about the number ten," I said, clapping the plastic hands, praising myself. "But why are you giving me ten presents on my birthday, Steve?" I hesitated, then added, "You barely know me."

He didn't flinch. "You're worth it. I'll explain later."

This frigid, inhospitable outdoors was Steve's comfort zone. Since I had agreed to be out of my element, I invited Steve into mine. I knew two things for sure: He was a good parent, and I respected him. But I needed to know one more thing.

"This is your world," I said. "Come and see mine."

I TOLD MY class we were having an important visitor—so important in fact that they could earn an extra recess if they behaved.

Too bad I didn't. I dressed in a tight black sweater, short black skirt, and high heels. Extra attention to makeup and hair rendered me unrecognizable. I overheard one of my students say, "Do you know who she is?"

Steve arrived, and I escorted him to a table in the back of the classroom. He saw an adult-sized chair and started to sit down.

"No, you can't sit there. Sit here," I said, offering him another one, not my Jesus chair.

He sat and observed my Norman Rockwell class, all on task, while visions of a long recess danced in their heads. The reading lesson was locating details, using Arnold Lobel's Frog and Toad series.

"Now, who can find the page that describes two things Frog did to try and make his seeds grow? The first person to touch the answers with two fingers and wink at me can choose our storytime book. Go!"

The challenge was on. My students dove into their readers. I meandered between the desks, among the sounds of whisking fingers and the excitement of stomping feet. Steve surveyed my students, my perfectly bribed students. With their noses inside their books, I had ample time to commit the cardinal sin—passing a note in class. I nonchalantly handed a folded paper to Steve. My kids wiggled in their seats, two fingers glued to their books, faces contorted as they tried winking at me. My classroom looked like a train crossing, eyes flashing at me like red warning signs.

But I spotted the deepest red coming from the back of the room. Steve's face flushed as he read my cursive note:

The first-grade teacher is wearing black panties.

This man deserved to know what kind of woman he was dealing with. I am not my first-grade teacher, Miss Wilcox, the portly woman who wore a gray checkered dress with a few inches of slip showing, the teacher whose thick ankles fascinated me for months. I also needed to know what kind of man Steve was. I had seen his kindness, intelligence, ambition. But... was he real?

Steve was not a simple box of eight crayons. His shade of scarlet faded into carnation pink, hovered in sunglow, then spread into peach delight. Good. He was at least a box of twenty-four. But Crayola makes a box of 120. I know. That's the only box for elementary teachers.

4

You Sing?

THE SPRING BEAUTIES BLOSSOMED IN LARGE DRIFTS OF pink-fringed white stars, their faces freckled with tiny red dots, speckling the arid Rocky Mountain foothills in a quiet explosion of March, new life, and new possibilities. Spring beauties, one of the springtime's first bloomers, blossomed into the first wildflower Steve introduced me to over the next month as we hiked and shared walks together, his knowledge a treasure trove of the delicate survivors of winter. With memorized precision, he identified each flower for me, detailing leaf structures, petal shapes, fragrances, and zonal properties.

I, in turn, shared my keen mind: "I've memorized every English spelling for the long E sound and have accurately recited the Pledge of Allegiance. Over three thousand times."

He introduced me to his daughters, Ali and Emmy, as we hiked up Deer Creek Canyon's mossy banks in search of rare fairy orchid pockets. "They approve of you, angel," he happily shared. Both Ali and Emmy were independently strong, like their father.

I drove Steve to Lisell Park, where 135 first graders found 1,200 Easter eggs in less than five minutes. Soon I learned to recognize wildflowers dotting the trails, the holly-shaped leaves of Oregon grape, the regal purple of buttercupped pasque flowers, and my favorite, mouse ears with low-growing, white perky petals, the species that has enough spunk to scurry and populate anywhere—sunny hillsides and stream banks and shadowy ridges.

Over the springtime months, the panoramic vistas of hiking together drew upon our palettes of experience to discover who the other was. We shared our lives' poignant moments that deciphered our individual flows and rhythms. Mutual interests converged into the least common denominators. Among them? Loves of music, writing, travel, and children. I specifically remember our first phone call when Steve learned about my band-playing college days.

"You sing and play music?" His voice electrified the phone line. At that moment, I realized that I could have been born a tuba and he still would have asked me out. Steve lives and breathes music. Guitar and singing are his passions, followed by any stringed object capable of producing sound—banjo, violin, piano, mandolin, ukulele. He plays his mandolin for respite, for weary travelers in airports worldwide. Once, a gate attendant leaped over a moving walkway when he saw Steve walking down a concourse and shared that, a year earlier, the uplift of Steve's music saved his life. The man had planned to commit suicide later that day.

My own musical debut began in first grade when my best friend Susan dragged me to the front of the classroom to sing "Those Were the Days," a Russian tavern song. I added piano to my musical repertoire, practicing out of human earshot on an

1896 upright grand with a cracked soundboard, the result of the one-ton beast slamming down our basement stairs, freestyle. In college, I performed summer stock, singing and dancing and playing keyboards at Elitch Gardens for the masses of amusement park aficionados.

We both loved writing. Steve's *10 Greatest Gifts* book birthed his company. While on his national book tour, a father said to him, "Your book saved my family. Do you have anything to save my corporation?"

Steve didn't, but he's an entrepreneur.

"Well...yesssss...I...do," and he built his leadership company between the ellipses, based on his book's tenets.

Steve got published late in life. I first published my poetry as a teenager for Blue Mountain Arts, an inspirational, free verse poetry publisher and greeting card company. My first publishing credit appeared in one of their inspirational poetry anthologies. In the table of contents, my name was just above Albert Einstein's. How did he get in? I remember seeing my words in print for the first time as a student at the University of Denver's bookstore. My blood rushed to my heart, imploding in self-consciousness. The writing was vulnerable and raw, my anonymous outlet of exploring romantic relationships, of which I had not one experience.

Someone anonymous said, "Language was born for the likes of us writers, so our pens might catch up with our hearts' expressions."

When Steve traveled, he did it efficiently, in style: first class, five-star hotels, chauffeurs. Katie and I did it in volume, in steerage, on foot. We ran out of interesting places to visit in the States and never had the money to venture beyond. A month after we met, in March, Steve's travels brought him to

Japan, coaching Ford Asia's top management, but I knew the real reason he booked the session—Mt. Fuji loomed nearby. Meanwhile, Katie, my mom, and I traveled close, to the Grand Canyon, over spring break. I blindfolded Katie on the South Rim Road and gingerly led her down the crumbly stairs to the metal railing overlooking the canyon, then removed the blindfold and told her to open her eyes.

"I don't believe this," Katie said, backing away from the railing, the sight too incomprehensible to stay in place. I snapped a photo of her face at that moment.

If only I could live my life, every day, with that magnificent awe on my own face.

When Steve was home, his office staff hosted a luncheon for me, and he introduced me to the employees of his company, Pathways to Leadership. Clones of his spirit and zest, eight of them drummed their hands on the conference table as if summoning rain, then shouting, honoring me in celebration, "Yohhhhhhhhh, Barbie, yohhhhhhhh!" We began having sophisticated dinners with his clients who had no concept of the value of name tags. Our dinner talk echoed with delightful repartee: them, about collaborating with the CFO from Hewlett-Packard; me, bantering about the most recent world events I read in Scholastic's *Weekly Reader.*

Dinners at Steve's included candlelight and hot tubs and the Denver skyline sparkling like glitter through French doors. Bachelor Steve always cooked, and it was always the same, Omaha Steaks—compliments of his ma—and sweet potatoes, hard to ruin. And the house was filled with music, ours and Il Divo, and repeated tracks of Andrea Bocelli and Celine Dion.

"Come and meet my ma in Lincoln next week," said Steve, one month after we met.

But our happy pandemonium and my reluctance to leave Katie morphed into last-minute laryngitis. Steve soloed to Nebraska, and I mimed for twenty-six children, whose behavior improved, a testament to the misnomer that children are self-absorbed.

While Steve traveled, I had slivers of time for important things such as watering his sunroom. And all his traveling gave me pockets of time—three months total—to clean my house. While Steve climbed Mt. Fuji, I deep cleaned my carpeting. While he rode elephants in Thailand, I cleaned grout and simply caught my breath. I was occasionally thankful for his travel.

My top priority, though, continued to be Katie's well-being. It was hard to believe, but my teenager accepted my dating. It helped that never once before did she have to compete for my attention. Her school and soccer schedule kept us close enough, plenty close, since she had attended my elementary school for seven years. I talked my principal into allowing Katie to be my first-grade student. We had the best year ever in twenty-three years of teaching; my parents were my girlfriends, and my students were like my nieces and nephews.

Our families went broke with over two dozen birthday parties that year, but the kids got a kick out of staying over at the teacher's house and seeing her in her robe serving them popcorn at midnight. They were so easy to teach because we understood each other as people instead of players. It was the year our exteriors rubbed away and everyone became real, loveable.

I had raised Katie with my family's support for thirteen years. Recalling my Girl Scout days when my mom sewed my Girl Scout badges onto my green sash years ago helped my single parenting efforts. It never dawned on me that my round badges would serve as the first emblematic, multitasking symbols of motherhood. I could build a fire! I could cook! I could apply

Band-Aids and take quality photographs! Katie and I lived on soccer fields littered with goose poop during the spring and fall, and Honey, the team mascot, ate that goose poop and threw it up in the dining room every Saturday.

Singing groups knit our friends together, sports practices divided our days, and our family get-togethers—my salvation—sweetened the years. We shopped at Kohl's, went to church every Sunday, read a story every night, and played Aladdin and Jasmine ad nauseam until their whole new world thankfully ended when Aladdin went down a pool drain.

Whenever Katie demonstrated brilliance in life, I would ask, "Who was your first-grade teacher?"

When she goofed, I made sure to ask, "Who was your second-grade teacher?"

Let's be serious. The principal wouldn't allow that two years in a row.

But with Steve in my life, my routine revolved in a tighter spin around a single parent's schedule, Steve's work schedule, and Katie's teenaged schedule. And after a month or two, Steve, Katie, and I learned to fit, like a dozen red roses in a spacious vase that just needed time to blossom.

5

The Ten-Cow Wife Story

MY BOYFRIEND OF TWO MONTHS SHARED HIS RENDITION of this Polynesian tale as he introduced me to his business partner, Craig, and his girlfriend, Amanda. First published in *Reader's Digest* in the 1960s by Patricia McGeer, it's a story Steve carried in his heart for decades:

> *There's an old Polynesian tale from thousands of years ago...Tradition held that if a young man wanted to ask for a girl's hand in marriage, he'd give her father two or three cows as a dowry. You see, in those days, if one of the children left the family, it would hurt the family's income. The cows would help make up the difference. Now, one villager had three daughters. Two of them were beautiful, each fetching three cows. But his third daughter, Mahana...well, she was homely and timid. No marriage offers.*

One day, a wealthy trader named Amaru traveled to
this distant island and offered ten cows for Mahana's
hand in marriage. Her parents could not believe
their good fortune. The wedding was the very next
day. The young couple sailed away, uncertain when
they would ever return. Years passed, until Amaru
unexpectedly returned to the island…with a different
woman, one who was radiant, dignified, self-assured,
Mahana. The village elders asked, "Amaru, would
you please tell us what has happened to Mahana?"

Steve the raconteur leaned into his kitchen table and delivered the punchline to the ten-cow wife tale: "Amaru answered, 'I treated Mahana like a ten-cow wife, because she is priceless to me.'"

Steve looked at me and winked.

Given our brief dating period, Steve's story initially put me off. First, that he could presumptuously row up and sail me away and, second, that my worth was measured against a cow, especially since I was born, raised, and fed in the Midwest.

But Craig and Amanda glanced at each other, held hands, and smiled.

"That's awesome, Steve, what a message," said Craig, leaning back in his chair.

I became the lone heifer, the landmark creature halfway between Sioux Falls and the Iowa border on South Dakota Highway 18. I stared ahead, masticating my mouthful of pie, my foot swishing back and forth, batting away pesky thoughts of Steve's pretentiousness and my disbelief that being compared to a cow was somehow elevating or endearing.

I preferred to think that, unlike Mahana, I was desirable.

But parts of her story rang true; friends my age were married. For four years, I had been the only single parent listed on Katie's team roster. For soccer. For basketball. For softball. I was Mahana, the last one standing.

"Now I'm sure Mahana had her quirks," Steve admitted, trying not to mar the story's luster, "but in Amaru's eyes, those quirks were treasures."

My foot stopped swishing, and the pesky thoughts invaded. Steve had his quirks and they were no crown jewels. Especially one. He flossed after every meal—at our first Italian dinner, at the table. I found used dental floss strewn everywhere, wedged next to my driver's seat, hanging off the kitchen counter.

I, on the other hand, had no quirks. Quirks require time, which most women have so little of.

Amanda piped up. "Oh, yeah, they drive you crazy, but it's a person's quirks you miss when they're gone."

She had a point. I confess I missed my dad's quirk of entertaining two-year-old Katie at church, his sport coat pockets laden with distractions like mini flashlights and Tootsie Roll Pops and carnival finger traps. During the offering, I especially missed his ritual imitation of a hockey fan getting hit by a puck to the face.

But amid Steve's ill-timed story, I began toying with the notion that he perceived me as a ten-cow person. Sure, my students usually treated me like one; I was right up there with the pope, considering my position, not to mention my title of Recess Giver. But this was the first time in my life when someone continually saw me in my purest form, the rainbow inside a prism, well before I deserved it.

Except for my mother.

Or any mother, for that matter.

We hold our newborn for the first time and sacredness becomes the perfect optical illusion. And I guess all that grace I gave to Katie over the years produced a surplus of understanding as she accepted my dating life.

"I can see how happy he makes you, Mom. I am okay with it," she would say. "But just remember what you've always told me: 'Treat your body like a temple of God, not an amusement park.'"

Her sacrificial stance meant everything to me, because I remembered how relevant my mom's love life was to me, too, when I was a pimply-faced thirteen-year-old obsessed with braces and mirrors and fat thighs.

Having a teenager is the best time to date, in my opinion.

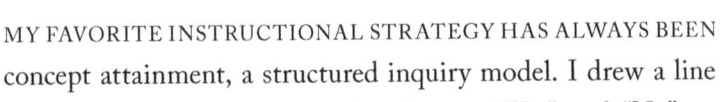

MY FAVORITE INSTRUCTIONAL STRATEGY HAS ALWAYS BEEN concept attainment, a structured inquiry model. I drew a line down the middle of the board and wrote "Yes" and "No" on either side. I told my students I was playing a game with myself that had but one rule; I welcomed them to join in whenever they figured out my rule, if they provided an example and didn't shout out the rule. I wrote this on the board:

YES	NO
United States	mac and cheese
Pacific Ocean	diapers
Grandma	fifty cents

"I know! I know!" shouted Tyler.

I didn't call on him. He raised his other hand silently.

"Tyler? Tell me something in the yes column."

"Tacos!" he said.

"Actually, that goes in the no column." I jotted tacos in the no column, then added the Declaration of Independence in the yes column. Another hand went up.

"JoJo, my dog, is in the yes column," said Dante.

"C'mon up, Dante, and whisper the rule to me. If you're right, you're the teacher."

He was correct. He usually was, and turning the reins over to him challenged his exploding intellect. I handed him the chalk and supervised his leadership, his rationale, his spelling. Half my attention stayed with him; the other wandered to a more private version of concept attainment, to the times I was not treated like a ten-cow person. I spelled a no in my head and began my list:

NO

- My eighth-grade lab partner eyed me as I poured vinegar into the test tube. I was careful not to spill anything on my Carmody Cobra cheerleading uniform. Perplexed, he asked, "How can you be so popular this year when you were a nobody last year?"
- As a high school sophomore, I tried to impress the student body president by eating a live goldfish. After some indigestion, my soon-to-be-ex-best-friend confided, "He said not to tell you this, Barb, but in the powder puff football game, he said you could play the entire defensive line."
- "This is your third name?" asked the Social Security clerk. "How is that even possible?" I took a big breath.

"Well, I was born in South Dakota and first I got married in 19—let's see—" He cut me off. "The shortest version, please."

Dante's voice summoned me back. "And what's the name for the nouns that always need capital letters?"

He called on Natalie.

"A person, place, or thing," Natalie said, since a noun didn't amount to anything much more than that in first grade.

I interjected, "Dante, look at how Cheyenne is sitting in her chair."

Dante paused and studied her. Next, he raised his hands into the air like a televangelist, cloning me. "Hey, now, everybody look at how Cheyenne is sitting so nice in her chair and..." He looked at William, who was about to tip backward in his. "And look at William!" William dropped his chair down on all four legs. "How is Cheyenne sitting in her chair? Compared to William?"

"Low blow, Dante," I said under my breath.

Natalie remained silent, her thoughts camped inside her brain for what seemed like forever; then her eyes cleared. She focused on a colorful chart ahead, but, because she was on my vision watch list, she squinted and sounded out something. A triumphant grin appeared on her face.

"Cheyenne is sitting properly. It's a proper noun. The rule of the game is proper nouns!"

"You're right, Natalie!" said Dante. Some students clapped and cheered. Others kept studying the board, figuring it out. Including William.

"William," I said gently, "do you always capitalize your name?"

"Yes."

"Why?"

He remembered. "Because I'm important."

So was I. Even when I was a nobody and big enough for an entire defensive line and had three names. At least I was trying to make a name for myself. Whatever my name was.

"Yes, you are," I said to William, "because you are so important in this world that you deserve to be noticed above all those other ordinary, common nouns. Come up to the board with Natalie and both of you write your names where they always belong. In the proper noun column. In the yes column. In the 'I Will Always Matter with a Capital Column.'"

Of course, we couldn't stop there. William wrote his name and gave the chalk to his friend Sam. Natalie gave hers to Olivia. Soon we had twenty-six scribbled names in the yes column, all underneath Grandma's and Jojo's.

THE TEN-COW THEME BEGAN MAKING SENSE TO ME WHEN I considered the herd of priceless people in my life and Katie's— my immediate family and the other one, my church family. And Easter provided the faultless opportunity for Steve to meet them all, my church family in the morning, and my immediate one afterward for brunch.

"Do they take yen?" whispered Steve, sitting next to me in the pew. The offering plate was getting closer. "It's all I have." He held up two bills with Asian faces, expressionless, exactly like the Lutherans sitting around us.

I shrugged my shoulders, so Steve tossed the yen into the plate. He was the poor widow who gave it all. Katie, my child who had so graciously met Steve a half hour earlier in the narthex, rolled her eyes at his question, so I kyboshed her by handing her a quarter, just like my mother did for me, and her mother before that. Katie heaved in high drama and plinked her quarter into the plate.

A bit about my church family. The congregation stared at Steve in surround sound, a stare seasoned rich in German stoicism. A protective clan, these Lutherans were: I was communed, confirmed, and married in these stained-glass walls. The most joyful, gentle woman I've ever met, Jan, taught preschoolers here decades ago. Her life sparkled and I wanted that, so I followed her lead and ended up teaching four-year-olds who, every year, would steal Jesus's Christmas thunder through their renditions of "Away in a Manger" as I strummed along on my brother Mike's guitar.

"How many chords do you know?" asked the church council president after the program.

"Three," I replied, "A, D, and G," which qualified me as the new children's music director. Preschool and elementary choirs followed, and attendance swelled because, next to God, parents worship their kids. Knowing this, we scheduled the choirs to sing at both Sunday services twice a month.

Being a children's choir director required tactical training, so I began playing Whack-A-Mole at local arcades to develop my peripheral vision, hammering random rodent heads back into the ground with a padded mallet. This fostered my ability to manhandle eighteen children sprawled across two long pews over half-hour stretches. My initials, BL, flashed across every Whack-A-Mole's highest-score ribbon in the Denver metro area, *without exception*—God as my witness. I was clearly the chosen one.

The kids' voices and laughter became mine, so middle and

high school choirs evolved, until I finally admitted I could sing and play keyboard and became the church's praise team worship leader. I had become the official worship poster child for Atonement Lutheran Church, that fan holding up the John 3:16 sign under the basketball hoops and ringside at all-star wrestling matches.

The church renovated and enlarged until the acoustics rang of heaven, no matter who opened their mouths. Children instilled in me the greatest gift of singing: By the nature of its structure, singing creates energy, forward movement. When you listen to yourself sing, unhappy thoughts can't enter—unless you're truly a pathetic singer. Children taught me that God didn't require vocal cords for praise or music, or even me, for that matter. Only heartstrings.

And speaking of hearts, for forty years, hundreds of other parishioners and I rode shotgun in a chariot led by a minister who wore out nine pacemakers, only to be shabbily sewn up, Velveteen Rabbit-like, and tossed back into the playroom. Lutherans are agreeable, generally docile Christians, but evidently high maintenance. Pastor Del was shepherdlike, but don't be fooled: His congregation protected him, fortified by church councils as thick as the walls of Jerusalem. He was someone who sensed people's comings and goings and would somehow slip in at the holy moment, retrieving them from their own wildernesses and carrying them to safety, either here or up there.

Pastor Del's arms caught me on a Valentine's Day years ago when my marriage crumbled. He taught us Lutherans the concept of grace, the concept repeated more often inside Lutheran walls than the concepts of the Book of Revelation or hell or cryptic passages. Grace is no-man's land and God's everyday land, a sacred shortcut.

But don't mess with Lutheran casseroles, I'll add. You might end up with some thoughts about that nailed on your front door.

After church, we drove for Easter brunch to Maggiano's, an Italian restaurant in downtown Denver. However, the location may as well have been Eisleben, Germany, birthplace of Martin Luther. Did you know that all Lutherans consider themselves to be saints? My family had it in spades, each member serving in high places in four different churches. Along with the joy inside all those churches was all the drama and heartache, so my family had to learn how to cope.

God invented this little thing called humor to help and generously dosed it to pastors; our family took humor to heart. It takes swings at the injustices of the world, giving goodness a chance to rekindle its light from the worst of circumstances. I love what the English writer G. K. Chesterton said about poking fun at faith: "It is the test of a good religion whether you can joke about it." And the most common place our occasional irreverence occurred was over a meal together.

I listened to my blissful, reserved boyfriend singing softly as we drove into Maggiano's. "Let's talk about my family?" I asked.

"Sure," he said, turning off the CD. "Now, Mom's name is Mary, and which brother is older, Mike or Steve?"

"Mike," answered Katie from the back.

"And Mike is married to Barb. And they're both the pastors. And Steve lives in Phoenix, right, Katie?" he asked.

I jumped in. "Yeah." Then, I paused. "Hey, sweetheart, have I told you about the time Barb did a memorial service without the body being there?" I was trying to brace him. "She'll probably tell you."

"No, you didn't."

AFTER INTRODUCTIONS AND SMALL TALK, MY MOM, MARY, aka Mother Mary, spoke first from the table. She'd been a church secretary on Martin Luther's payroll for decades. "Steve, you were raised Lutheran too? Is...that...right?" she asked, her voice trailing off into ecstasy.

"We're all saints, you know," said Dr. Barbara Lemke, my sister-in-law, the pastor. She's the saint who took my maiden name as her married one and stole my identity.

Mike asked, "Are you a Bronco fan? Did Barb tell you we have season tickets? You should come with us."

"You better be a fan," warned my other brother, Steve, who skipped seminary but still ascended to sainthood on church councils.

Abruptly, Mike and Steve fell silent as the waitress placed our plates in front of us, giving them time to size up my new boyfriend, a common urge of older brothers, a sweet perk for little sisters.

"Careful, those could be hot," said the waitress.

Barb laughed out loud. "Boy, I've heard that before." She turned to my boyfriend, Steve. "I once did a memorial service at church for someone who wasn't even there."

My boyfriend stopped chewing.

"The funeral director called that morning and said the deceased wouldn't be ready for her service. Her body was being cremated." Barb glanced at Mike, who looked down, grinning, so she continued. "Only me, the funeral director, and her husband knew."

My boyfriend wiped his mouth with his napkin.

"Finish it, Barb," said Katie.

"So we went to pick up her remains on the way to the burial, and the funeral director said, 'She's still too hot to handle.' So we pretended to bury her so we wouldn't hurt the family's feelings, and then I went back and did it for real the next day."

Then Katie joined in, memorizing liturgy from her years in the pew. "Honey, Cooper, and every one of our nine foster puppies were baptized with water, holy words, and oil, sealed with the cross of Christ forever." She grinned at me, and I could sense the spark in her that I love igniting. "Mom, what date was my baptism?"

"Same day as Honey's birthday, December 28."

"Mom, when was Honey's baptism?"

"April first," I answered automatically. "April first, 2000. On April Fools' Day. To keep things kosher."

During Easter brunch, Steve retold the ten-cow wife story to my family, scoring brownie points. My family members are fans of cows. We'd come home from Sunday church to the aromas of pot roast and mashed potatoes.

Between the successful Easter introduction, the love of beef, and the shared border of South Dakota and Nebraska—and Steve just being Steve—I began to seriously wonder if herding some cows might be in order.

How does one become a good wife? How does a good marriage work?

6

Taking Chances

STEVE SAT ACROSS FROM ME AT HIS DINING ROOM TABLE with his Epiphone guitar in his lap, strumming it absently. Then his energy changed; he lifted an ear and plucked individual strings, testing their pitches against each other, tightening and releasing the strings, satisfying some soundless harmony in his head. He strummed a chord with conviction, quieting the reverberation by pressing his palm into the strings. His eyes met mine. Finally, he said it.

"I wrote a song for you," he said. "Wanna hear it?"

Nobody had ever written a song for me, let alone performed it for me.

"Of course I do."

His gaze returned to his guitar of forty years—the instrument that paid for his college when his bands played at frat parties and dance halls in the '60s, the guitar he would strum in cornfields under Nebraska stars. His fingers began moving between the frets. He sang his lyrics.

Chilly nights, morning dew
Pet names and silly games
Harder to catch my breath...

Good morning, my love, I've been waiting for you
Dreaming and praying and waiting for you
Teach me to run to your joy...

Music had never told me it loved me before, but today it did. Steve's emotions hid behind the mask of beautiful resonance, of chords forever escaping into new inversions. I knew music was Steve's language. He loved me but couldn't say those three words; instead, they transposed themselves through the lift and tumble of stanzas. But it had only been two months, and he was afraid to say *I love you.*

I wasn't. After twelve years of divorced life and vicariously learning about building relationships and love by watching friends and family, my epiphany arrived. I heard the echo of the trusted sage in my life, a counselor named Barb Dalberg. Picture a Norwegian Maya Angelou.

"You are not the same divorced woman you were, and you never can be again," she had assured me many years ago. "It's not possible because you keep evolving. So love and let go of the outcome."

As Steve sang, I stepped into the truth of her words. I trusted myself; I was not the same woman whose marriage blew up, and I never could be again. I could once again trust my instincts, a requirement for trusting someone else's. The necessary platform for trusting Steve.

And I let go of the outcome. I was free to care for Steve with no expectations for tomorrow, let alone the future. We were so enthralled with the moment that we didn't have the time for expectations to dim our future. With Steve being divorced twenty years, and me, twelve, we were grateful for the day's joy—and that was enough. Telling him I loved him wasn't a risk; it was a certainty that I wanted every good thing for his life, whether we ended up together or not.

When he finished his song, tears filled his eyes. I reached for his hand and spoke my words with newfound understanding; the love I felt for him didn't belong to me, but rather flowed through me, like wind.

I moved closer. "I love you, Steve."

His body reflexed briefly in surprise, then relaxed.

"And I don't expect you to say anything to me," I assured him.

DURING THE MONTHS OF APRIL AND MAY, I HID FROM MY students and went to the movies. The movie title didn't matter; what did matter was that I wouldn't hear my name repeated. Think of a world leader in a press conference, where journalists' voices pile on top of each other like football players surging for the end zone. I once kept a tally of how many times I heard my name in school in one day: seventy-five. I multiplied seventy-five by 175 school days and discovered I heard *Ms. Lynn!* an average of 13,125 times a year. A perk of divorce is that I got to change my name.

The most stressful time to teach is springtime, when the state shortchanges learning and beleaguers us with premature, looming deadlines for student accountability reports. The rotten part about these reports is that their early deadlines shave off about two months of the mythical nine months of learning. So we had to work fast, hard, and smart. I tried to pass myself off as being the pedagogue, while all along I preferred the loosey-goosey approach, but the paradox worked: The kids knew when to tip their hats and respect themselves and their work; the rest of the time, we fell in love with a magician called Learning.

Collectively reading a million words in seven months wasn't uncommon in our class. It was expected. Completing a thousand extra math facts in sixty days for a Pluto Pizza Party caused writer's cramp but promoted brain gain. Yet, we had to show accountability, too, so we hunkered down and fast-forwarded lessons on filling in those stupid, standardized bubbles.

"Yeah, yeah, yeah, we know," my students would say.

"Anyone not get this point?" I would ask. If they didn't, class helpers stepped in. Children helping children: the best use of tax money ever. No waste.

Fortunately, our school consistently ranked among the top in the state. Traditions of a strong principal who had our teaching backs, seasoned cohesion of teachers and parents, and academic rigor enabled our middle-class, high free-and-reduced-lunch student population to compete with the rich schools, year after year.

But keeping seven-year-old students engaged in the school year's homestretch proved challenging, even at Bear Creek. So we found reasons to celebrate anything good to sustain us.

Every now and then, my lessons turned to toast. During a math lesson one stormy day, springtime snowflakes began pirouetting in April, titillating off-task students.

Enter celebrations.

"It's snowing!" my kids would say, with a freshness you never tire of.

So I went with it.

"Hey, everybody!" I yelled. Over the squeals and the squeak of fingers rubbing foggy windows, I lured them in. "There's only one thing to do." I paused, dramatically. "Time to go outside and catch snowflakes on our tongues! Forget your coats!"

In 8.2 seconds, the class sort of lined up and flew out the door. Little did they know we had just completed our fire drill practice for the month.

I countered the academic rigor with, yep, you guessed it, more celebrations, particularly *the* underdog holiday of May Day, which celebrates spring's newness and anonymous showering of candy and flowers on neighbors' doorsteps. My brightest student, Brandon, took his post at the intersection of School Office and Third Grade Hallway. His reconnaissance mission, should he choose to accept it: cough loudly enough for me to hear him if the principal decided to leave her office and head our way.

Our principal, Dr. Doll, had attended Catholic school and triumphantly led her public school in Mother Superior fashion, complete with two parochially educated assistant principals, Sisters Wagner and Costello, whose combined leadership crammed the school's waiting list in the hundreds for two decades. To her staff, Dr. Doll's office felt as safe as stained-glass windows, but to her students, it was a confession booth.

She would not appreciate me, Maria von Trapp, running through her abbey with twenty-six children delivering May Day baskets to third-grade classrooms, baskets stuffed with playground dandelions and candy scammed from home. It became the only day my class could move soundlessly down a hallway without touching any walls.

On May Day, I reviewed division during our math lesson, and we figured out that having twenty-six children in our class translated into posting five clandestine kids at every third-grade door, with Brandon the lookout as the remainder.

I commanded with military hand signals, counting down on my fingers, mouthing, "Five! Four! Three! Two…One!"

Discerning children pounded the grains out of the 1950s wooden classroom doors, then nonchalantly sprinted around the corner where I stood (we had to practice and practice the nonchalant part). Next to me, school secretaries surprised my kids with May Day Milky Ways and jawbreakers.

Steve asked me, "Why do you carry on this tradition every year?"

I explained, "It's because I don't want May Day to be forgotten. It has a tradition of hidden joy. I teach my kids to be on the lookout to uncover the fun, steal it, then share it." I thought how I could explain it further to this worldly jetsetter. "It's like Amaru, paddling his canoe back to Mahana, recognizing the significance of something precious."

.... ‿ᕲᕲᕲᕲᕲᕲᕲ ....

AFTER THREE MONTHS OF HOUSE CLEANING, I FINALLY granted Steve permission to visit my home and my bourgeois life—my tract home, a home with a stamped sidewalk, a proverbial single tree in the front yard, and symmetrically matched fence lines with ninety-eight other homes crowded into the subdivision, all equally endowed with outrageous HOA dues.

I easily cleaned the downstairs. I washed windows, wiping away doggy nose prints on patio doors, erased Katie's fingerprints on the walls. The upstairs was another matter—namely, my apocalyptic bedroom suite. My walk-in closet had morphed into the junk drawer's close cousin. But now, like when Queen Elizabeth arrived in one of her colonies, all was ready.

Steve rang the doorbell.

Honey greeted him with warm wags. Our leviathan pup Cooper, however, responded by leaping over the couch and spooking our house-trained bunny, Ellie May, who came out as a male when we brought him to the vet for constipation. He zigzagged two laps around the kitchen table legs.

The next thing you know, Katie took charge.

"Honey! Go get Ellie!" she commanded. Ellie May froze in the familiarity of the sing-song order. My rabbit darted back toward his cage in the dining room, with Honey army crawling closely behind.

At least this gave Katie something to do during that awkward rite of passage when a boyfriend comes over to your house for the first time.

"Hi, sweetheart!" I said, giving Steve a hug, but not a kiss, because I had to demonstrate the epitome of class. The household commotion—my life in translation—seemed to startle this bachelor of twenty years. Steve was speechless, but his face gave away his words. Who is this woman? he confessed to me later.

"Outside, Cooper!" I barked, pointing toward the garage door in an attempt to calm things down. He obeyed, thankfully, by squeezing through Honey's doggy door, a 12-inch x 8-inch rectangle, his body slamming against metal and wood. He looked like a newborn squirming through the birth canal, only louder.

I proudly showed Steve our home. My divorce left me with two mortgages on my first house, but thanks to a successful weekend garage sale that netted me $600 in coin rolls, I covered my earnest money check before it bounced (knowing how the Federal Reserve system worked during my banking days helped). With a diet of mac and cheese and the dot-com economy, I built our current house and happily gave Steve the tour.

Showing him certain objects didn't mean as much as the stories that happened nearby: The kitchen where I graded papers. The recliner that played "Rudolph the Red-Nosed Reindeer" when you laid back because a musical Christmas card was stuck somewhere inside its upholstery. A litter of nine lab foster puppies had obliterated our backyard, with Cooper leading the pack. His littermates hung from tree limbs and chewed down the maple tree and deck lattice in one afternoon. Once we replaced the maple, Cooper ransacked the laundry basket and flung my bra high in its branches, dangling beyond my reach, a permanent windsock.

On the staircase, I showed Steve where Katie pretended to be Esmeralda from *The Hunchback of Notre Dame* movie and tied herself up at the stake.

"Oh, Mom, I can't believe you told him that!" Katie said, mortified.

"I have pictures," I told Steve.

He didn't laugh.

My pride continued. Now it was *my* turn to draw attention to some stairs. "Remember that dead fly of yours? Well, you're standing on the very stair where Honey dropped a coy fish from our neighbor's pond. It was still flopping."

Everyone knows it's awkward showing a man your bedroom. Mine, sweetly feminine, dripped with ivory drapes, an ivory bench, angels, and white candles around my bathtub.

"This took her a month and a half to clean, just this room here," Katie said, paying me back. "She even cleaned her closet for you. First time ever."

This time I didn't laugh.

I could tell Steve liked the peaceful aura of my bedroom. If his mind began to fantasize about being there, I popped his thought bubble right out of the air.

"Now, I don't have views like yours, but…" I took his hand and together we stepped into the bathtub. "The best view I have is from the tub. See?" I asked. "You can see downtown Denver. But you have to stand up to see it."

As if Steve hadn't had enough of my world, more of it spilled out before him when I invited him to an elementary school's equivalent to Mecca, field day. For all his client dinners and work events I had awkwardly attended over the past months, it was his turn to blend in again.

Steve must have been expecting polo as an event, because he arrived fashionably dressed, wearing an expensive fitted white coat and a wide-brimmed, cream-colored hat for the sun. He also toted a black umbrella for the rainy forecast. I politely introduced him as a friend to my students. While the parents grinned, Gail threw her head back and gave me yet another thumbs-up.

Nepotism reared up. "I got Ms. Lynn and him together!" yelled Gail's daughter.

My student Charlie tugged at me. "Ms. Lynn! That man with the black umbrella reminds me of the man in the yellow hat in that book we read yesterday." Charlie tilted his head up at Steve and smiled, waiting to be noticed. I loved it when kids did that. People want first to be noticed, then known. Charlie asked Steve, "Hey! Do you know Curious George?"

7

So This Is Nebraska

ONE WEEK LATER, WE DROVE TO LINCOLN, NEBRASKA, TO meet Steve's ma and to throw her a surprise eighty-eighth birthday party. Steve and I were getting serious.

To be sure, Nebraska is the close country cousin to two savagely boring states while driving through them—western Kansas and, occasionally, South Dakota. But no worries. Steve stashed a surprise in the glove compartment to break up the trip: four harmonicas. So instead of the monotony of cornfield after cornfield, I listened to him play "Oh Susannah" in four keys. For five hours.

But Steve is a master at pointing out hidden beauty. Slowly, timeworn barns became masterpieces, framed inside auburn fields, chaff teeming from the late sandhill crane migration. The Platte River meandered into trickling waterholes for calves trailing their mothers. Steve pointed out what Ted Kooser noticed in his 1980 poem, "So This Is Nebraska": "a meadow-lark on every post."

The drive reconnected me to my Midwest childhood, its carefree roots tangled in unsophisticated brilliance of simplicity.

My dad used boxcars to teach me to count. He'd roll his window down and wave a friendly hello to the engineer, signaling him to blow the train's whistle, a thank-you for the kindness.

We kids took swimming lessons in lakes, not chlorinated pools; my first swimming lesson involved a toss from my dad's arms into Lake Okoboji. My head submerged and I was terror-stricken, only to feel his mighty arms swoop me up, his laughter sifting between the heavy drips of water off my head. He comforted me, then chucked me back into the water a second time. This time I knew he'd be there, and I instantly lost my fear of water.

On October nights, my brothers and I watched crisp leaves burn and turn to ashes on our neighborhood streets at dusk, sweet-smelling smoke lingering on our fingers, the only time of day children hushed in the glow and wondered how their friends' faces could look so different in shadowed light. We treated every Sunday like Christmas Day, when Sioux Falls stores closed shop for church, the day I would add my silver attendance star to Jesus's paper cross, proving to God I was present, since He didn't have enough stars to think about already.

And I'd smell the lilac hedges in spring and snip a bouquet for my teacher, wrapping it in a wet Kleenex. In the summer, we'd blow away ants' piles between sidewalk cracks and watch them rebuild a day later, grain by grain. Over the Fourth of July, I'd fearlessly throw Black Cats over a country bridge into the Big Sioux River, sparks popping and fizzing, their lines of smoke dragging inside the breeze. But the state fair's double Ferris wheel, an alluring stairway to heaven, petrified me.

Like these Nebraska cornfields, the rows of South Dakota fields whizzing by mesmerized me as a child. Their steady, perfectly straight parallels entranced me, and I often found my vision blurring into vacant stares, into nothingness, as it did on Nebraska's I-80, its ribbon drawing me back into my Midwest childhood days, memories Steve and I shared for hours.

Now, since Steve was a Renaissance man—a writer, leader, musician, singer, rock climber, gardener, entrepreneur, CEO, world traveler, hang glider, skydiver, and scuba diver—what could a Renaissance man's mother possibly be like? Possibly the Virgin Mary, laced with steroids. On the 500-mile drive, I learned a lot about Ma, the type of woman who could do everything better than anybody. Anybody referred to me.

I admit Steve's ravings about Ma attracted me to him. He loved everything about her, what a perfect farm wife she was— raising three strapping boys while cutting off chicken heads and cooling homemade apple pie in the kitchen window, churning butter and serving trays of freshly squeezed lemonade for the hired help on afternoon break, branding cows, birthing calves, laying irrigation ditches, canning vegetables, and baking bread with an old sourdough recipe from the Garden of Eden.

As class valedictorian in 1936, she excelled while surviving a polio outbreak. An accomplished singer, ballroom dancer, and published writer, Ma's most prized collection was Papa's love letters, penned on hotel stationery as he courted her while working as a traveling salesman for Kellogg's before the outbreak of WWII.

Ma was very much alive and literally kicking. She worked out twice a week at the gym. She sent birthday cards to every farmer in Lancaster County and every member of her church, including illiterate infants. When milo prices soared, Ma stepped up and commanded, "Sell!" Even her paintings had recently caught the attention of the University of Nebraska. They wanted to enroll her.

This woman experienced the Depression, World War II, the Dust Bowl's grimy mantle, the untimely death of Steve's brother, Eddie, her husband's dementia, and a pitchfork through her foot—and what do you suppose were the first words I heard her say over the phone?

"We are fun people!"

There was absolutely nothing about her I couldn't love.

True to form, I met Birthday Girl Ma in a sea of thirty fun friends and family. Her farmhouse resonated with Midwest flair—potato salad in the fridge and half-assembled Memorial Day artificial bouquets. A tasseled pink birthday hat topped the head of her old black lab, Marshall, his whitened eyebrows and snout hinting of heaven's glow seeping into his face. Tied to the balcony, wind-whipped party balloons danced in the prairie gales that swayed the oak tire swing near the porch. Ma and her favorite niece, Myra, took a bogus errand so the rest of us could make the party arrangements and pass out the songbooks for the traditional sing-along, a persistent bough on the Vannoy family tree.

Cousins and farm friends gave me a neighborly Nebraska greeting. Ma and Myra returned, and the crowd hid behind bookshelves and inside bedrooms, the excitement palpable.

"Surprise!" the group cheered as Ma entered. I stood next to the front door, certain that after spotting Steve, she would want to see me most of all. He had raved about me and told her that I was "his keeper."

Covering her mouth in delight, she immediately scanned the room for Steve, her true north after Papa had died of dementia five years earlier. Steve walloped and crowned her with a Happy Birthday tiara atop her snowy curls. He kissed her and hugged her with that embrace reserved for mothers and sons only. Clothed in flowered pastels, Ma's energetic laugh discounted her white hair and shuffled steps. Just like her son, behind her glasses twinkled hazel eyes.

She strolled right on by me, intent on embracing her nieces and nephews and all the other buttercups in her field, the Otleys, who leased her farmlands, along with their daughter Lucy and her pit bull, Chopper. Lutheran pastors, the Senior Diner's cotillion, and her best friend of seventy years, Jane, standing in a walker, got the first fifteen dibs on her. She finally hugged me, exclaiming, "I'm so glad you're here, Barb!"

After the party and sing-along, we made the rounds to seven cemeteries the following day, starting at Rose Hill where Steve's papa lay in the old district, and we placed the last wreath three hours later in a homesteaded field fenced in century-old wire. At eighty-eight years, Ma's memory of a dozen graves over two counties was remarkable, except for one plot. A splintered, wooden cross stood crooked against an obelisk headstone belonging to Ma's grandmother, who had been accidentally shot to death by her own child in the 1880s. Ma replaced the faded carnations caked with clods of dirt with a vibrant red, white, and blue bouquet. Each grave, every name, a lifetime of story weaved the Vannoy tapestry into a braided rug I began to visualize.

Ma talked incessantly. Her patient son drove on, past her childhood town, Firth, population 516, where knee-high grasses grew between the train rails and railroad ties, and a decaying grain elevator towered, succumbing to its last memories of life half a century ago.

Steve's patience disappeared. "Ma? We've been talking for hours. I need some quiet. Can we all please stop talking for ten minutes?"

"Yah," Ma answered with her German lilt.

So she tuned to the radio station inside her head, the Vannoy radio frequency of music, KZ80. Her body seemed to sway to some inaudible beat. Soon her head bobbed. Gradually, she hummed aloud, filling the car with a happy melody reminiscent of honeysuckle and daisies. The hum escaped through her pursed lips, shaping delicate words drifting through her vocal cords and floating into an outright song, sweetly thin as a springtime wren.

"You are my sunshine," she crooned, "my only sunshine... you make me hap—"

"Ma!" Steve stiffened his arms against the wheel.

Her fragrance of honeysuckle overpowered Steve, the yellow of her daisies too bright.

Ma glanced at me in the back of the car, then grinned at her son.

"You didn't tell me I couldn't sing."

I handed Ma the remaining memorial wreath from the backseat, the one belonging to her parents. She had arranged red and white artificial mums inside the Styrofoam wreath and affixed tiny blue bows and wooden crosses around the edges. Her parents' headstones used to be in the graveyard of St. John's Lutheran Church, their old country church outside of Firth, but the building had been relocated years ago, leaving behind an unpretentious array of grave markers in the middle of an ordinary pasture.

She held the wreath close to her bosom and pointed left, left, right as Steve navigated through dusty ribbons of gravel county roads. After twenty minutes, Steve glanced back at me in the rearview mirror and I understood.

Clinging to her handmade memorial, Ma could no longer locate her parents' gravesites. At first, she acted composed and pretended to take the confusion in stride. We joked about seeing the same yellow railroad crossing signs as we slowed down to get our bearings.

I prayed, *Please, God, help us find Ma's parents*, looking over the sameness of short corn stalks and fence posts.

Five minutes later, we spotted an old, rusted Chevy with fins waiting at a stop sign ahead.

"Turn there, it's just down that way a little bit," Ma said, repeating a line we'd heard several times.

Steve turned and drove past the Chevy, still idling at the stop sign. He stopped the car and kicked it into reverse, opening the window to address the driver.

An unkempt old man sat behind the wheel, frizzy haired under a John Deere hat, his white eyebrows bushy with age. His car's interior was as beat up as he was. He sat upon a foamy cushion piled with junk. Cigarette smoke wafted into our car.

"Excuse us, sir," Steve said, "but we're trying to find where the ol' St. John's Lutheran Church used to be. Do you have any idea where that is?"

The man thought a bit, trying to decide if he knew. He nodded his head slowly, easily. "Yes, I do," he replied, and pointed behind him. "It's about two miles from here. Down that road to County Road 5, then take a left, go for...I'd say, a quarter mile, then take a right on, dagnammit, what is it? Anyway, after that quarter mile, go right a while and it'll be on your left."

Steve tried to repeat the directions. "So, I go ahead down to County 5, take a left then go—"

"Do you want me to show you where it's at?"

I looked hard at this creepy man in an old Chevy sitting at a stop sign in the middle of nowhere. I looked at this vulnerable, elderly mother in the front seat.

"That'd be great, thanks," said Steve. He closed the window.

"Leave that window up, sweetheart," I said, "and lock our doors."

The man made a U-turn and, pulling in front of us, drove away, dust choking the road.

Sure enough, he led us to the headstones, about two dozen of them.

I could only imagine Ma's relief.

The man stepped out of his car and approached ours.

"Stay here," Steve said, getting out.

I locked us inside as the creepy man briefly visited with Steve, who nodded for us to get out. I left our purses inside the car. The man followed us to the headstones, puffing his cigarette, and watched Ma place the wreath between her two parents. He smiled in satisfaction.

"Thank you for your help, sir. Where are you from?" asked Steve.

The man thought again, as if plucking some name out of a fishbowl. Taking another drag of his cigarette, he waved his hand indistinctly. "From around here," he answered, glancing toward the horizon.

"What do you do?" asked Steve.

"Oh, I've done lots of jobs. I've been a plumber, a driver, foreman. Construction worker."

Really?

"What do you do now?" asked Steve.

"Not too busy these days," he answered vaguely. "Not too many jobs."

Steve kept pressing. "Got a wife?"

He glanced around, stepped back. "Nope. I'm a loner."

"Kids?"

"Two."

Steve shook his head. "So what are you doing here in Nebraska, here in Lancaster County?"

The man grinned, slightly. "I'm just a helpin' you folk."

"Sorry!" Steve said suddenly, extending his hand, "I should have introduced myself. I'm Steve."

The man shook hands and held the grip.

"And you are…?" Steve asked.

The man thought a long time, considering his answer. He pressed into the handshake and spoke deliberately.

"My name is…Steven. Steven Van…Nord," the angel answered.

STEVE AND I walked the family fields, hundreds of acres, beginning with the north eighty that Papa and Ma bought in the '40s by picking and shucking one hundred acres by hand. I understood how the land mirrored Steve's peacefulness. Papa and his three sons spent twenty years together memorizing each contour, fingering new seedlings brilliant with life, occasionally pulverized by one night of hailstorms. Milo, wheat, soy, and alfalfa took their seasons upon this land. Cows stared, and chickens ran for their lives. Farm dogs Scot and Louise patrolled for coyotes and flung rats against grain bin walls like helicopter blades.

Steve took my hand and led me next to the creek through the thicket of trees his family had planted decades before—walnut trees, trees that invited meadowlarks and cardinals and the family crow named Elmer. And I wondered how farmers crafted rows of cornstalks among curved hills and how fallow fields rebirthed themselves.

Back in the farmhouse, Steve wrapped his arms around me and kissed my neck. He abruptly stepped back.

"There's a tick on your neck, angel," he said, picking at it.

Excuse me. This compared with the times the school nurse inspected me for head lice. But here, I had already tested positive.

Ma was no help. "Oh, Steve, check the rest of her out. There's probably more." She waved her hands dismissively. "Look inside her ears. They like to crawl in there, y'know. Nice and warm."

"Where did I get these from?" I demanded. I pictured a tick up close, its snapping incisors, peppercorn eyes. I didn't want to be me.

"Most likely from the trees we walked through," Steve said.

Blood rushed from my face. "You let me walk through trees knowing there were ticks in them?"

Chink. Chink. Steve was losing his regality. Like the Sphinx, minus his nose.

"Angel, this is Nebraska," he replied.

Ma pulled a tick jar from under the sink and handed it to Steve.

As if they didn't have enough ticks, they collected them here too?

He parted my hair and found one more.

.... ~✺~ ....

THE NIGHT BEFORE WE LEFT THE FARM, I LAY ON THE porch swing, listening. The coal train skirted outside nearby Prairie Home; I heard its distant yawn. As a little boy, Steve said he listened to the wind blow through the spruce trees by his window, to the calves' bawling, to the frogs near the creek. So I listened for those echoes too. My ear caught the frogs' calling. I listened for cows and heard none but grinned anyway.

My thoughts became the country swing, shifting gently under the sigh of the prairie breeze, rocking me, back and forth, back and forth, then back…pushing back my years, where I am once again a Midwest child, free and pixie-haired, trusting the world's goodness answers to me. I lie in the back of our '67 Galaxy, daring the moon to peek its face between cornstalk shadows as we cruise home, delighted when its glow dances through my eyes, the wind whipping my bangs against freckles I want to hide, the cadenced rhythm of concrete seams lulling me as sheep to be counted, the cricket song rising, corn tassels buzzing in the prairie breeze, now returned, blowing away the chaff from the years between my childhood and this swing where I am once again, whole. Here in Nebraska, inside this brush of innocent magic—who I was back then, who I am this night—I feel no difference. I am finally, fully, me.

8

Vertical Marathons

IF HIKING IN THE FOOTHILLS WARMED UP OUR RELATION-
ship in the springtime, climbing the tallest Colorado mountains
in the summer brought our love to new heights. In June, I
looked forward to packing in more memories with Steve and
unpacking the tangled labyrinth of students' needs orbiting
inside my head.

Being in a gravitational pull with masses of children for
the better part of a year leaves teachers spinning and disoriented and downright loopy. Our summer vacations unshackle
preoccupied, concentric thoughts about our students. We all
struggle to think in a straight line again, as opposed to zigzagging and seeing stars. I needed a singularly straight path
in June. And I shared this insight with Steve as I surfed the
internet at my house.

"I have the perfect solution," he suggested. "Let's climb a
fourteener. Angel, all you have to do is follow one trail in front
of you. Let's climb Pikes Peak."

"Isn't that the longest one-day hike for a fourteener in
Colorado?"

"Yes, it's twenty-six miles round trip. I've done it a couple times before."

"But I haven't. What's the elevation gain?"

"Oh, I think around 8,000 feet."

"So it's an uphill marathon. How many stories is 8,000 feet?" I asked, doing some mental calculations while typing a Google search.

"Um, I don't know off the top of—"

"Ten feet equals one story, so 8,000 feet is equivalent to an eight-hundred-story building." I kept typing, searching.

Steve pulled his head back, surprised. "An eight-hundred-story building?"

"Yes, hiking up Pikes Peak is equivalent to climbing eight Empire State Buildings stacked on top of each other." I leaned into my computer screen. "Or seventeen Great Pyramids of Giza."

"Angel, you can do it," he answered.

.... ༄༅ ....

AT 1:00 A.M., STEVE AND I SIGNED IN AT THE BARR TRAIL-head in Manitou Springs for our ascent up Pikes Peak, the crown jewel of Colorado Springs. It was 35 degrees, crisp enough to see each other's breath in our headlamps. We had trained for three weeks in Denver, Steve meticulously preparing our gear for safety. About 7:00 a.m., groups of two or three fit men and women wearing only T-shirts and athletic shorts began passing us by. They pranced up like mountain goats, smiling as we stepped off the trail for them: Air Force cadets in training. I was proud to be an American.

Halfway up, we stopped at Barr Camp, a primitive cabin painted brown with green shutters and a welcoming sign: "Barr

Camp, Elevation 10,200 feet." We still had six miles to summit. Inside the cabin we ate ham sandwiches while Steve added chlorine dioxide tablets to filter water in our bottles. He noticed a dusty guitar hanging on a wall and asked the forest ranger if he could play it.

"No one's played that thing for years," she said, shaking her head, "but you're welcome to try."

He tuned it as best he could, then turned to me. "How about you sing a little Dixie Chicks?"

I sang the song "Godspeed," a lullaby of dragon tails and Superman pajamas and a mouse. Awkward it was, singing of moonbeams and angels' wings with mud-caked feet and a bear whistle around my neck. Self-conscious, I closed my eyes and finished the ballad.

When I opened them, I discovered we had an audience. Four hikers peered through the cabin door, leaning on the wooden porch, listening. Tears trailed down the cheeks of the forest ranger. She blubbered something about how beautiful the song was, but our impromptu performance wasn't the takeaway; the takeaway was recognizing the power of the music that Steve and I had created together.

We didn't summit. Lightning strikes shattered the susurration of raindrops on lodgepole pines. Unrelenting rain turned us back two miles short of the summit. We hitchhiked a ride down on the rail cog taking tourists back from its "America the Beautiful" vista. Later that day we wolfed down dinner in Colorado Springs, where Steve gave me a blue box. I opened it.

A ruby ring with diamonds glistened.

His explanation was simple. "I was going to give this to you on top of Pikes," he said. "It's a promise ring. I promise I'll always love you and be here for you."

I felt a little old for a promise ring, but since it was a ruby with diamonds, I didn't mind. A few months back, I had told him I loved him with the three magic words; he told me that day he loved me with gems.

I love how love keeps recreating itself.

.... ~~~~~ ....

AT LEAST HALF OF STEVE'S MANSION WAS UNDERUTILIZED. I walked into one bare room, much like a classroom looks when its teacher retires. The room needed...life. And Inspiration tapped my shoulder: Ma and her nieces would be driving in for a visit over the Fourth of July.

"Let's turn her bedroom into a 1930s farmhouse bedroom, so when she comes, she'll feel right at home," I suggested to Steve.

"Sounds great, but she arrives in one week."

"Sweetheart, teachers get two days to fix up their rooms before school. Watch and learn." We decorated the room with authenticity: Antique stores provided 1934 editions of *Life* magazine. We added a country quilt for her twin bed and refinished her antique secretary's desk, complete with clothes she sewed for her three sons. Braided rugs and lacy chintz curtains accented the era.

Steve had always been the guardian of her heirlooms, from his baby coat worn by five generations of Vannoys to Ma's 1936 high school autograph book, with precise cursive. A hand-painted landscape of the Vannoy farm, crafted by Ma, served as the focal point of her new room.

Ma arrived with nieces Myra, Arlis, and Judy. Ma liked holidays as much as I did. Out she stepped from the car, stitched in full raiment of spangled glory: a red, white, and blue–striped shirt, white pants, royal blue tennis shoes and jewelry, red beads, white post earrings, and a blue seashell brooch. Once she stood up and gave us a hug, I stepped back from her and, putting my hand over my heart, saluted her.

"I pledge allegiance to the flag of the United States of America," I said.

She laughed in delight exactly like my first graders did, unspoiled, pure.

Steve led her to the bedroom, her eyes closed. When she opened them, I knew she belonged to the mammal family because I heard every variation of sounds that animals utter—squeals, shrieks, and howls. Her laughter turned to tears as she eased herself into a rocking chair. She glanced up at her blue velvet dress hanging on her closet door.

"My wedding dress!" she said with delight. She nodded her satisfaction at her son, and turning to her nieces announced, "It wasn't on long." Ma touched everything—her Victrola, her 1936 high school scrapbook nibbled by mice, her piano sheet music from the '20s and '30s. "I loved playing this." She began to sing, "You are my sunshine, my only sunshine," and giggled, abruptly stopping. "Warren's love letters!"

Next to the sheet music, three neat stacks of yellowed envelopes contained every letter her husband had written to her during their courting days. The address was simple: Helen Pape, Bryan Memorial Hospital, Lincoln, Nebraska. The envelopes had been sliced open cleanly. Purple three-cent Washington stamps and green one-cent Jefferson stamps, postmarked from 1939—1941, seemed to whisper the beauty of the envelopes' contents, like time in a bottle. Warren wrote her every day on hotel stationery, the return addresses embossed on the envelope corners: Hotel El Dorado, El Dorado, Kansas; Walcott Hotel, Shawnee, Oklahoma.

So that was why Steve saved all my love notes.

We started a bedtime tradition with her whenever she visited. Just before bedtime, Steve would grab a stack of letters, and, sitting at her feet, we would listen to her read Papa's life story, listen to her commentary, listen to its sacredness. Afterward, we would tuck her into bed, sing her a lullaby, and kiss her goodnight. We'd see her face, a sweet child inside a woman's heart, her smile of gratitude slowly fading into a serene countenance, illumined by not one, but two, three, four night-lights.

The next morning, Steve discovered a surefire way to bond Ma and me: take us to the mountains, set up two lawn chairs next to a bubbling Colorado brook, then leave us as he hiked three hours over Guanella Pass. Now Ma could do many things, but hike at 10,000 feet was not one of them. Our first time alone, she talked and I listened, her captive but willing audience.

Half a century passed in her life before I was born, enough time for her to teach that acceptance made life easier for everyone, and optimism's shelf life was longer than life's trials. I discovered we both sang alto, always trying to find harmony between the lines of life, preferring the limelight instead of carrying the tune.

On the Fourth, Ma taught Ali, Emmy, and me how to make the family recipe, the all-American apple pie. Ali and Emmy's pies baked to generational perfection; mine awaited naturalization just outside Ellis Island, a pie not quite ready for citizenship. Its crisscrossed strips looked as if a spider spinning its web pooped out.

We added whipped cream and topped the night off with apple pie and A&W root beer floats as we watched Denver's skyline cascade into willowy branches and bursts of rainbow-sparkled displays up to fifty miles away. We lit bottle rockets and ground spinners and kept the punks alight, and Ma spelled all our names in golden sizzling sparklers until they all echoed out.

Ma and her nieces returned to Nebraska the same day Steve and I headed to Estes Park to summit Longs Peak, the tallest fourteener in Rocky Mountain National Park. Steve invited twenty of his business clients throughout the States to join us, providing another ambitious opportunity for me to prove myself worthy in his world. I wanted to look the part, so I spent hundreds of dollars color coordinating myself in a white, metallic Patagonia raincoat, tight hiking pants, and hat. I met his clients at 2:00 a.m. at the trailhead in their hodgepodge hiking gear—linty caps, faded scarves. They looked comfortable, I was as stiff as an Apollo astronaut.

Longs Peak is a behemoth mountain at 14,259 feet. The standard Keyhole Route requires fifteen miles of hiking with an elevation gain of 5,000 feet. The potential for fatal falls is high, and scrambling among boulders the size of small houses is but one of many risks. (It's considered to be one of the top ten most difficult fourteener hikes.)

After an hour of hiking, we turned around on the trail and saw a train of headlamps ascending the mountain behind us. Denver's city lights twinkled in the east, backdropping a moonlit night with piercing stars. At 3:30 a.m., the wind picked up and began to blow, knocking me off the trail. Steve's hat flew off into a canyon abyss below. We finally reached some rocks for a bathroom break.

Finding a secluded place to go to the bathroom is challenging above timberline, especially in a group of twenty. Keeping your balance as you do it in 40 mph winds could be considered an Olympic trial. I waited until everyone had peed, then meandered off behind some rock outcroppings. I heard voices nearby, but headlamps had been turned off, so I was safe. Due to frigid winds, I kept my gloves on and dropped my three layers of pants and squatted. I went, well, all over, because when one urinates on rocks during a squall, urine splashes the rocks like grease in a frying pan. Attempting to pee faster made the splashes sizzle higher.

I heard Robert's voice, the president of Ford in Russia, approaching me, talking to Steve.

I stopped peeing instantly and started pulling up my pants, except that I had my gloves on. With gloves on and three layers of pants rolled inside each other, I couldn't pull anything up.

"Where's Barb?" Steve asked. He yelled louder. "Barb? Barb? We're ready to go."

Oh please, God, keep the headlamps off.

"Robert, have you seen Barb?" asked Steve.

"No," Robert replied, a few feet from me now, and I heard a click up high and saw a light down low.

Robert's headlamp shined brightly now, spotlighting me.

"Or rather, yes, I see her," he told Steve, awkwardly. But Robert kept staring.

Steve clicked on his own headlamp once he saw Robert's shining orb.

Let's all wonder where Steve looked too.

Let's just say I had no choice but to live through that.

At 13,000 feet, winds whipped through the Continental Divide at the narrow aperture called the Keyhole, entrance to the final ascent. The wind blew hikers off rocks like paper kites in a hurricane. We stayed long enough to have a few laughs, sticking our heads up and rippling our lips with g-force winds, then turned back.

On the way down the mountain, I dawdled along the rocky trail, feet dragging, so I stopped and hung back to rest. The next thing you know, I spotted Robert back there, too, turning his back and peeing right on the trail. A hiking no-no.

Just so we're all clear, Robert spotted me too.

Now we were even.

We continued on and passed a group, still ascending.

"Hey, where'd you get that hat?" Steve asked a buff hiker.

"I found it in a crevice a few miles back," he answered.

"Give me my hat back," said Steve.

Once we got to the car after the strenuous hike, we heard a voice mail from Ma:

"Steven? We just wanted you to know that we are staying in North Platte tonight. We missed a turn in Denver and went too far—to Kansas instead. How many miles did you say we went, Arlis, before we realized we made a mistake?"

We heard Arlis's faint voice in the background. "About three hundred."

Ma's voice continued recording. "Yah, three hundred miles, so the trip is a little longer than we thought, but we are okay. Well, son, didn't want you to worry. I love you both."

9

Bringing the
Goodness Out

STEVE TURNED AROUND ON THE TRAIL. "EVERYTHING FITS with us, angel. We both love music, we both love to write and travel. We believe in kids. And," he said, "you're...geographically desirable."

"I'm what?"

"Geographically desirable. Twenty minutes away."

"Isn't that a romantic thought, thank you," I answered. "But it's not true of you, especially when you're thousands of miles away from me."

"I actually thought about that, being away from you. Now look, what kind of flower is that?" In August, the wildflowers bloomed wide, sapphire lupines and ruby-colored columbine and primrose paintbrush speckled the mountainsides, carpeting the high meadow near his house.

"That's—a vetch. I recognize the leaves," I said. "They look like Palm Sunday branches."

"Yep. Anyway, if we ever did get married and lived in the same house, what would we do together all day?"

"You mean that? Are you worried about that?"

"Not worried, just...wondering. A lot, actually."

Occasionally, our conversation drifted toward a future together, but never stayed there. We continued allowing our gratitude of being together to ground us in the present. I knew Steve well enough that I could finally trust him with Katie's life, a major feat. But like him, I didn't spend too much time projecting my life ahead of his next trip overseas. I'd been single for twelve years. What was six months?

On that late afternoon hike, Steve paused and sniffed the air.

"There's elk around here," he said. "I recognize that mating scent."

I stared at the man who recognized the sexual pheromones of an elk. I decided I could wear whatever perfume I wanted, if this aroma was his basis point.

I also found it peculiar that my nondrinking, nonswearing, goody-two-shoed boyfriend noticed things like a penis-shaped rock and libidinous scents of enormous mammals.

We hiked another fifteen minutes.

"I have to pee," said Steve, speeding up on the trail.

He's quite private, so I stayed behind as he walked over the ridge.

Above me, I heard something crashing through the brush and tall grasses, and I felt the ground shake, then heard a snort. I glanced up about thirty yards into the glazed eyes of a five-point bull elk. His nostrils were the size of golf balls, but even more frightening was the white foam dripping from his mouth. He adjusted his head as his foggy eyes focused on me. He froze.

I thought of two useless things. One, did elk get mad cow disease? Two, I couldn't interrupt Steve's privacy.

The elk charged straight at me, thundering down over the steep foothill, dislodging rocks and dirt along the way.

I tried to scream but nothing came out except air. I shook my hands, which somehow kicked my voice into gear. I screamed louder than ever before in my life. "Steve! Help! Help me!"

But amid my panic, I couldn't run up toward Steve in case his pants were down.

I took the idea of respecting his needs to a moronic level, I get that now. I turned around and did another moronic thing, raced for my life back down the trail, the sound of the hoof-beats clomping at an angle toward me.

And I felt Steve's hand grab my arm and lurch me down the hill, through clods of cactus and rabbit brush until we reached a ponderosa pine with a wide base and low-hanging branches. He whipped me into its trunk.

"Stand behind it!" he yelled, keeping his eyes on the elk as it bulleted toward us.

It didn't stop. His antlers slammed into the branches, becoming entangled in the limbs and twigs. He shook his head violently, white foam splattering the air. His woody, musky scent rose up under the tree. Stacked up behind the trunk, Steve and I watched this crazed beast thrashing its body at the skirt of the tree. It stomped the ground in fury, releasing its antlers. Disoriented, it backed up the hill, its head rolling in circles, panting so hard his ribs heaved. Its frenzied gray eyes ran amuck.

"Don't move," whispered Steve. "Don't move."

We barely breathed as the elk attempted to catch our scent but failed. He stumbled up over the ridge. Steve grabbed me and wouldn't let go. "I don't know what I would do without you," he whispered.

STEVE CONTINUED FLYING around the world, reaching children and their families through corporate meetings. As an eighth grader, Katie headed back to school, as did I, standing in front of yet another group of fledglings—wide-eyed, mute first graders. This lasted one day. The next day, overwhelmed by their new lives, a few would fall asleep. Their closed mouths would slowly open wide like baby birds waiting for a worm, chirping over each other, their squawking marred with speech delays, a cacophony of fresh springtime newness.

"Teacher! Fat boy is asweep!" my tattler James announced, my adorably immature former student who was repeating first grade in my classroom because he deserved another year of childhood—and also because his mom failed to tell me he never finished kindergarten.

"James, remember? I have a name, and it's not Teacher, it's Ms. Lynn," I said. "And th-th-that boy's name is Andrew, and it's okay if he sleeps for a little while. He's getting used to things."

And James taunted me in his mocking voice, "So if I faw asweep, what wiw you do?"

Count my blessings came to mind.

"James, I'd let you sleep, too, and keep going with our schedule, and you'd miss snack time."

And later, during that first week of school, I read a story for James, and for every other uniquely created child in my class: *Leo the Late Bloomer* by Robert Kraus. It's a reassuring story about how children all bloom at just the right time, a first-grade favorite. James teared up. He knew he was different.

I pressed his hand into mine. "Patience," I whispered into his ear. "Trust me."

Being a first grader can be tough. My Amaru approach of seeing someone's goodness, a child's goodness, didn't require chapters of explanation like Steve's *10 Greatest Gifts* book does. Steve studied countless research findings. My classroom is my only laboratory. I require only number charts, shark teeth, confetti, and Jesus's chair.

I've watched hundreds and hundreds of first graders fall out of their chairs for almost twenty years. I was a first-grade teacher in a school that couldn't afford first-grade chairs. Instead, we inherited leftover second- and third-grade chairs, which left us with dangling feet and no grounding. This would be akin to adults sitting on bar stools with no footrests for six hours a day. We'd squirm. We'd be uncomfortable. We all knew that a few of us would fall out of our chairs.

At first, I thought my mismatched classroom furniture was a result of being low on the totem pole. But after fifteen years and the fact that the other five first-grade teachers shared my problem, I knew I belonged to a tribe. Our perpetual budget deficit continually created our endless shortfalls and distracting sideshows in class.

For the first few years, I honestly did feel sorry for my students who fell. Their MOs were universal: panicked faces, desperate eyes locking into mine at that point of no return, flailing V-shaped legs unceremoniously flipping backward over their heads. The crash followed, an avalanche of limbs, chair legs, and crayons. Frozen in time, the embarrassed child absorbed silent stares of classmates, who in turn stared at me, searching for hints of compassion—or my verdict. After witnessing hundreds of tumbles, my patience sometimes grew slim.

The constant interruptions took their toll. I already competed with short attention spans and the creation of the Game Boy.

One year, everything changed; actually, I did. It was mid-October, and I learned acceptance. I accepted the fact that children falling out of their chairs was a fact of life, like flies being attracted to flypaper. I gave up control. I shared my epiphany at lunch with my first-grade teammates, my best friends, the unannounced reason more people should go into teaching.

"I'm done fighting it," I declared as I swallowed a mouthful of ham sandwich in the teacher's lounge. "I'm not gonna let kids falling out of their chairs ruin my day anymore."

Diane grimaced. "I know the feeling. I had two fall out this morning in my room."

Stacy piped up. "I had one!" She dropped her cookie on the floor. "Now you see him, now you don't."

Dixie laughed. "I had two, and one of 'em brought his desk down with him. The inside of the desk was such a mess that the kid basically disappeared."

"Does it count if he acted alone?" asked Terry.

I was curious. "How many kids fell out of their chairs this morning in all our classes?"

My teammates bobbed their heads, repeating their past.

"Two."

"One."

"Two."

"One. But he got pushed."

And my two made eight. It was 10:45, and we still had four hours of school left.

I was inspired.

After school, I drove to the teacher store and bought a hundred number chart, typically used to track our days of attendance. However, the next morning, I hung the extra one in the back of my room above the first-grade copy machine. My teammates frequently used it during the day. I shared my plan. My team fine-tuned the guidelines:

1. One number is added to the chart every time a child falls out of a chair.

2. Two numbers are added (double points) if a child grabs and brings down a desk as well.

3. No number is added if a child is hurt (clinic trips were rare but did occur).

4. Children MUST fall out of the chair independently and naturally. No interference from mean children.

5. Rules of the game must be kept confidential.

6. Once the 100 chart is filled with numbers, we celebrate our patient tolerance with a special lunch for the teachers.

It was a good week. We filled in forty-two numbers. I noticed my attitude warmed up. One of my top students, Lindsey, fell out of her chair. Every classmate gawked at her.

"Lindsey," I said, "do you want to do that again for the class? But in slow motion?"

Her self-consciousness disappeared and a grin replaced it. "Okay!" She happily reenacted her mishap, delighting her friends.

I noticed the enthusiasm. "Let's ALL fall out of our chairs in slow motion!"

Yes, you are imagining the scene and hearing it correctly. We continued the simulation several times that week until the kids got sick of it, thereby extinguishing its distracting power.

Meanwhile, as I taught, my teammates came in to make a few copies throughout the day. They would grin and inconspicuously add a few numbers. Our spirits soared as the kids nosedived.

Dixie sang, "Another one bites the dust," adding another number while making copies.

The two different hundred number charts confused parent helpers. They would ask, "Why are the numbers on these charts different?"

"Oh, that," I replied, as indifferently as a flight attendant reciting safety instructions. "It's some research we are working on."

Before the winter break, we had two lunch celebrations. Our students had fallen out of chairs 253 times. But after the Christmas holiday, sad, miraculous things happen to first graders. They always mature and grow into their bodies. Consequently, in January, their clumsiness declined. Spills were down.

So were our celebrations.

We decided to give the children a chance to join our celebrating. We challenged all 135 students. For every three days (not consecutive, good heavens, we're not perfect) that no student fell out of a chair, an extra recess would be awarded for all. Now understand, for a first grader, a fifteen-minute recess equals a beach vacation. We transformed body awkwardness into body awareness. The kids sat up straighter and worked harder. They ended up playing harder at recess for the rest of the year. We all learned to go toward the flow instead of fighting it. We didn't try changing the kids until they wanted it.

Another handy panacea for molding children involves shark teeth. One tooth will do. I dangle it in front of the class and swing it like a pendulum to hypnotize them.

"Do you want this?" I would ask my class.

They salivate. I feel like Pavlov, but instead of using a bell to whet their whistles, I use shark teeth. Pavlov had a dominance issue, it was contagious, and I caught it.

Dirty classroom floor? I use shark teeth to clean it. Offer a shark tooth to landlocked children and in less than one minute they sit taller, fall out of chairs less often, and improve math accuracy by 40 percent.

Another convenient tool to make first grade easier begins with a handful of confetti: Throw it on the floor. Then put out party food—cupcakes, Fritos, Twinkies, Capri Suns. Give children the choice: confetti or food? Confetti wins. How do I teach a child reading fluency? Toss confetti inside the pages and promise it's theirs if the reading is smooth.

My student Jamie, notorious for picking and peeling scabs, followed me around, beseeching me for a Band-Aid to stop the bleeding. Not surprisingly, Jamie also preoccupied his time with peeling crayons and picking his nose. Consequently, I would send Jamie to meet his Maker in my time-out chair—Jesus's empty chair. It gave me permission to completely ignore his behavior because he was in Holy hands.

A Chatty Cathy in class? *Oh, Jenny, talk your heart out in that empty chair.* A cheater? *Try to pull the wool over that guy's eyes over there.* When I thought about my student sitting on a makeshift throne of God Almighty, my discipline response cooled down, to the point I might forget about the child entirely because teaching days get demanding.

And my favorite use for the empty chair? An open invitation for students to seat themselves when they knew they needed to wind down, or take responsibility, or work without being disturbed. My students would ask me, "Can I go to the time-out chair?" or they would invite themselves into it.

Steve made his living by understanding how to respect children, then up-leveled the concept for adults. I made my living by acquiescing to childish antics, then twisting the rules to empower the darlings.

CHRISTMAS ROLLED AROUND, and I didn't know if I should be happy or miserable. My family celebrated Christmas as if it were the longest, most important birthday party on the planet. We had so many yearly traditions they turned into OCDs. My brothers and dad had always strung lights on our house. With two pastors in the family, halos formed over our family's heads after attending three Christmas Eve services—in three different churches.

Afterward, we'd track St. Nick's whereabouts on NORAD as Katie wrote her marathon letter to Santa, requesting gifts not only for herself but also, during one year, for twenty-four family members and friends and dogs throughout the country. "Dear Santa," she would write, "Pleaz leav prezents for:" (I knew I was in trouble when I saw the colon). While Grandma arranged cookies and milk, Grandpa carried Katie up a ladder at 11:00 p.m. to leave reindeer food on the roof; in cahoots, Pastor Mike and Uncle Steve threw rocks on the roof.

"Listen, Katie! It's the reindeer! Better go to sleep!"

Then the family would leave, and Honey and I would slog into the basement at midnight, scrounging up gifts for Uncle Jim in Virginia and for Teddy our guinea pig to preserve Santa's magic. The sweet reward of single parenting is on Christmas morning, when you are the only one in the audience, sleep deprived, yes, yet witnessing the moments you were born to live.

On this particular Christmas, Steve wrote me a beautiful song as his Christmas present, a beautifully sad, lonely song. Unlike my family, which created more holiday friction than fireworks, a December melancholy hung over Steve's. Both his brother and father passed years before during the holiday season. And his divorce, like so many others, meant fragmenting and sharing family time with his daughters' mom. The first Christmas I spent with him felt like Good Friday. I honestly didn't know what to do except sit with him on his couch and dry his tears. And vow that, as his friend, this kind of Christmas was over for him.

10

The Australian Proposal Song

IN JANUARY 2007, AFTER A YEAR OF DATING, STEVE ASKED me to join him on a business trip.

"I have a session in Australia next month. Come with me," Steve said. "I'll fly you there after the session. Melbourne. A week of exploring, maybe Tasmania too?"

I was troubled for three reasons.

Reason #1: Inconvenience. My paraprofessional had already cut six hundred red and white links for my valentine chain. I had to be there. It was tradition.

Reason #2: I had never crossed an ocean. I explained that Pluto was closer and could we please go there instead.

"Angel, the pilgrims crossed the ocean."

Reason #3: I was most troubled about leaving my fourteen-year-old daughter for the first time. Katie shared her concern with me too.

"Please stay longer, Mom," she said, flipping through television channels, "and take advantage of that extra day."

It was decided.

My mom, Katie, and Honey dropped me off at Denver's airport. The plane trip to Melbourne took twenty-nine hours. Steve's chauffeur handed me two dozen roses as I exited customs. I fawned over the roses, profusely thanking the handsome chauffeur.

"Those roses are from me, not him," Steve said playfully, behind my back.

"Oh!" I said, laughing and giving Steve an internationally large kiss. "I'm here! I'm here! Can you believe it?"

He pulled me close, inches apart. "I love you," he said, grinning. Motioning toward the chauffeur, he added, "This is Theo, the man who did not give you roses."

Theo stuffed my suitcase into the limo's trunk, pulled my door open and stiffly waited. I couldn't believe Steve traveled in this style. No more okey dokey Nebraska. In his world, chauffeurs and five-star resorts were as ubiquitous as my empty gas tank and Twinkie lunches.

We arrived at downtown Melbourne's five-star hotel, the Grand Hyatt, prestigiously situated on Collins Street, the city's heartbeat of high fashion and dining. Concierges whisked away my luggage. Steve was unusually giddy with enthusiasm, unlike me. I'd been awake forty-eight hours.

"I need to sleep," I pleaded, heading toward the nearest horizontal furniture, a lobby couch. Disoriented, my surroundings fogged in heaviness.

Steve held me back. "Angel, whatever you do, don't lie down. You'll get over your jet lag faster if you just treat the day normally and go to bed tonight."

We shuffled upstairs to a twenty-ninth floor suite, as spacious as my 2,100-square-foot home. Floor-to-ceiling windows framed Melbourne's skyline, its angular skyscrapers mirroring surrounding buildings, clouds, and blue skies. Dotted between the buildings were green pockets of city parks. A nearby cathedral's twin spires softened the urban starkness. It was a view I'd seen only in movies.

Steve plopped me in a chair, then sat on a nearby ottoman and stared at me. I smiled with a hint of oncoming hibernation. He reached for his guitar and placed it gingerly on his lap. "I'd like to play a song I wrote for you, angel."

I squinted, then opened my eyes wider, pepping them up. I had patiently sat on a plane for nearly thirty hours; I could sit another four minutes for this wonderful man. Besides, the only body part that had to work was one ear. I nodded.

He smiled as peacefully as I had ever seen. He began to strum a lovely melody, but abruptly stopped and shook both hands. "Sorry, I get nervous when I sing in front of you."

I'd heard that many times before.

"That's okay, sweetheart," I said reassuringly. *Why be nervous? A zombie doesn't respond to anything.*

"I'll start again." The guitar struck an arpeggio, then another, and Steve drew a breath to sing. Again, he stopped, flustered in embarrassment, and rolled his eyes, his thoughts seemingly in knots. Laughing nervously, he tried again.

And again.

I sat and waited.

On his fourth attempt, he sang to me with his heart embroidered in his words, his voice occasionally cracking with emotion:

Yes, I'm head over heels, and I don't know what to do,
When you look at me, when you smile at me, I want
  you more.
Could it be, do you agree, I was made to be with you

I can't catch my breath, when I look at you
I love you more...

What a beautiful song. *It was so him.* His head dipped into the body of the guitar and his words became satin, caressing my body, enveloping me in warmth, each note carrying me further into this blissful dream of mine, a man singing a love song he wrote. I allowed myself to relax even deeper, closing my eyes to soak in his love.

What woman wouldn't want this? Yes, tell me more!

Oh please say yes, you're in love with me
You can't wait to spend your life with me.
You want my hand, you want my heart,
You want to hold me evermore...
Lala la la...lala la...

My body jerked, but my eyes remained blissfully closed, at peace.

Oh come with me, I'm in love with you
I can't wait to spend my life with you.
I want your hand. I want your heart...

Funny. My dream went silent for a while. But I wanted it in technicolor. I wanted this dream to continue, so I rewound his words in my head, willing them back with awakening consciousness. I remembered hearing a line, "I can't wait to spend my life with you...I want your hand." *Wait a minute. What's going on? Is it what I think it is?*

I popped my eyes open. My dream—was real.

In front of me, I saw Steve, his eyes welled with tears, a man unable to utter the next life-changing lyric. In front of him was a woman who snapped to attention like a matador facing a charging bull.

"Won't you please…" Steve whispered, "please…" his voice trailed away, the song's melody lost in his love, "marry me?"

My mouth gaped open. I didn't see it coming. An international trip was enough, with no expectations for the future, just gratitude for sharing today.

His shoulders relaxed slightly, his mouth curved into a smile. He squinted his eyes to look at me more carefully, his awareness of the past few seconds coming into clearer focus. The man who had just waited twenty years to propose woke up too.

"Were you just sleeping?" he asked, incredulously.

"Yes! And…yes!" I squealed deliriously. Even though I'd never met any woman who slept through her marriage proposal, I was not going to be known as some loser who lied. My vision fogged through tears amped with a rush of adrenaline, pumping me out of my chair like a pogo stick into his arms.

Steve shook his head, laughed hard, and resigned himself to this life he had chosen. He took my hand and led me over to the room's safe and took out a ring box. And leading me back to the proposal site, he sat me down, bent down on one knee, and handed me the box. He wanted to do it right. And I suppose he wanted to make sure I was awake.

I opened a square, velvety, purple box with curled ribbon and was immediately confused.

I saw two rings.

One was an offset solitaire diamond ring with enough glitter to make a preschooler jealous. The other was another solitaire ring, highlighted with glistening square diamonds on the band.

Steve took one ring out, looked into my eyes and asked *the* question.

"Will you marry me?" he asked, sliding a ring large enough for a bull's nose over my size four finger. "Oh, we'll get that sized once we're home. I guessed," he said, softly. He stood and pulled me close to him.

I WAS STILL speechless.

"I had it all worked out to ask you to marry me when we were done hiking to Half Moon Bay on Tasmania next week," he explained. "But when I saw you at the airport, I just couldn't wait. I just couldn't."

My attention still fixated on the mystery of the other ring.

I asked awkwardly, "Who is this other ring for?"

Steve looked down at the box, perplexed. "Ummm," he began, "I didn't think about it. That's how the engagement ring came. Boxed like that."

I softened. The swirls on my engagement ring matched those on the band. The two solitaires interlocked. "Sweetheart, I've never heard of a woman getting two rings. I think this is my wedding band too. That's a first for m—" I began, but remembered it wasn't. I held his face in my hands, then I began shaking at the realization that my life would never be the same. My face flushed with emotions and tears. "I love you. Yes. Yes. Yes!" And I kissed him with the half century of love I still had inside of me to give.

"Can we pray?" asked Steve.

He prayed many things, I think, gratitude above all, and finally for God's guidance. And I'll never forget the words he said for the first time, words I would hear in his prayers repeatedly through the years: "God, help me be a good husband for my angel."

It was the sweetest prayer a single mom of fourteen years could hope for.

To keep me upright, we celebrated by sightseeing in downtown Melbourne, beginning with our favorite venue, a cathedral. Inside St. Mark's Irish Cathedral, on the bank of the Yarra River illumined with frosted streetlamps, I asked the priest's permission to sing my favorite praise song, "Jesus, Let Us Come to Know You" by Michael Card, knowing that the acoustics of the church's soaring transept would perfect my joy.

Afterward, Steve yodeled out his hymn, "Down by the Riverside."

Eight hours later, I stood in front of my bed and announced, "Timber," and crashed into the best dream of my life.

11

The Magic of Ten Wedding Vows, One Yacht, and One Wombat

STEVE DIDN'T WANT TO WAIT; HE WANTED TO GET MAR-ried in Australia. I needed to wait. He'd had a few months to ponder it. I was still living in the past, a full day behind, on Denver time. And I had to get it right this time.

We decided to tell our families in person when we returned. We agreed to get married in one year, to make the most of the engagement period, to make the vows solid. I'd read some-where that the word *marriage* is translatable in every language. That's how significant it is. Steve and I chose to live apart until the wedding day, because somewhere, deep inside us, despite what the world told us, love in its grandest sense is best not reflected in an experiment. The two of us, bastions of preserv-ing marriage, chose to claim its glory, its merit, its imperative

necessity of preserving that functional, oft-forgotten corner-
stone of humanity known as civilization.

My belief in marriage, in particular when children are
involved, is anchored from many places: to honor God, to
uplift Steve's understanding of his permanence in my life, to
demonstrate its merit for my daughter, to validate my students'
experiences.

Inside my memory are the faces and eyes of Katie and
my young students, classroom after classroom, as we ice-break
during our first week. Children with married parents talk
about their families and keep the cadence of their discussions
steady; some who don't have married parents (like my child)
occasionally lie and make up stories. Other times, their voices
trail into softness or vanish altogether, as if their silence
could make the conundrum disappear. And many of their
sparkling eyes glaze over and dart from me self-consciously, in
the awareness that they are different—blowing Piaget's theory
of egocentrism out the window. My erudite first graders know.
Children know. My students, overall, love the idea of parents
being married.

While the world tries to water down the value of marriage as
being obsolete or antiquated and touts freedom of expression as
its defense, waving its hand disparagingly in knowing better, no
one ever steps into my classrooms to film the faces of babies who
all too well know better. Our world spins faster than the slow-
roasted values that molded its cohesiveness, that continue to mold
our children. It seems we've lost the skills to maintain marriage's
integrity and wait for its rewards, and that is unsettling.

And, on a more pragmatic note, I had a house to sell, including an entire backyard I needed to landscape, after our litter of
foster pups uprooted every figment of foliage. Katie would be

starting high school that fall. I wanted her to get settled before we moved into Steve's house. Besides, she was only fourteen. I needed every second of maturity we could muster.

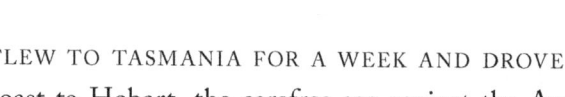

WE FLEW TO TASMANIA FOR A WEEK AND DROVE DOWN the coast to Hobart, the carefree sea against the Australian bush staging the possibilities for our future, and we started writing our vows. With a fresh legal pad, we drafted them, scribbling phrases sideways in the margins, inside the lines, across the headings.

Steve and I decided to write ten vows, the ten greatest gifts we could give each other. Plus, we left space for an extra unwritten vow that we knew we'd need later, because life likes to play tricks on people. Harnessing the power of well-defined, individual promises would fortify our marriage. I believe there must be some good karma associated with the number ten because it's the dominant numeral in human history: Ten is spiritually universal—the Kabbalist, Hindu, Jewish, Muslim, and Christian faiths honor its force. Almost one-third of the world spends a lifetime rising and falling to the call of the Ten Commandments.

Not to mention there's ten fingers and ten toes and ten bowling pins and a rocket countdown. Do you know how many words rhyme with ten? Ask my first graders. Seismologists gawk at the Richter scale that records tenfold measures of energy. Parents of toddlers, myself included, garner its might by showing off their children who can count to that profound number.

And there's this book this guy wrote called *The 10 Greatest Gifts I Give My Children* that turned into a best seller and slipped some magic in my life.

Steve and I committed to memorize our vows for life. During my divorce counseling years ago, my therapist Barbara Dalberg asked, "Do you remember your vows? You said you wrote them yourselves."

"All I remember is unfolding a piece of notebook paper while we stood at the altar," I answered, then smiled.

Barbara's smile erased mine. I found a big part of my problem.

So I asked my friends if they remembered their vows. They remembered the part "for better, for worse, in sickness and in health," but not much beyond. And I began wondering how much easier this whole idea of marriage would be if we could commit the vows into our memories instead of just pulling them out on our big anniversaries like the tenth, or the twenty-fifth, and fiftieth if we make it that far. If, as musicians, we can recite a thousand song lyrics instantaneously, if we can memorize multiplication tables and two handfuls of website passwords, we could certainly commit to memory the words that provide the scaffolding for our most intimate connection in this world.

We decided to get help from people who had been there.

Steve emailed his friends around the world, from Fortune 500 leaders and CEOs to frontline steelworkers and glass bottle assembly line workers and shared our news with a request. In part, his message asked this: "From your experience, would you please share one of your nuggets for building and nurturing a great relationship and family?"

THE WORLDWIDE NUGGETS of wisdom turned into a gold mine for us, an online counseling service. The replies flooded back, immediate and countless, from Thailand to Russia to Canada to Spain, from the armchairs of homes to factory breakrooms and from airport lounges and soccer fields, emails piled into his inbox, hundreds and hundreds of them, the writers blessing us with the gift of themselves and their hard-earned lessons of keeping and treasuring marriage. They shared timeless words rich in experience, their lives delighted in our decision to defy a complicated world and fill it with marriage.

Some wrote thousands of words back, treating Steve as a professor for some thesis project. Others wrote short-answer essays; some, a powerful line or two, but all types, equal in conviction. We printed every response and highlighted each tidbit of advice, compiled a book of quotes and bound it. Let me share some excerpts:

From Prairie Home, Nebraska: *Pull the weeds when they're small, that way you get the roots.*

From Moscow: *I'm no expert but I'll share one thing that I think is important and has sustained us: Always look forward to something together, planning a vacation, building a new house, a party, making a photo album, anything involving the two of you and those around you whom you love and hold dear.*

From Geneva: *To have a great marriage, not only do you need to love your spouse, but you also need to love your marriage.*

From Hong Kong: *I can tell you the one thing that lacked in my marriage that was profound enough to cripple it and therefore dissolve it was the lack of communication.*

From Toledo: *A marriage made in heaven is made by you.*

From Bangkok: *Hold hands and stick together.*

From Mexico City: *I don't think there is any advice I could give you that I haven't heard you speak of or seen in your writings. My one and only request is you name your first child, girl or boy, after me. Any child born after that can be yours and Barb's call.*

From Rio: *It comes down to both managing your emotional triggers. We made up some silly code words to say when we see it happening.*

From Toronto: *You and Barb have had months to get to know each other and earn each other's love and respect. Give your family members time to go through the same process.*

From New Jersey: *Don't lose the mystery. Never think it is something you just do. Of all our life experiences, marriage is the most unfathomable. It is the single human event that we can spend a lifetime experiencing and still only scratch the surface of the depths of the mystery.*

And my favorite, from Frankfurt: *Buy her flowers, every month of your anniversary date. It's a monster hit, especially with her friends. Major brownie points.*

What better marriage counseling could we receive than worldwide wisdom?

⁂

WE ARRIVED IN HOBART, A MARITIME PORT AT TASMANIA'S southern tip, and were surprised to encounter a few other unexpected visitors: 70,000 of them for the biennial Australian Wooden Boat Festival. The weekend gala brought together the most stunning wooden fleet in the southern hemisphere. The waterfront delivered a flotilla exhibition of 620 wooden sailing ships, with vibrant banners draping this quaint seaside town, a cacophony of fishy aromas, and sticky cotton candy and carte blanche merrymakers slogging Aussie Hop Hog beers—Australia at her finest.

Only bar seats were available for dinner at the Pub in the

Paddock on 12th Street. We inquired about rooms, Mary and Joseph-like. Steve liked winging it on vacations; I preferred nonrefundable reservations.

Steve addressed the bartender. "Where's the nearest hotel?"

"Dunno." She glanced over her shoulder, raising her voice, her accent mesmerizing me. "This ding-a-ling's lookin' for a room. Today. Any left in town?"

"Iffy," replied a customer. "Real iffy."

Other customers shook their heads, then grinned with knowing smiles.

"You're Americans, yes, mate?" asked a middle-aged woman in stretched-out overalls, sipping her wine.

"Yes," Steve replied proudly, expanding his chest to emphasize his Lincoln Memorial T-shirt.

"Everything's been sold-out for weeks, mate," said a man behind us. His polo shirt and khakis suited him, a gentleman with weathering gray on his temples. "You won't find anything in town for the next couple days." He paused. "But tell you what. Me and my wife," he pointed to a salty dog woman next to him, "we'd be happy to put you up on our boat."

His wife smiled, nodding in agreement—or nodding off from beer, I couldn't tell—nursing her Carlton Draught bottle.

The nearest town was two hours away, and it was already dusk. Steve stared at me, egging my thoughts. My thoughts envisioned the USS *Minnow*, Gilligan, and Lovey and Thurston Howell.

"Okay, that's very kind," Steve replied, his eyes dancing with hopes of a new adventure.

"No worries," the man said, offering his hand. "I'm James. My wife's Anna."

James and Anna polished off their drinks. They led us

to the waterfront, where we pulled out our luggage. It wasn't much. Steve's business trip was only three weeks long, and I wanted to look my best on my first international flight: three large suitcases, two carry-ons, two backpacks, our doggy bags from the bar, and a mandolin. We dragged our mountain of luggage over a crossword puzzle of patchwork docks until we reached James and Anna's boat.

It wasn't a wooden *Mayflower*. It was a sleek fifty-five-foot fiberglass yacht.

James and Anna must have missed the memo about wooden boats.

Anna teetered on the edge of the dock, three sheets and a quarter to the wind. She hurdled down onto the starboard bow and clambered aboard, the current ebbing her yacht two feet from its slip. Slightly less inebriated, James managed to help us transport our luggage across the chasm, except for Steve's large suitcase. Marked with a United HEAVY tag, the ugly green monstrosity contained all his clothes, business documents, and computer. Before Steve could stop him, James hoisted the suitcase against his knee and aimed it at Anna, swung his arm like a pendulum, and heaved it. The suitcase, having zero inertia, grazed past her fingertips and started heading south. Somehow, Anna grabbed the suitcase with her other hand as its weight jolted and molded them together like a marble carving.

Because our mound of luggage required one entire cabin, we squeezed into the one single berth remaining. I huffed and grumbled at the compressed inconvenience, having to shuffle my feet when moving around because I was unable to bend my knees, penguin-like. Finally, all tucked in, the gentle roll of the Tasman Sea lulled us to sleep. At 3:00 a.m., an intermittent, muffled melody roused me. I listened, confused.

"Steve, wake up, do you hear that?" I whispered.

"Hear what?" he mumbled.

"Listen."

He propped himself up. A familiar melody repeated itself. "Is that 'Santa Claus Is Coming to Town?'" he asked.

"That's not possible. It's February," I countered with holiday knowledge.

The little ditty replayed every thirty seconds. Disoriented, we both got up and rummaged through stuffed closets and cabin holds full of rags and tools. No luck. The melody continued to haunt the room.

"Maybe it's in the room next to us," I whispered. "I'll check. We'll never sleep until we find it."

I opened a hatch and stepped through it. A single bulb lit a large gray metal room. Gentle hums reverberated inside, and pressure gauges hissed quietly, needles steady. I relayed what the room looked like to Steve.

"You do know you're standing inside the engine room," he whispered. "And that the captain's quarters are on the other side of the room."

We finally found the culprit: a musical Christmas card, still sealed, farting off the last of its battery. Just like my recliner at home.

The next morning, James and Anna cooked us a magnificent egg breakfast, including my first serving of muesli, a sophisticated cereal with birdseed tendencies. Their dog gobbled leftovers. A shrine took center stage outside the galley; a single ivory candle burned in the center, surrounded by relics, twinkling lights framing a small bottle of sand, bamboo shoots, dainty bells, a fuzzy catnip toy, and a red collar with the name Toby. A tabby cat's photo, inside a golden frame, said it all.

Noting my interest, Anna, now fully coherent, filled in the blanks. "That's to remember our Toby," she explained, removing our plates from the table. "One afternoon when we were gone, he fell outta the boat. He must've swum around the boat for a couple hours tryin' to get back on. We found 'im floatin' next to the slip when we got back."

Now, I'm an animal lover, but I did everything I could not to picture that poor cat doing laps.

In the first two days of our engagement, Life did step up as our teacher: Together, this married team's example of generosity began suggesting some vows for us.

After Hobart, Steve still didn't want to call ahead for reservations, so we drove for a day and didn't spot even one of the island's mascots, the Tasmanian devil. Alive, that is. Tasmania has more roadkill than any place I've seen. Maybe no one cleans it up because the roads are so desolate. We drove well into the night, past midnight, into the bush of the East Coast Highlands, desperate for a night's lodging. We drove in blackness, save the Milky Way's stars and the reflective eyes of deer, for a solid two hours—no porch lights, no towns.

Finally, a dark, dilapidated billboard caught our eye. We backed up and shined our headlights on it. We struggled to read the rusted sign, with its jagged plywood edges and sun-soaked letters: "Lake Leake Chalet, 5 kilometers." An arrow pointed toward a narrow lane into the bush.

Fifteen minutes later we arrived upon an empty parking lot. One lightbulb glowed above the chalet's entrance. On the moonless night, Lake Leake Chalet, barely visible, looked like a 1950s YMCA camp frozen in time—cedar siding, warped picnic tables. Should we approach? What other choice did we have?

Steve pounded on the door and waited a few minutes. He

pounded again. No answer. He shrugged his shoulders and turned away toward our car.

The door creaked open an inch. We looked down and saw two eyes studying us.

"Can we stay here tonight?" Steve asked.

The door didn't move. Neither did the eyes.

"We would appreciate it, it's late and there's no other place around here," he pleaded.

The door opened. Before us, a young girl appeared, her face in the shadows, hair matted. Perhaps twelve years old, she wore faded Superman pajamas with footed feet. She didn't speak but stepped back, allowing us inside. She turned and motioned for us to follow her down a dimly lit corridor, where she turned a corner. She pointed to a door, slightly ajar, and motioned us inside. She began to leave.

"Wait!" said Steve. "Where's the bathroom?"

The girl walked down a few doors and stopped. She touched its handle, she left.

I turned on the light. A single bulb lit up a metal bunk bed with sagging coils and thin mattresses. Threadbare quilts topped the sheets with linty balls. Musty summer camp memories flooded me. Steve walked over to a window.

"These curtains might disintegrate if I touch them," he said, fingering them lightly.

After he knocked down the cobwebs in the shower stall, we each took quick showers and put our clothes back on for the night. He turned off the light bulb, and I prayed the scaffolding of the bunk wouldn't collapse as he squeaked himself into the divot of the bed above me.

"Are we safe here? Will we be alive in the morning?" I asked, half joking, half not.

"I don't know."

I reached up my hand. "Hold my hand."

Hand-holding can never be underestimated.

The next morning, as Steve searched for the girl to pay her, I waited outside. Splintered split rail fences outlined three corrals long unused, with dried tangles of rocks and weeds confirming its unkempt condition. The bush began where the corrals ended, with eucalyptus branches casting heavy shadows over the corrals and the chalet's A-frame roof. Weathered wagons, wheels missing, slumped near the corral gate, and I imagined a vibrant horse ranch here years ago. Overgrown in spotty patches of rye grass, a narrow gravel road disappeared into higher, healthy fields of golden tufts.

Against the farthest fence, something caught my eye, a gray streak scurrying along the ground. It stopped. I walked several paces right for a closer look. The grayness bolted to my right also.

What was it?

I stepped up on the split rail fence for a better view. This time, the gray shape, about the size of a loaf of bread, hesitated, then shot straight toward me. It didn't stop.

"Steve!" I screamed as I ran toward our car. "Something's chasing me!"

The gray streak didn't stop. It toddled low to the ground, fast as a rabbit.

"Steve!"

"Scooter!" said the girl's voice.

The gray blob stopped abruptly and shuffled toward her, standing next to Steve at the chalet's entrance.

"Scooter!" she called again, laughing.

Scooter chugged along as fast as his three-inch feet could

carry him until the girl scooped him up in her arms and held him like an infant, on his back, nuzzled into her chest, his two-inch-long claws skyward.

"What is that?" I asked.

"This is Scooter," the girl answered.

"What is Scooter?" I repeated. I had heard some folklore that after God created all the animals, he took all his leftover parts and created the Australian ones.

"He's a baby wombat, and he's mine. His mom got hit. I found him on the side of the road."

"A baby wombat?" I turned into one of my first graders who squeal when they see a picture of puppies in a basket.

Steve interjected. "Can Barb hold him?"

This was better than kissing the pope's ring. Or summer vacation.

"Sure."

I watched her gently place Scooter into my arms, like a baby. I marveled at his claws.

"How old?"

"About seven or eight months. He sleeps with me." Her face brightened. "And—his poop is cube shaped!"

"No way!" I said. I couldn't wait to tell my students this useless, fascinating fact.

"Barb, this is Tara," said Steve.

And I relaxed and asked my go-to teacher question: "What grade are you in, Tara?"

Tara smiled but didn't answer. Tara lived in the middle of the bush. She didn't go to school. She just shares her wombat with a dingbat like me.

Her father had left for a few days on a lumberjacking trip. Scooter broke her shyness barrier, and Tara showed us the rest of her menagerie behind a gray barn: two joeys, a pasture of deer, a litter of kittens, and a couple Australian cattle dogs. Her zombielike personality became authentic and alive with our questions about her life and what she loved; no longer would I remember Tara's Superman pajamas first. I would remember who she deeply was, the young girl who unselfishly dropped Scooter into my arms and left an indelible stench on my sweatshirt.

I wanted my vows to Steve to be that freely given, minus the odor.

I flew home on my birthday. Steve upgraded my seat, wangling the system by playing a ditty on his mandolin for the ticket agent. I took a picture of the Sydney Opera House from the plane's window and crossed the date line so I could celebrate my birthday twice, once with Steve and again with my family back in Denver. No surprise, Steve gave me another ten birthday gifts as we parted ways—this time as he parted toward Spain.

I was going home to get married.

12

The Unexpected Gifts
of Engagement

AS WE WERE SEATED AT MY KITCHEN TABLE, I TOLD KATIE and my mom the news.

They had different reactions. My mom threw her fist in the air and yelled, "YES!" like she had won an Olympic medal. Katie began to cry. Unlike me, Katie and my mom had predicted the Australian engagement, but the reality of Katie's changing world caught up with her.

"I saw it coming, Mom, and I'm happy for you," she said between sniffles, cuddling Honey, "but for so long it's just been you and me. That's going to be hard."

I hugged her and assured her we were waiting a year, largely in part to give her time to adjust to the news, and to enable her to begin high school in our own home. I also pointed out that she personally would have as much room to herself at Steve's home as she did in our entire house. We would decorate it any way she'd like. Steve and I had already discussed that.

"But this is our home, Mom. Honey. Cooper, Ellie May. Our dirty kitchen," she sputtered. "All our memories are here. Our parties, our sleepovers, our Christmases. Everything."

This was harder than I thought. Katie had acted like a strong young lady for a year. Now she was a porcelain doll. I realized she had been putting on bravado because she wanted me happy.

"Trusting Steve with *your* life came long before I trusted him with my own," I explained. "That fact was my number one determiner. And now, I can trust him with mine."

"But where's your ring?" she asked. My mom raised her eyebrows too.

"It's getting sized for a few weeks. Katie, you won't even have to change schools," I added.

"Can Honey sleep with me when we move in?" she asked.

Not a problem.

"Yes. Steve doesn't want Honey on any furniture."

We all laughed.

WHEN THE VANNOY FARM FIELDS BEGAN SPROUTING THAT spring, Ma welcomed me into the family with the most unusual engagement gift.

"Barb. Barbie. My Barbie doll!" Ma's voice ripped like sunbeams through the phone's speaker. "Well, Barb, I have some great news. Oh, yes, I do! The beans sold today for a great price, so I have enough money now for the down payment on your headstone. For your engagement! Isn't that wonderful?"

I stared at Steve. *Welcome to the family*, his eyes answered back.

"Now, Barb, what is your exact birthday?"

My future mother-in-law was plotting my death, in every sense. I already had plans for my death. Three of them. Compliments of my dad, the first was in serene, Mt. Pleasant Cemetery in Sioux Falls. When he bought plots for my mom and himself, he bought up four more surrounding plots.

"To keep the riffraff out," he had explained.

The second plan, of my own volition before meeting Steve, involved my ashes being scattered over Monterey Bay. Steve and I had briefly talked about the third one. We would be buried together atop the lighted cross in Denver, the one we saw on our first hike.

But now, my future Nebraska mother-in-law played her trump card—the family cemetery in Waverly, Nebraska, home of the Waverly Vikings, as evidenced by the horned head on the water tower guarding the cemetery.

What Ma had put together, let no one put asunder. I couldn't disappoint her. How could I put this woman's zeal to rest? I sighed. Her ulterior motive, above all, was love. With Ma's plan for the rest of my life, I did what many women are programmed to do: I spread myself thin.

Literally.

I agreed to four resting places.

"Wow, Ma, that's great news!" I stammered. "What a...surprise! I don't know what to say. It's generous and makes me feel, well...like I'm part of the family already."

"Tell Ma your birthday, angel," Steve said.

"My birthday, Ma, my birthday is February 19, 1962."

"Just let me write that down. February 19, 1962," she repeated. I pictured her sitting at her kitchen table, her shaky hand recording the date on an AARP notepad. "There. Perfect! How wonderful!"

Thank God the beans sold, I reminded myself.

"Now, Barb. What name do you want on your headstone?"

That was a fair question. I had three names to choose from already, not including the name I would pick when I married Steve. I hadn't even said "I do" yet, but Ma decided to set my next name forever in stone with her son's surname.

Smart lady.

"Oh, Ma! Umm, let's put BARBARA LYNN VANNOY." I felt strangely powerful. I wondered if anybody else ever had inscribed their name on their headstone before their name existed.

"I'll get this to the mason first thing in the morning. You and Steve can see your new headstone when you come out over Memorial Day. It's so wonderful!"

I acquiesced, and Steve grabbed my hand, celebrating the heart of this gracious, giving woman. *The apple doesn't fall far from the tree.* I liked this tree, this giving tree, of Ma. And I learned that her son bears her fruit, living in her shade all these years.

A few months later, Steve and I traveled to Waverly's Rose Hill Cemetery. I saw my new headstone feathered in Kentucky bluegrass. I did three things.

1. I pulled a few dandelions and sprigs of clover that had sprouted in front of my name, then compulsively pulled all the other weeds from the family plots surrounding mine. Their farming roots had already settled into my bones.
2. I hugged Ma, thanking her for the inexplicable engagement present.
3. I touched the rough granite edge of my headstone, trying to make sense of the weirdly eternal moment, and noticed

something familiar. The granite was the same stone, with the same typesetting, as my dad's headstone in Mt. Pleasant.

I belonged.

AS WE STARTED WORKING OUT OUR VOWS, ONE OF THEM became obvious:

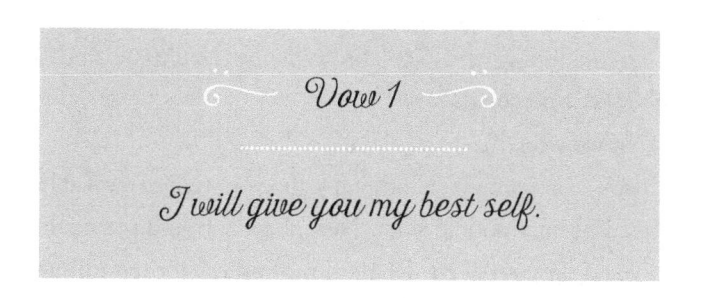

Vow 1

I will give you my best self.

Easy enough, so I decided to start living that one right away. Since my fiancé thought I was beautiful, I began viewing myself through his eyes and committed to treat myself that way. I ordered some new makeup from Amazon and noticed a "Gift message" box, so I clicked the square and wrote a complimentary note to myself for when it arrived. I typed: "Barb, you are such a beautiful woman, inside and out, and you deserve this."

When my makeup arrived, I realized Amazon charged me $8.95 for my sentiment.

Steve deserved to have a woman with beautiful legs. The spider veins in mine looked like a road map of California, with a prominent varicose vein snaking south like Interstate 5. So I made an appointment to get rid of them with sclerotherapy, with Steve paying for the procedure, since I couldn't afford it.

The dermatologist opened the door, her assistant on her heels. Their combined positive energy spun Einstein's atom out of orbit. Waaaaaay too many protons.

"Hello! I'm Dr. Wilson!" She offered her hand and her smile at the same time and motioned to her assistant. "This is Jan!" Both looked young enough that they shouldn't be driving. Dr. Wilson had a blonde bob and Jan had shoulder-length pigtails that reminded me of that Hush Puppy dog.

Since I wanted to be respectful of Steve's generosity, I only made a ten-minute session, which still cost hundreds. I confessed, "I'm nervous doing this, so I brought my earphones and iPod. Don't take it personal."

"Oh, we won't!"

If you've never had sclerotherapy and you want to try it at home, do this: Put on a poodle skirt. Next, have a friend place a living beehive under your skirt. Remain motionless for ten minutes.

I turned on my earphones and started listening to Jim Brickman's soft piano ballads, for exactly three seconds. Dr. Wilson injected Sotradecol, a failed experiment of rat poison. Its sting headed straight up that blue varicose vein into my cerebral cortex. I needed music that would cover up the pain my brain registered. I needed hard rock. I knew an artist's name but couldn't focus enough to find him on iTunes. And the doctor kept poking.

What's his name? What's his name? What's his name? my brain pleaded.

My brain didn't know. But God answered. Rick Springfield.

"I'm gonna play Rick Springfield," I announced, fumbling through my iTunes.

"Jessie's Girl!" the duo shouted simultaneously, their voices louder than Rick's guitar inside my ears. I took a hit of Rick as I pressed the title on my iPod.

The song blared and soothed like a Bible verse in troubled times. It didn't wash away anything like a Bible verse, though. The sting kept flowing.

I thought joining Rick's song would help. So I sang—well, I shouted—because like a child I thought singing loudly and a little faster than the song would make the sting hurt less.

Oh Lord, they wouldn't…they couldn't…but they did. They chimed in, wishing they had Jessie's Girl, too. Dr. Wilson lifted the needle into the air and squirted a few drops of the rat poison. Then she let me have it again.

I refused to sing the chorus. Who were the adults here?

When the doctor finished the procedure, Jan asked what kind of Band-Aids I wanted—flesh colored, Scooby-Doo, or Disney Princess. I thought hard, not wanting to make a mistake. I chose Disney Princess and counted twenty-two of them on my legs. Jan rolled on compression hose, uncomfortably snugger than the tights my mother rolled on my first-grade legs during South Dakota's blustery blizzards.

My next stop was next door, my first trip to a spa for microdermabrasion, another procedure Steve bankrolled for me. Microdermabrasion is a synonym for exfoliation that's been exponentially amped up. It's like vacuuming your face. When I decided to have microdermabrasion and a facial, I had called the spa and asked for an appointment. They asked if I'd like to try a new esthetician. I said yes.

I showed up at the spa, with no makeup, of course, hair pulled back, ready for a soothing facial and, later, microdermabrasion.

My esthetician greeted me in the waiting area, the person assigned to view every enlarged pore on my nose, squeeze every blackhead out of existence, and add serum inside wrinkles induced by single parenting and first-grade mobs.

This beautiful young lady with flawless skin, exquisite makeup, and model-high cheekbones was none other than my former fourth-grade student, Ashley, whom I taught fifteen years before.

"Ms. Lynn!" Ashley exclaimed.

"Call me Barb," I answered. Anything to gap the time warp.

"Oh, I couldn't do that, it would be too weird."

Like this wasn't.

She was pleasant but remained professional. I, on the other hand, became self-conscious and acted like I had forgotten my homework. Just like she couldn't call me by my first name, I couldn't blot out the fact that, as an adult, she prepared to embark on an excavation expedition across my face. I could only think of her as My Former Fourth-Grade Student.

She escorted me into a dimly lit facial room where Gregorian music of flutes and chimes beat softly. We small-talked about her family. My Former Fourth-Grade Student asked me to undress from the waist up.

"You can keep your bra on if you want," she offered.

Let the relaxing begin.

A note about My Former Fourth-Grade Student. She was the Chatty Cathy of my classroom, a major feat considering I had a whopping thirty-five kids in that class. Her Siamese twin was Karen, and together they ruled my classroom like Sunday morning talk shows. My Former Fourth-Grade Student also had the audacity to slip out of my class and walk home in the middle of the afternoon. She bolted as we moved desks from one classroom to another. My principal entered my classroom after receiving an outraged phone call from the girl's mother.

"Barb, did you know that Ashley walked home fifteen minutes ago, across ten lanes of traffic on Kipling Street?"

Nope. I had thirty-five children in my class, including four children diagnosed with ADHD. Another student was suspended for setting his desk on fire. How about the boy who brought in a double-edged serrated knife for show-and-tell? Or the girl who ended up in juvenile detention before she was fourteen? Not to mention—well, I will mention—the child who needed counseling because he drew pornographic drawings on his Friday spelling test. I proved it by retrieving his test from the school's dumpster Saturday morning, his F grade stained with pizza sauce. I had to outwit a combative, hungry squirrel to retrieve it.

Mind you, this was a fourth-grade class in 1989, way back when teaching was easy.

(As a trivial aside, the school district couldn't afford to pay a paraprofessional aide to help me keep track of my darlings until after Thanksgiving, so, nope, I didn't know that My Former Fourth-Grade Student went AWOL.)

Yet, I must state that every single one of my students passed their fourth-grade proficiencies in reading and math requirements that year. Because I polished off my first whole bottle of beer that year at age twenty-eight, that's why.

And also because I belong to a miracle network of game changers known as American public elementary teachers.

So how My Former Fourth-Grade Student, this spunky spitfire of a girl, found a career inside soothing music and darkened rooms is beyond my comprehension, but suffice to say, she had some karma coming.

Braless, I heard My Former Fourth-Grade Student enter the dimmed room. She sat behind my head and slowly began massaging my temples and proceeded to wash my face with an astringent specifically designed to enlarge my pores for her to see. She shined a spotlight on my face to illuminate me like a full moon, craters and all.

My Former Fourth-Grade Student proceeded to rub lotion on my face and neck. Next, she massaged between my eyebrows, where the wrinkles she gave me were born.

"You're very tense," she whispered.

Finally, my feelings mattered to her.

"Now, I'm just going to clean your nose up a little bit, Ms. Lynn," whispered My Former Fourth-Grade Student.

I'd recognize that whisper anywhere.

She took out her mining pick and excavated all the filth on my face, unclogging pores, the papules and pustules exploding and thick sebum leaping out for joy, her fingertips gently brushing away the excrements.

"You have lovely skin, Ms. Lynn," she said.

"Thank you," I replied, keeping my eyes closed for fear I'd discover this was for real. "But how do I get rid of the dark circles under my eyes?" I asked, trying to change the subject.

My Former Fourth-Grade Student recited a litany of products and vowed to leave some samples for me at the counter. I listened to her speech, checking for correct syntax, and wasn't surprised that it was beautiful because she had had so much practice speaking the English language in my classroom.

When she finished my facial, My Former Fourth-Grade Student prepared to vacuum my face and neck.

"Have you ever had microdermabrasion?"

"No."

"Well, this suctions the dead layers of skin and reveals your healthy layer of skin underneath. It will be a little pink for a couple of days, so avoid sunlight."

I planned on avoiding life, in general, for at least a week.

My Former Fourth-Grade Student turned on her minia-ture Hoover vacuum. "If this is too much, let me know. It feels like a gentle carpet cleaning."

She began sucking my face, carefully plowing row after row, like a John Deere tractor in a cornfield, removing the topsoil of dead skin. Afterward, it felt so clean that I could have run to confession and bared all my transgressions as easily and carefree as a butterfly might visit a flower, linger in delight, and flit away. I felt as if all my sins had been sucked away.

Not to mention my pride.

My Former Fourth-Grade Student's voice was velvetlike, completely contrary to the riptide of undercurrent continually pelting me for nine months in the classroom. She was a bright student and, now, a poised, beautiful adult. I wondered if My Former Fourth-Grade Student went home afterward and told her mom about me.

At least she drove there this time.

.... ⁊⁊⁊ ....

AT THE END OF MY SCHOOL YEAR, MY CLASS CELEBRATED my engagement and threw me a bridal shower. Thanks to my room moms, corrugated wedding bells, white linens, punch bowls, and mints filled my classroom. My kids played a pin-the-veil-on-the-bride game on our calendar bulletin board. Metallic silver and gold gift bags topped the reading table in the back, near the spot where I passed a note in class to Steve.

My newly bloomed James, wide-eyed, handed me his present, his enthusiasm spilling over into the bag as my class sat crisscrossed, apple sauced on the floor beneath me, their attention glued to my present. I shuffled through pink tissue paper until I found a white tissue taped neatly in a square, like a large note. I opened it delicately, then pulled it out, higher and higher.

My face raced through every shade of Crayola's box of 120, finally landing on apricot with a smudge of wild watermelon. I kept pulling out a peach gown, a lacy, silk Olga nightgown. Lowcut. James's mother grinned. My kids covered their mouths in shock, then squealed.

"Fat's aw wight!" James cried out, speech impediments still intact. "You's owd...," he said, eyeing me sideways, "you's owd to be a bwide, but you's just a wate bwoomer too!"

ONCE SCHOOL WAS over, I took advantage of the summer vacation and cleaned out my house, since it would be put on the market six months later, after our marriage. Katie and I would move into Steve's home. Simultaneously, my mom decided it was time for her to downsize her own house, my childhood home of thirty-four years.

Looking back now, the timing makes perfect sense. When my dad died in 1999, my mother joined my ranks and became a single parent also, a reference usually reserved for younger women. But like any parent, she would have liked to have someone to talk to about her children's complications as adults, because I had heard that one never stops being a parent. Together, my mother and I had weathered single-mom challenges on our individual home fronts, making repairs on fixed budgets, attending events alone and pretending it didn't bother us, filling our own Christmas stockings.

But after Dad died, Mom's house became Katie's second home. My mother stepped in full-time and co-parented Katie with me for over thirteen years. At Grandma's house, Katie enjoyed every necessity (and luxury, having a grandparent) a child deserved—a bedroom that answered to her changing interests, closets stuffed with clothes, soccer balls, a school desk. Being engaged to Steve translated into an unchartered life purpose for Mom, as well as a new relationship with me as I began navigating Katie's life with Steve.

I liken mothers who help raise their grandchildren to the empty pages and white spaces inside a book, the extra pages at the beginning and end of the books, the white space found at the end of chapters. Readers flip through these sections, unaware of the necessary roles these spaces play in the construction of the story itself, these vital, invisible parts that hold the story together. Most readers unconsciously disregard these blank spaces, choosing instead to focus on the story's visible drama and characters, unaware that empty pages and spaces serve to mold a story into a meaningful retelling. White space in a book frames its story.

Without my mother, my engagement wouldn't have happened. She rounded out my confidence, back to a bona fide woman after I was barely human, sprawled on a bathroom floor, heaving into the toilet when divorce papers were filed. She showed me where to put my foot on a staircase when tears made it impossible for me to see. "Mom! All I want to be when I grow up is a stay-at-home mom!" I wailed—fully aware that being a stay-at-home mom was harder than being a teacher. She was the one who showed up at every soccer game, assembly, sick day. The silent one who created scrapbooks for Katie when I didn't have time to sit down. The one who made duplicate photos of Katie, boxes and boxes of them. The parent every child deserves.

As Katie and I watched the moving van leave my childhood home (and Katie's), she said, "Mom, there go my moving boxes of memories."

My forever mom gave me the courage to stand up and enjoy life again, as Ma, my new mom, loved me enough to plot my final resting place.

A FEW WEEKS before our wedding, Steve and I sat down at his dining room table and finalized our wedding vows. Because we had to unravel all our years of single living, one year of writing vows seemed barely respectful for the privilege of it. Over several months, we emailed drafts back and forth, refining them over numerous dinners, editing each other's work. We had two versions of vows: our short version consisted of ten sentences. I penned them in calligraphy, ensuring I left space for that extra, elusive eleventh vow at the bottom. We sent them to Ma, so she could embellish the vows with her artwork around the borders. The long version is what we would recite on our wedding day.

It was 725 words long. We tried not to cut corners.

Unbeknownst to our daughters, we had also created ten vows we would share with them.

We wanted to build an intentional life, and our vows were our lifeline in creating it. We had to get it right this time.

BECAUSE OF STEVE'S allergies to dog hair, Katie and I interviewed families, loving but clueless enough to take in Cooper, and we got lucky in rehoming him. Ellie May died in my arms, the only rabbit I knew who loved sunning himself on velvet couches.

Hypoallergenic Honey, on the other hand, would move with Katie and me. I introduced Honey to her new digs as Steve traveled. She sniffed every corner of Steve's house, scurrying from room to room, then she jumped on the couch.

"No!"

Confused, Honey jumped down, ran a few circles, then sprinted upstairs to Steve's bedroom and tried out his recliner.

"No! No, Honey!"

She cowered, feeling guilty, not knowing why. I felt guilty, too, and did know why, because my dog and I were codependent. "No, Honey, you can't do that either." I picked her up and patted her new dog bed. "Here, baby, try this," I said cheerfully. "Here's where you'll sleep." Honey stared me down. She jumped off the recliner. She sniffed her bed, walked across it, and leaped onto the nearby loveseat. She curled up in its corner, eyeing me, testing me.

I plopped down next to my girl. "I know the feeling, Honey. Living in someone else's house will take some getting used to."

AN UNEXPECTED MELANCHOLY arrived with the impending end of my single parenting days. On December 31, the day before our wedding, Katie and I decided to spend the day together, just the two of us, soaking in the last of life as we knew it. That night, we pulled out the hide-a-bed, popped popcorn, and watched our favorite movie, *Ever After*, a French Cinderella movie starring Drew Barrymore, an ironic nod to my life. We'd memorized the movie, but one quote particularly struck home, the one where Prince Henry asks Danielle de Barbarac to be his wife.

"Is that what it was like when Steve proposed, Mom?" asked Katie, tossing popcorn to Honey next to her.

"Hard to know. I was barely awake."

"Mom, I really am happy for you."

I loved this girl more than my own life. She had been my reason for getting up, for doing a good job teaching, for giving my life purpose. When she was one and saw me weeping on the stairs after my divorce, she toddled over to the kitchen, grabbed the dishtowel, and returned to wipe my eyes. *She was one year old.*

"Kay, this marriage is going to last this time," I promised her, squeezing her hand. "And I know it's going to take some time getting used to Steve." I shook my head. "I don't know of any other girl who has so many amazing father figures in her life." Katie had my dad, Pastor Del, Mike, and Steve. "This is as big of a change for you as it is for me, and you've been great." I paused, collecting all my humility, and stuffed it into a tea-cup-sized voice. "I'm so sorry I brought you into a broken home."

"Mom!" She jerked back defensively, shocked. "Mom! It never was a broken home with you. The only home you ever gave me is a full one, loving...compassionate...whole." Adamant, she added, "Never say that to me again."

I kissed her cheek. "Thank you." The climax of *Ever After* interrupted us.

"Wait for it, Mom, here it comes, here it comes, say it, say it—"

We chorused the part that we knew so well, the best redemptive line of this Cinderella movie, the underdog line in movies that made all the wrongs right.

ON NEW YEAR'S Eve, Katie and I took Honey to the nearby greenbelt one last time, the place where Steve had phoned me two years before. And we honored our single-parent family traditions: ate at Einstein Bagels, added a stocking cap to a Kohl's lingerie mannequin, took in a movie, shared hot chocolate at Barnes and Noble, and sucked on Tootsie Roll Pops from the Safeway.

I had kissed her at midnight on New Year's Eve, and we lit bottle rockets and spelled our names with sparklers. And when I climbed into my bed for the last time, I called out to her, "Katie? You are the light of my—"

"Life," she called back from her bedroom.

"Child of my—"

"Soul." Her voice grew softer.

"Angel of my—"

"Dreams, Mom."

above left: Steve's home, perched high in the Rocky Mountain foothills, overlooking Denver. *above right:* Professional photo of Steve Vannoy, featured on the website of his company, Pathways to Leadership, 2006. *below:* Me, in my elementary school class picture, where I perpetually began repeating first grade. Sioux Falls, South Dakota, 1968. (I'm second row from the front, fourth from left, the only girl with a fountain on the top of her head).

above left: Class picture day portrait of my daughter, Katie, in her middle school yearbook. *above right:* The free J.C. Penney portrait of Katie and me (2008). *below:* The unbiased first-grade teacher with her favorite Teacher's Pet, Katie, Bear Creek Elementary, 1999.

above: The Lemke family. From left, Jillene, Mom, me, Mike, Barb, Steve in Puerto Vallarta, 2015. No family picture exists where we aren't eating. *below left:* Honey, heartbeat at my feet. *below right:* Helen (Ma) Vannoy, 2012. Photo taken for Lutheran church directory.

above: Cooper (front and center). Our foster puppies, the scamps who chomped down the maple tree, 2005. *below:* Me, ready for my first lunar walk on Colorado's fourteener, Longs Peak, Rocky Mountain National Park, 2006.

above: Me, the newly engaged fiancée sleepwalking along
the Yarra River in downtown Melbourne, February 2007.
below: Steve on Wineglass Bay, Tasmania, 2007.

above left: Scooter, the baby wombat, Lake Leake Chalet, Tasmania, 2007.
above right: At my headstone in Rose Hill Cemetery, Waverly, Nebraska.
We raced to see who would put flowers on my grave first. Steve won.

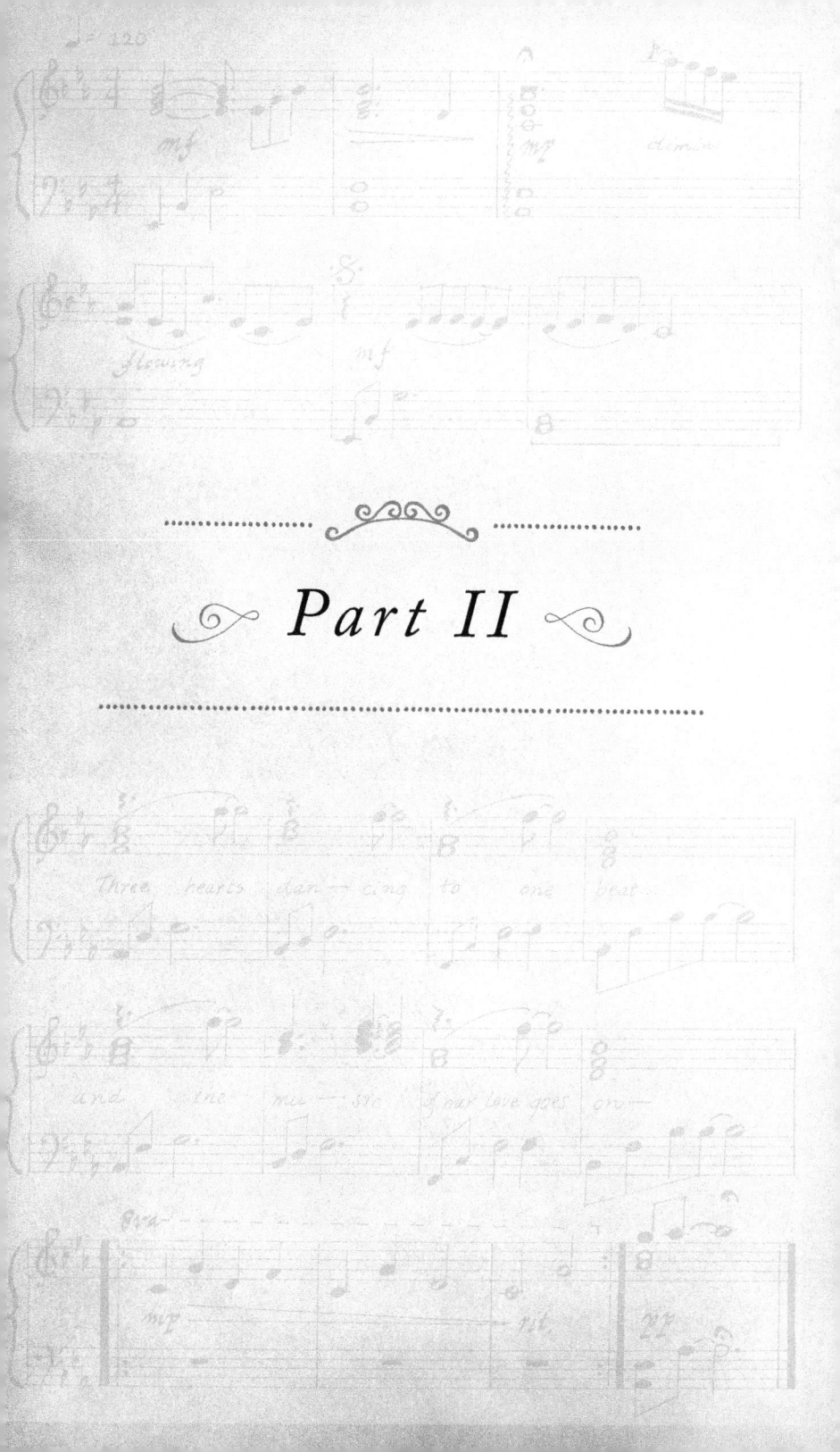

Part II

Our Vows

- I will see and trust your sacred goodness
- I will put you and us first
- I will renew our love daily
- I will forgive myself and you to protect and nurture us back to wholeness
- I will use our union to serve and build our family
- I will give my best self to you
- I will step into our moments with gratitude
- I will celebrate and support your unique unfolding
- On essential points, I will ask for special requests
- I will welcome God as our partner through daily prayer

13

DIY Wedding Day

I WENT ALL OUT FOR MY WEDDING DRESS. I BOUGHT IT ON eBay for $50. It promptly arrived in a 9-inch x 12-inch manila envelope. At first I was appalled, then appreciative; the seller had the professionalism to bubble wrap it. It was my dream dress, featured in an old *Brides* magazine, late season from Nordstrom, and by some dumb luck it appeared in my size on eBay.

I opened with a bidding price of $25. But some other fun-sucking bidder had the audacity to outbid me by $20. With only four hours left in the pricing war, I summoned the courage to leave my competition in the dust. My ivory gown hangs before me now on my armoire, just outside our bedroom. When I see it, I relive my wedding day.

"Where's my dress?" I asked Katie as we sat inside our SUV, loaded on the morning of the big day. Packed inside my Escape, I'd stuffed last-minute essentials one needs to permanently move into another home: your child, your dog, houseplants, canned vegetables, makeup, ungraded papers, and dirty underwear from the previous day.

And a man's wedding ring.

"Mom, I packed your dress. It's in the back," Katie answered, impatiently. She checked her watch nervously.

Who was getting married today?

I grinned. My smile brought us both to the present moment, to the time between the ticks of a clock. Her eyes softened and filled with amusement. Time stood still as we sealed the significance of the moment, the three of us (don't forget the dog), one last time. Katie surveyed the Beverly Hillbillies' mound of belongings behind us in the SUV, rolled those beautiful teen-aged eyes, and confirmed what she regretfully suspected from the start: *Yes, this is my mother.*

"Only you and me," she said, referring to the method in which we operated for thirteen years. "I love you, Mom. Let's do this."

What she didn't know was that the night before, at 2:30 a.m., I knelt at her bedside, praying. *Thank you for being there for Katie and me for thirteen years, God. I found a good man. I'm a good woman. Make our marriage worthy in Your eyes. Protect us all.* That was the second time in my life I knelt next to her in the middle of the night, praying for the two of us. The other time was when I stood over her crib, the night before her dad and I appeared in court and finalized our divorce.

Steve helped us unpack our final load. We reviewed the ceremony details as Pastor Del arrived. He would also serve as our photographer. Katie and I went upstairs to prepare. Honey, the ring bearer, followed.

Steve and I both had large first weddings. My first wedding included five bridesmaids, four banquet lines, three pastors, two children's choirs, and a groom in a white tuxedo. Steve's wedding included 400 guests in the bride's family mansion, with one room designated for hundreds of high-society gifts. One of two bands even flew in from out of state for the gala. Because of this, Steve wanted an intimate ceremony, a ceremony that highlighted vows and family. Only our daughters would attend. Plus Honey.

Steve felt so adamant about a small wedding I prayed I would be invited too.

This request was difficult for me. I wanted my immediate family to attend. My mom, brothers, and sister-in-law had helped me recover into single-parent living and raise Katie—celebrate her life, kiss her owies, teach her bike riding, sing karaoke with her. It was my first test of putting my husband's needs above all others. The last time I married, I followed tradition and had it my way. This time, I followed my husband's desire, and Steve agreed to my request to hold a large, formal reception in our home later that summer.

Ten minutes before the wedding, I called my mom.

"Mom," I began with a lumpy throat, "I love you. Thank you for being here and sacrificing for Katie and me for thirteen years." We cried, and my heart broke because I knew I was breaking hers. At 11:30, with Honey at our heels, my beautiful daughter, my maid of honor, walked me down two flights of stairs into a fairytale.

In the sunroom, a thousand twinkling lights welcomed me, their sparkles hyphenating blossoms of pink- and peach-fringed hibiscus and redolent jasmine flown in from Hawaii. Every expression of color greeted me: white-tipped lilies with yellow-fingered stars, laceleaf blushing through its shiny petals, rosy bougainvillea vining the stairs, angel wing begonias' frosted leaves trimming our wedding table, with two dozen long-stemmed white roses next to a small, aged treasure box in its center. Dozens of candles glinted against colored vases, enchanting the room like a holy place, the iridescent lighting and blooming colors swirling into living stained-glass windows.

I saw Steve's eyes. The rest of him blended into some magical figment of my greatest expression of hope, desire, a lifetime prayer that had landed squarely three feet in front of me. And he wasn't going anywhere.

My handsome husband's eyes filled with tears when he saw me.

Steve wasn't the only one who cried. Honey began whining also, because she must have sensed life wasn't about her any longer. As I introduced Pastor Del to Ali and Emmy, Honey began upstaging the ceremony by disappearing behind palm trees and refusing to join us. I insisted that Katie strip our rings from Honey's dress and remove her from the ceremony itself so she wouldn't overshadow my moment. Pastor Del begrudgingly put my dog in our SUV inside the garage on that cold January day.

He opened the Lutheran Book of Worship, bookmarked for the Order of Service of Marriage. "The grace of our Lord Jesus Christ, the love of God, and the communion of the Holy Spirit be with you all."

He paused, listened to the silence, and resumed. "Eternal God, our creator and redeemer, as you gladdened the wedding at Cana—" He closed the Book of Worship.

"Excuse me, I'm worried about Honey out there." Technically her shepherd, having baptized her on April Fools' Day, Pastor Del left us, the ninety-nine sheep in the wilderness, and went after the one sheep that needed rescuing. He briefly put our nuptials on hold, then returned, exclaiming, "Rejoice with me! For I have found the one who was lost and placed her in Steve's warm library."

"Alone? With my $6,000 carpeting?" Steve asked, blankly.

We continued our service as our daughters shared readings, from Gibran's *The Prophet*, from Psalms ("Oh magnify the Lord with me, let us exalt His name together"), and from John 17 ("Father, let my followers be One as we are One"). Pastor Del delivered our marriage sermon. Since Del and I had conducted dozens of weddings together (with me as the wedding singer), he pleased me when I heard him include his signature quip, "And just remember, Steve, the woman is always right."

Steve laughed. Nervously, though.

I laughed too. I had God on my side.

It was time for our music and our vows. Steve pulled out our two-page, single-spaced vows, the 725-word long version. Pastor Del stepped back, alarmed.

"Those are your vows? They look more like a manifesto." He shook his head. "All right, let's—"

Steve and I asked everyone to leave the sunroom.

They couldn't believe it.

Steve and I wanted to sing our wedding music to each other, privately. We also wanted to exchange our wedding vows privately.

As awkward as a pastor would be up and leaving in the middle of a wedding he was conducting, Pastor Del and the girls plodded up the stairs and closed the sunroom doors, granting us complete intimacy.

With Steve on guitar, we serenaded three songs to each other: "I'll Still Be Loving You," "Longer," and "I'm Head Over Heels," Steve's proposal song. Celine Dion's and Andrea Bocelli's "The Prayer" would wait for our reception.

The vows came next. Steve started. He read our long version, the 725-word edition, pausing after each vow to reflect on what it meant to him.

Fifteen minutes passed.

Then it was my turn.

Ten minutes passed.

Through the closed sunroom door, Pastor Del yelled, "Can we start to eat?"

I heard Honey, presumably barking for scraps.

Katie didn't wait for an answer. "Yes! Yes!"

Our wedding party began chowing down hors d'oeuvres.

After our vows, we presented each other with the small, aged treasure box on the wedding table. The box represented our marriage, but the inside was empty. We needed to fill the box, our marriage, every day, with loving actions, intentions, newness.

With our vows and presentation of our box completed, we invited the family and Pastor Del back inside the sunroom. Honey pranced in too. Pastor Del was irritable. "What could possibly take that long?" he asked. "I don't even want to know what you were probably doing in here."

"We're ready for the rings now," Steve said.

With our daughters present, Pastor Del blessed the rings. I remember how Steve's ring glinted over his masculine hand. I remember worrying how my size four ring would fit over my size six arthritic knuckle.

We surprised the girls with a candelabra centerpiece with five candles, one for each of us. The candelabra would be lit at holiday gatherings. We lit it, signifying the unity of our new family, and again surprised our daughters by reciting our vows to them, ten of them. Vows of being their champions, of being their sanctuary, of honoring and encouraging the relationship with their natural parents.

Pastor Del pronounced us husband and wife.

I didn't know a man's lips could be so gentle.

I didn't know my spirit could be so full.

I had a hunch that Honey had done a number on our $6,000 carpet.

ON OUR WEDDING night, I tucked Honey into her bed on the floor next to our queen bed.

"Angel, can you please turn up the heat to 52? I'll finish lighting the candles and turn the music on."

I licked my finger and held it up, checking for wind direction. "I can't tell. Is that 52 below or above zero?"

So this was married life, going to bed together in the refrigerator crisper box with another human being instead of a dog at 9:30, a far cry from the single parenting nightlife of *Star Trek* reruns and lights out at midnight.

With the lights off, I expectantly waited for my lover's response. Instead, I heard noise pollution. Steve had reached behind a lamp and turned on a hidden fan.

"What's that for?" I asked, a little louder now.

"I need a fan to help me sleep."

"Tonight?"

"All nights, it's white noise," he explained, "and the extra noise will help with Katie being here now, you know."

"Katie's at my mom's tonight. That's why Honey is up here," I reminded him.

He wrapped me in his arms and whispered, "Hello, Mrs. Vannoy."

The first female to respond to Steve's advances was Honey. She whined and tap danced at my bedside, desperate and confused. Her ultimate booby prize was her bed on the floor, the lame reward for faithfully sleeping next to me for ten years. Her whines turned into cries, cries into yips, and yips finally exploding into a full-blown bichon blitz, a breed-specific behavior where dogs blow off steam and seek attention by tracing large figure eights at dizzying speed.

We listened to her dramatic huffing in the darkness, the rhythmic chugging of her legs, churning faster and faster, her metronomed grunts rising as she rounded the corners, her grunts falling in the straightaways. She stopped abruptly, panting loudly, white noise-like.

My heart couldn't bear it. "Sweetheart, can we pl—"

"Barb, she's *not* sleeping with us," Steve insisted.

14

Marriage Hell

OUR FIRST THREE MONTHS OF MARRIAGE WERE HELL; ALL vows were off. Now, hell has elevators, the top floor fittingly being the ground floor, with subterranean levels—P1, P2, P3, and infinitely more, I discovered—descending into its abyss. When the elevator doors open at ground level, the entrance to hell displays a sign over its lintel, "We're not in Kansas anymore." Its ambience radiates and heat rises.

Such was the case with Steve's 102-degree forehead one week after our New Year's wedding. I was the carrier, the petri dish, cultured to perfection with first-grade germs. For the first several weeks, this debonair, jet-setting CEO heaved into my mother's favorite pot roaster with my hand on his shoulder, rubbing his discomfort away, unwittingly breathing more pathogens into his airspace.

Did I mention the lice?

Underneath the lobby level of hell, the P2 floor is crowded. Everyone is thrown together in cramped spaces and expected to deal with it, starting with our queen bed. During our first week, Steve rolled over in bed around midnight and elbowed my eye, blackening it. We had to undo our collective thirty-five years of single adult living, coupled with a sliver of a fourteen-year-old's vibe. Steve the farmer was diurnal, an early riser. I was nocturnal, as most single moms are. My biggest challenge in moving into my new husband's home was that I had no room to call my own, a surprising problem considering we now lived inside a 6,000-square-foot house. Steve had his library, and Katie had her 1,500 square feet of lower-level luxury, privacy, and familiar belongings.

I had my car.

Most of my household furnishings remained in my old house, up for sale in 2008, the worst housing market in US history. Steve jockeyed for space as he watched his own kingdom shrink, beginning with a battle over closet and drawer space.

"Are you actually measuring how many inches of clothes racks I have?" Steve asked, seeing me with a tape measure inside the bedroom walk-in closet. He retaliated by counting my dresser drawers. Even Honey, my pampered, baptized bichon vied for territory. No longer allowed on furniture, especially our bed, she pooped and peed like the house was one huge hydrant, a canine form of *Hey, remember me?*

My hairspray and perfume gave Steve headaches. I counted 153 energy bars of his; where would my Oreos go? The house's dim lighting challenged me; I once tried telling Honey goodnight and kissed the wrong end. We got into spats about keeping lights on. I had never paid for a mansion's electric bill, and men forget how multitasking women revisit rooms frequently because we can't remember what we were last doing. Steve tried to accommodate my femininity in a house previously utilized as the headquarters for his company.

In our great room, I asked him, "What's the point of a

single snowshoe hanging on the wall?" He studied the room, testosterone rising.

"All right, but the Indian lamp stays put."

"Both of them?"

The next layer of hell, P3, sizzles with the undercurrent of maladjusted relationships. He wasn't comfortable with honey-do lists. Because of our unpredictable work schedules— Steve traveling half the month and me teaching and chauffeuring Katie everywhere—the advent of our marriage somehow brought an exit to the housekeeper, and I inexplicably defaulted to the subservient June Cleaver housewife of the 1950s. This, in turn, incited Katie's snarling charm in protecting me. Not to miss the fun, I joined the brouhaha, alienating Katie when I defended Steve, then proceeded to backlash him by protecting my perfect daughter from his newly wedded, unwarranted comments.

Enter my mother. She could hardly wait to tell me this story.

She picked up Katie after school and brought her home.

"Hi, Mary!" Steve had said, warmly, opening his arms for a hug.

Katie stuffed her hands into her pockets and swayed, silent.

My mom and Steve small-talked in the stairwell until the smallness disintegrated into nothingness. Not yet at ease with my mom, he became nervous, and believing the dog could resurrect the awkward, flustered moment, Steve yelled back inside the house to demonstrate his helpfulness, recalling the command I had taught him—with a slight faux pas.

"Katie? Wanna go outside and go poopie and potty?"

Silence.

Katie's eyes disappeared up and over her brain.

Honey never came.

No one wondered why.

My mom, the church secretary steeped in Martin Luther's cloak of grace, patted Steve on his shoulder and smiled. "Now dear, we all make mistakes."

Steve, the introvert, the homebody, stayed home. I loved daily doses of Burger King. Whenever I—the soccer mom, library-loving, "let's get decorations for another class party" teacher, "how 'bout a movie" kind of gal—left Honey home for some father-daughter bonding, she rebelled by throwing up. Steve would leave the carpet cleaner and paper towels next to her barf when I returned home.

"She's your dog," he would say.

"It's your house," I would answer.

It's easy to lose sight of eternity in other people.

I guess it was a teeny tiny bit hard for Steve, but compared to us girls—Honey included—Steve had it easy. After all, his life didn't change much. Except that after two decades of bachelorhood, he would never have a house to himself for the rest of his natural life. A generic messiness of his home crept in, streaked kitchen countertops and scummy shower doors, testaments to my previous life of single parenting.

Preparing the lower level for Katie roused the mice and voles out of their London Tube tunnels beneath the house, directly into her bedroom and hallways. The work also coaxed thousands of boxelder bugs burrowed inside the house's cedar siding to join the rodents. Stepping outside was no use; neighborhood sightings of bear and mountain lion, not to mention their scat by the dog run, kept us all cozily inside.

Out of the woodwork also came the quirks. Marriage delivers quirks, recycled habits, like a dump truck raising its hydraulic rams and depositing its payload at your doorstep. I sat on the kitchen floor pulling out gunk from the bottom of the dishwasher.

"Can you please not leave your dental floss on the plates?" I growled. "It gets wrapped up in the paddles down here."

When expecting company, I swept the kitchen floor. Steve swept the garage. (My friend's husband helped her by blowing leaves off the sidewalk and cleaning the eaves troughs.) I heard the crinkle of granola bar wrappers at three in the morning. Who does push-ups between cereal bites? Who claps their hands after every successful email that is written?

Hiking clothes are Steve's staples, appropriate for every social occasion. According to his sense of style, hiking boots are acceptable footwear for the gym, church, weddings, and biking in public.

To be fair, Steve noted a few quirks about me he didn't know before. He watched me page through my notebook of poetry I'd written as I thoughtfully and intermittently placed classroom stickers on certain ones.

"Angel, aren't those for your students?" he asked gently, gesturing to a sheet of space rockets.

"These are my leftovers from last year," I explained ever so patiently, "but still good enough for me. I earned them."

Two decades of teaching represented about 500 students. I calculated I have graded about 800,000 first-grade papers. That does not include the thousands of "DO OVER" assignments where children's handwriting didn't dress up well enough to greet their Maker, or the thousands of math papers with backward 7s. That also does not include one week's worth of ungraded papers Cooper pulled off my kitchen table and chewed up while Katie and I attended church. I forgave the dog. He was lucky he did it on a Sunday. Besides, he did me a favor. It cleared my afternoon schedule.

Grading close to a million papers changes a person; it creates an overdriving sensation to reward good work. So it's not too surprising that when I edit my writing and deem something exceptional, I comb through my heap of old stickers. My work is littered with sayings like "YOU ROCK!" or baby lambs bleating, "BRILLIANT!"

I'm also quirky about providing my students with excellent children's literature. I checked out hundreds of library books from the suburban Denver area; therefore, I created a revolving, twenty-year line of credit for overdue books in three counties. When I was a commercial loan officer before my teaching days, I required my clients to zero out their lines of credit for one month per year. I circumvented this prudent requirement with the handy perk of divorce—name changes. On library cards. Three times. And surely, I wouldn't be expected to take the time to track down my students and turn them over to the authorities for stealing my books and enrolling in other schools. How could I hand over my angelic pilferers (crooks) to the authorities? But my fines piled so high I had to be creative.

So when Katie was seven months old, I bundled her up, took her to the public library, and sat her on the librarian's desk.

"How old do you have to be in order to get a library card?" I asked the librarian.

"Oh, there's no age requirement," she answered.

Katie began accruing fines as well until she demanded that I pay them off before her sixth birthday.

One might ask where this quirk came from. Overdue fines run in my family. In 1971, when I was nine, I found an overdue book of my father's titled, *How to Survive an Atomic Bomb*, with a due date of "Aug 7 '55" stamped on the inside cover. I calculated he owed $273.50, a nickel a day. And since he was still alive, I must have subconsciously deemed that library fines were inconsequential in the long run.

Another time, as Steve walked around a pile of library books next to our bed, he pulled a baggie of half-eaten cookies out of my nightstand. "Angel, why do you hide cookies? I find these everywhere. Yesterday I found one of these inside your sock drawer."

"What were you doing going through my sock drawer?"

"Looking for gum that you stash in there too."

"Well, you always hide your cool pens from me," I reminded him. (Writers leave pens in their wills, you know.) "And I know where you hide that nail clipper, just so you know. Top drawer of your roll top."

He shook his head, exasperated. "Why, Barb, do you hide cookies?"

It was complicated. "I hide cookies because I see how hiding things works for Honey. If she saves the bones, she won't eat as many and she won't get fat. I hide cookies so I can eat more of them?"

One evening, as Steve sat quietly reading his *Wall Street Journal* in our bedroom, I bebopped in and out, each time bringing up a new topic as I passed by: Honey's bad breath, current events, Katie's music concert, a Visa bill. He finally closed his newspaper and sighed.

"Angel, sit here for a moment," he said, patting the loveseat, and Honey jumped up. He pulled her close to his side, stroking her.

"Just for a minute. I have grading to do next. What's up?"

"I'm just wondering," he began. "How do you—do it?"

"Do what?"

"How do you—exist? Your mind jumps around from one thing to the next, like a pinball. I mean, really, how do you function like that? One minute you're soft and feminine and the next—" He stumbled for meaning. "The next, you're—you. Scrambled and overwrought, occasionally manic. How can you possibly be all those people at once?"

I was confused. "Sweetheart, aren't all women like this?"

But that night in bed, Steve whispered, "Angel, can you take your Ambien now?"

The merits of his quiet mind did, nonetheless, prompt me to attempt meditation. After all, his calmness attracted me to him. Across our street in the foothills is a labyrinth, so I tried to meditate there; but after going around and around to the center, I had to check my pedometer and was disappointed that the labyrinth required only 200 steps of my daily recommended 10,000, and my mind still had so many places to go and many, many people to see.

I retraced my steps back to the outside, with a dawning déjà vu that I backtrack 20 percent of my daily steps because my mind is too crammed to live life in a straight line. Intrigued, I further calculated that I could lose approximately ten pounds per year by preserving my monkey mind when I revisit places. One can easily conclude that having a quiet mind makes you fat.

Although the labyrinth didn't provide much perspective, its surroundings did. Years ago, someone had carved its place next to a grove of cedar and cottonwood trees, towering over the ruins of a turn-of-the-century country club that had burned to the ground in the 1940s. Remnants of that bygone era remain frozen in time. Hints of stone staircases appear and disappear into the foothill. Gnarly dead cedar limbs conceal coyotes, rats, snakes. Unearthed footpaths, edged with crumbling stone walls, twist around and up slopes, with a single black lamppost marking a junction. The scene reminded me of Narnia, its unsettling mystery, that clandestine place as Mr. Tumnus said where it's "always winter, but never Christmas." The winter of my marriage.

Steve couldn't recall a windier winter at his home than the season I moved in. One of those towering cottonwoods in the grove had toppled onto one of our hiking trails, its roots dangling high, its crown crushed in a ravine. I didn't know if our marriage was going to be blown over or blown out.

15

See the Sacredness

AFTER THOSE FIRST THREE MONTHS, MA FINISHED PAINT-
ing her embellished flower border and mailed the framed vows
back, remembering to leave space at the bottom for the vow we
hadn't figured out. Her work added beauty to our promises I
had penned in calligraphy, as well as a dimension that I could
only describe as a mother's love.

Steve and I decided to display the vows in a prominent
place for maximum impact. The door leading to our garage
was used frequently, but we dismissed the location because we
would hurry by it. We decided to hang the vows in the most
frequented place in our home: We pounded two nails into the
walls opposite of the master bedroom toilet. One nail was high
behind the toilet and the other was halfway down the wall in
front of the toilet. First, we hung the vows high on the nail
behind the toilet for Steve's benefit, then agreed to move it
halfway down the opposite wall for me, and agreed to rotate it
monthly. To be fair.

The funny thing is, after our vows were posted, our marriage started showing up.

I woke up on April 1, April Fools' Day, and slogged into the bathroom. The vows, bordered with Ma's cheery hand-painted petunias, seemed to stare at me authoritatively, like I did when my students didn't take me seriously. I mumbled each of my vows out loud and realized that during our engagement, Steve and I had spent two years practicing Vow #1 on the list: I will give my best self to you. It's the obvious yet essential vow that flows from dating. We already demonstrated that we knew how to dress up our physical, emotional, spiritual, and mental expressions for each other. We knew the importance of providing joy, of taking responsibility for developing our most positive sense of self. So I looked at the other vows on the wall and realized two of them vied for my immediate attention, so closely related they could have held hands:

Vow 2

I will see and trust your sacred goodness.

Vow 3

I will forgive myself and you to protect and nurture us back to wholeness.

I mentioned the vows to Steve. We decided to post a vow or two on our refrigerator also, to emphasize their importance in our lives and to give a space to switch the vows out on an as-needed basis.

Toba Beta says that "sacredness inspires respect." To me, sacredness is anything that gives life. I pondered many familiar places of sacredness such as cathedrals, cemeteries, nurseries, the crosses on roads marking where loved ones have died. And I thought about where sacredness leaves a trail, like inside a spider's first bridge thread cast into the breeze where it spins and tethers its silk, grounding its existence.

Seeing sacredness in people is taking a long, second glance into their souls until their purity, beauty, and goodness come into focus and remembering that no matter how high our egos build mountains to block that light, one's soul, by nature, remains immovably intact—precious, unblemished, untouched. I easily loved children with this truth for two decades before I met Steve. I could excuse and forgive children's precocious nonsense because I knew I had an upper hand. Children wake up in the morning hoping one person might recognize their sparkle.

When my students went bonkers because frigid days meant inside recess, I would turn the classroom lights off and begin scrounging in my room. I'd peek inside empty desks and lunch boxes and rummage through the trash cans. Curious, the kids would notice and stop their batty behavior.

"What are you looking for, Ms. Lynn?" their eyes would ask, followed by the one student who, needing even more attention, would verbalize it.

"I'm looking for gremlins," I answered, knocking out the shavings from the pencil sharpener, then blowing into it and sticking my eyeball into one of its holes.

They giggled.

"Anybody seen one? Those little furry tricksters sneak into my classroom and make all of you look and act really bad. We need to find them and get rid of them." I pulled an imaginary gremlin from the pencil holder and smashed him between my palms. I smelled my hands, then rolled my eyes in disgust. "Ew! Help me get rid of 'em."

My students upended every learning object and found gremlins and stomped on them and held them and ate them. Some tried to take them home by zipping them in their backpacks. After a few minutes of rounding up the critters in the darkness, I turned on the lights and invited my kids to the front.

"Those gremlins are mischievous," I began, "and take no sides. They make you forget who you truly are. But I know who you really are, and now I want you to remember who you are. Show me."

The kids knew I had just called out their unhinged behavior and rescued them from themselves. The classroom's silence would hush into a deep serenity. They straightened their backs, closed their lips, and became freckled angels disguised in pigtails and buzz cuts.

I grinned at them. "I was going to ask our principal if she had seen my class, since it had seemed to disappear, but I see it's showed up again."

Boy, were they pleased with themselves.

I leaned in closer to my children, my priceless darlings, and gave my speech. I saw their ten-cow greatness. "When things get tough in your life, remember how you feel right now. Calm. Powerful. In charge. Full of goodness." I touched Ryan's arm, a boy who had earlier disconnected the phone while the principal tried calling his parent. His brown eyes stared into mine. I looked at his friends.

"This is who you truly are. Remember who you are."

STEVE AND I woke up hoping the other would recognize the sparkle too; we hadn't mastered the lesson yet. And while gremlins aren't real, I had, for a time, believed in their destructive abilities more than Steve's sacred goodness. I remembered who Steve was, and who I didn't want to be any longer. As Thich Nhat Hanh wrote, "In the sunlight of awareness, everything becomes sacred." I told Steve about my intention to live out our second written vow.

So on our third-month wedding anniversary as an unhappily married couple, I tried infusing some sacredness into our relationship by giving Steve the ultimate expression of love: a $74 NIV leather-bound Bible with a six-inch spine, a colossal anthology resplendent with commentary at the bottom of every page, complete with an atlas of the Holy Land in technicolor. It didn't matter that he owned four Bibles already; none were as noteworthy as my gift, which had his name inscribed in golden letters on the cover. I admit it was heavy, four pounds, Ark of the Covenantlike. But, in my defense, Steve had kept repeating that he wanted to get closer to God.

His response to my thoughtful gift surprised me.

"What the hell am I going to do with this enormous Bible?"

I glanced around for gremlins. Seeing none, I snarked, "Ask for forgiveness, for starters."

I guess Steve also took that vow to heart, because on the same day, he reciprocated with a thoughtfully written anniversary card. He also slipped in a new $34,000 grand piano. It was a handmade Estonia, nicknamed "Essie," and only one of 250 crafted that year. Essie is a lovely piano, a bit like a thoroughbred horse, living the life of a carnival pony, circling round and round with an immature yet charming rider. Essie will never be free, forever chained to my style of playing, with my finger memory slowly losing consciousness.

I took piano lessons for eight years—first, from Mrs. Rabe, who would slap my wrists with a ruler when my hand position slacked, and later, Mrs. Stokes, who became the first living metronome, nodding her sleepy head in rhythm as I played until she fell asleep, or died. I often couldn't tell, because there were several seconds of silence after I finished my sonatas. But God even used Mrs. Stokes's weakness for His good, because she covered my piano books with stars and stickers, igniting my teaching career.

Essie felt out of my league. Because Steve bought such an exquisite instrument, the store owner ushered us into the private concert hall and invited me to play a fifteen-foot black satin Bösendorfer Grand, whose sound is deeply richer than a Steinway. As I sat down to this $183,000 piano, I noticed it had six extra bass keys, a feature designed to capture the tones of Bach's organ works.

This piano had been crafted with delicate precision, painstaking pride, smoothed over a thousand times, over a thousand hours with the tenderest of hands. Built for beauty, for expression, for joy, my fingers pressed into its keys and awoke its purpose. Its tone and the stringed fibers reverberated, and something ethereal transcended my ability. The piano's magic overtook me, and I became one with it, my fingers lithely caressing a new melody across the keyboard and into my ears, its echo swelling inside the concert hall.

Steve approached the piano bench when the song ended. Enchanted, I closed my eyes, blinking back tears. My hands dropped into my lap. "This piano would turn anybody into a virtuoso," I said, "even if you've never played before."

He touched my shoulder and leaned over and whispered, "This is the only way I see you, angel."

When you see someone's sacredness, everything changes.

A NOTED *NATIONAL GEOGRAPHIC* PHOTOGRAPHER, DEWITT Jones, celebrates what is right about the world. He's a master at capturing the world's goodness, delight, and beauty.

As a first-grade teacher, I've watched my students enter my classroom numbed to their innate ability to see the world's miracles as naturally viewed through the camera lens of Dewitt Jones. What I often found were children unable to sit still in their chairs for more than three minutes. Their attention span could be likened to a leaf blowing to the whim of the most prevalent wind. Surface conversation was common, because too few of us had the time to slow down and feel our own breaths, let alone explore the real depth of our children's pure, powerful understanding of the day.

With this in mind, I began showing my six-year-old students Dewitt Jones's photographs. I wanted to remind them of what they already brilliantly knew—how to notice what is truly remarkable about life and put it in their writing. Of course, it took practice. Society's rushing tempo had already taken its toll.

I'd begin with the basics. We started with pictures of wild animals, like a sea otter.

"What do you see?" I asked. I expected anything and everything as an answer.

"Ohhh! How cute!" they said, which is the universal response to every animal picture.

"An otter!"

"A seal!"

"No, that's not a seal, silly!"

"Is that a baby one?"

"I saw one at the zoo. It swims good."

I would show a few more pictures, then stop. Before holding up the next one, I'd say, "Now, hold your breaths quietly when you see the next picture. Look for three things you notice in the picture that no one else will see. You'll see more in your silence. And don't raise your hands. When you can share exactly three details of what you see, you can give your breath to me without a sound. I'll notice, and I'll call on you. Everybody ready? Take your quietest breath."

I'd hold up, say, a lion picture. And the gift of childhood, of noticing things we adults don't see anymore, surrounded me for those precious seconds. Only by stepping inside their quiet stillness did they unwrap their own gift:

"I see a lion with long claws. His whiskers aren't even. And he's furry."

"I see a lion who is looking somewhere else. I noticed his nose is black. He looks strong."

"I see a lion. That's a cat. I saw a lion at the zoo last summer."

(I told you practice was important.)

And so it went, our practice of noticing what is good and right about animals, about nature, its details, having the awareness of delighting in what's around us, purposely lingering in silence as a class to understand what else life was teaching us about it. And we'd share our thoughts together, yes, often trying to outdo the others with our observations, but always ending up celebrating the unexpected responses. Our world became bigger and we began living inside it.

Once our observation powers improved, we started looking for the hidden goodness inherent in each day. We'd start and end the day with my question, "What is right about the world? What deserves celebrating?"

I kept a list of hundreds of my favorite responses they gave over the years, these six-year-old savants of mine:

"The pattern on a butterfly's wing." "Hearing a baby bird learning its song." "Martin Luther King Jr." "A bee's buzz and fuzz—hey, that rhymes!" "An empty swing at recess." "People saving the rain forest." "People who write books." "My hamster in heaven." "The courage of the pilgrims and how the Indians helped them through the winter." "Bad hair days after I had cancer." "Catching snowflakes on my tongue." "Clouds that are animals." "My violin." "A shark tooth."

But my all-time favorite response? It came from one student with sixty-seven absences and twice as many instances of being tardy, my little girl whom I had referred to social services for neglect three times, including being high on meth.

"What is right about the world?" I asked her class.

With quiet conviction, she boldly raised both arms in triumph and respectfully proclaimed to the class: "I AM!"

Her classmates giggled and added silly laughter. Then they clapped their hands in agreement, stood up, and celebrated her.

MY FIRST MARRIAGE TAUGHT ME THERE ARE THINGS WE humans can't do on our own. One of them is to forgive the big stuff. This lesson took me eight years to master, when, finally, in a moment of overdue insight, I realized Jesus had literally taken a time-out from heaven and showed up here to teach us how to do it. Some things are so infected inside that we can't be expected to pick up a garden shovel and dig it all out. Forgiveness was a massive concept for me to conquer, so I finally took the pressure off myself to accomplish it independently and opened my heart like a butterfly sailing on a breeze—and asked God to do the rest. He did.

Second, I had always read that forgiveness isn't about another person, but sometimes it is. The impetus that brought me flailing and kicking toward forgiveness's feet was knowing that my daughter would need an idea of how to do it later in life, too, and she was watching me now; realizing that made me shake off the dust and ask God to be a man and show me how to do it. I struggled to reconcile and embrace the incongruity that such a crummy first marriage could emerge with the magical swirls of heaven I saw every day inside my child's eyes.

The worst thing is to leave all your love behind, buried in the muck of your mistakes and others'. That's no place to live.

And actually, it was my ten-year-old Katie who challenged and cured me of one of the hardest conundrums in teaching: finding the goodness in demanding children with chronic behavior issues. All teachers have a handful every year, the ones who short-circuit our brain waves and enable us to climb walls without ropes and give up countless teaching breaks known as recess. One student, Tristan, became my consummate first-grade star, his name flashing across my mind's marquee like a ticker tape. Tristan! Tristan! Tristan!

"Tristan did this! Tristan did that! Tristin tried to do this and that!" I bemoaned to Katie on Monday. Then Tuesday,

Wednesday, Thursday, and Friday. I replayed Tristan's weekday antics on our weekends too.

I did this for weeks. For months.

While driving home from school one afternoon, I brought up Tristan's name again with Katie. She lost it.

"I'm sick and tired of hearing about Tristan, Mom. I don't want to hear his name one more time this year," she said angrily. She added, "Try forgiving him instead of complaining about him all the time."

No one had ever been that direct with me before about one of my students. Not even my teammates; sometimes, when things got bad in our classrooms, we'd have verbal competitions about surviving our students' stunts, like on reality TV shows.

But, finally, I could understand how stressful my reactions toward Tristan had been on Katie, day in and day out. I decided that Tristan's name would stay where it belonged. At school.

It was hard. His name tried to leak out of my mouth after school. But I refused to allow his actions to affect my family life anymore. I directed my conversations toward a new horizon. And because my focus changed, Tristan's behaviors slowly took a different direction too. By the year end, he finally rejoined the fringes of the human race instead of my rat race.

Inside my marriage, Steve's barrage of annoying quirks kept coming at me too. Yes, I forgave his dental floss epidemic and his curt comment about my magnanimous Bible offering. But the crackling of his granola wrappers still woke me up at three in the morning. He neti-potted over my dishes in the sink. I couldn't watch a Broncos game without listening to the same mandolin riffs I'd heard for months.

And yet, in those three months, marriage began to teach me that quirks aren't all bad. His best quirk was surprisingly awesome. Whenever we would get into tiffs and need our separate space, he would do something I had never seen anyone do before. He would return and do something outrageously loving for me instead of giving me the silent treatment. If we disagreed about one of our daughters, for instance, he would leave and return with tickets for a movie later that night. The only downside to his kindness was that it was harder to stay mad at him and therefore get my way.

One afternoon, we got into such a bad disagreement that I grabbed Honey, left the house, and stayed overnight in my family's cabin seventy miles away in Fairplay. Just before midnight, I heard a car's tread on our gravel driveway outside the front door. Petrified, I didn't turn on any lights and hid in a closet for ten minutes until I heard the car drive away.

The next morning, I opened the kitchen blinds and spotted a vase of Dutch irises in full bloom on the deck railing. Attached to the flowers was a handwritten sticky note from Steve, scribbled with the words, "I'm sorry. I love you and miss you. And Honey." Inside another envelope was a page he had ripped out from his *10 Greatest Gifts* book, with the following highlighted:

> *An episode a young couple shared during one of our seminars probably sums up this concept best. A couple was visiting their priest for some premarital counseling. As the priest came into his office, he asked them if they had noticed the beautiful Oriental rug in the vestibule. They had, and indeed thought it was outstanding. "Did you also notice the spot in the corner?" the priest asked.*

They hadn't. "Well," the priest said, "I know that spot is there and I always see it when I look at that rug. If you want your marriage to work, remember to always look for the beauty and not the spot. Whether it be a spouse, a child, a neighbor, a boss, or a friend, you can find as many spots as you want to look for."

Don't ask me what our argument was about. I can't remember.

16

The Vows Fight Back

I SAW OUR VOWS AGAIN AND AGAIN EVERY DAY, TOWELING myself off from a shower, in the corner of my eye as I looked in the mirror putting on makeup. Seeing them three or four times daily—and reading just a few of them—gradually began improving our trajectory.

If they weren't in front of me, they would have simply blended into my wedding day memories of my dress, the candles, the rings. But now, we were learning to assume the best about each other instead of the worst. I discovered that giving Steve the benefit of this truth—that he's not trying to rub me wrong—saved us days of grief. And I began to see him in his fullness again. I saw firsthand how his dedication to serving humanity pulsed through his company, his employees, clients, and us.

Steve's primary mission, all along, was to touch and ignite families into their magnificence, for parents to see their children in their greatness, and for children to live inside their joy and goodness each day. Living to serve children united us. I saw the massive energy it took to travel across the world twice a month, to train and to transform the lives of high-powered leaders, leaders whose reach could touch a thousand employees and individual children's hearts. Not to mention the synergy of new possibilities and new self-expressions that would also bolster bottom-line profits.

But our tight schedules kept isolating us, negating the potential in our marriage, so I concentrated on another vow:

Vow 4

I will put you and us first.

We took this vow to heart and sought ways to honor our union. Friends invited us to a couples' group for dinner. Our host, Daniel, nestled his home in sprawling acres of foothills in a communal setting near Evergreen. Renters were typically New Age and spiritually entwined, drawn together by an electromagnetic veil vortex on the property. In short, a veil vortex is, according to Einstein, a location where the absence of electromagnetic fields creates altered states, which can increase IQ, enlightenment, and cosmic awareness of extraterrestrial life.

As we walked into Daniel's house, my only earthly concern was whether my apple pie would taste good.

In the front room, the conversations oscillated in small talk until a man mentioned the vortex and tried explaining it to the newcomers, Steve and me. The closest translation I could concoct was the theme music from *The Twilight Zone*. Each couple was asked to provide a brief introduction as to how their relationship came into being. Steve and I would go last.

The swirling vortex beneath us pulsed with truth serum at its core. Couples nodded their heads in agreement as they shared accounts of LSD and psychedelic drug use in the sixties and seventies and how these experiences brought them together. Hallucinogenic tales were as common as tying shoes or smoking pot.

The conversation made me reminisce too; when I was six, I collected pop bottles at the railroad track and traded them for candy cigarettes, but never puffed any since.

The couple next to us, the fifth couple, mentioned animals. I liked animals. So I kept staring at the floor but began using my peripheral vision to notice the husband gesticulate with wavy arms. "I was out at sea when I sensed a presence, but I couldn't understand it. Then an eel, or something like that, approached our boat. The eel lifted his head out of the water," he continued, stretching his neck higher, "and I listened carefully, to the eel creature."

Steve circled his foot and brushed it against mine. I held my breath.

The man continued. "The eel told me...and I should have known! The frogs and dolphins could understand their language, the aliens' language, and the dolphins communicated the aliens' message to me," he explained evenly. "The aliens spoke...they spoke..." And he stuttered, lifting his eyes, searching the open galaxy for the right word, "You know—"

He found it. "They spoke Reptilian."

Four or five members nodded their heads in universal understanding. They'd been there: been stoned, met E.T., and taught ESL to amphibious creatures.

Steve's shoulders heaved, and he tucked his chin to his chest, coughing. My foot circled back to brush against his.

Now it was my turn. I figured I'd start with a simple list. Lists would be safe.

"Well, I'm Barb," I said steadily, noticing the twisted skeins of green shag carpet by Steve's swirling foot. "I grew up Lutheran, have two brothers, and one is a pastor. My mom is a church secretary, and my dad was best friends with our pastor."

Where was I going with this?

I babbled on, my thoughts spinning freely as a pinwheel. I tried to fit in by mirroring the existential thoughts I'd heard before my turn. "My sister-in-law is a pastor too. I like laughing gas when I visit the dentist. I like how sounds become crisper, fuller. I hear lots of new things but never an alien's voice. Yeah, root canals are much more relaxing for me than a massage. Ah, what else do you want to know? And I love dolphins, too, but eels give me the creeps."

They laughed at me; Steve, who finally had the opportunity to unload his fifteen minutes of stifled, carbonated cackling, laughed the hardest. Leaving the apple pie behind, we didn't stay for dinner. How could we? We chuckled about our bizarre evening. But as we drove away, the vortex's electromagnetic power seized us, altering our understanding.

"Sweetheart, all those couples seemed really happy, didn't they? And comfortable with each other."

"Yes, angel."

"I don't think any of them have been remarried. They're on their original spouse."

Steve blinked several times. "I think you're right."

"Maybe the vortex really works. Really does enlighten." I suddenly felt chagrined. "What do they know that we don't?"

"How to accept people like us. And," he grinned, "foreign languages."

TO STEVE, PUTTING US FIRST, AS OUR VOW SUGGESTED, meant protecting me, especially since he traveled frequently. He devised an impenetrable defense for our bedroom, beginning with two bear spray cans ("His" and "Hers") on our nightstands. He rationalized that no intruder—be it bear or burglar—would expect that. Under our bed, our arsenal included two baseball bats, assorted hand weights equaling nearly seventy-five pounds, and an exercise step that could be used as a tripping device. I might add the decoy at our feet: ten-year-old hearing-impaired Honey.

Steve also purchased an emergency rope ladder and stuffed it under the bed. Men don't understand how we women use underbed storage, so during practice fire drills, not only did we rescue ourselves but also saved tangled stowaways such as blankets, sweaters, and *Reader's Digests* to peruse until the fire trucks might arrive.

Because of our work schedules, we didn't have time for a honeymoon after our wedding. Because of our marriage vows and because we wanted to start liking each other again, we made time for us by squeezing in our trip to Rio, piggybacking off Steve's business trip to São Paulo. Before we left, Steve handed me a tiny piece of paper.

"These are our vows. Put them in your wallet. I put a copy in mine too." He had scotch-taped the edges, so they'd last.

I had never flown in first class before, and once again, Steve's world of the haves and my previous world of the have-nots collided. My leather seat looked like Captain Kirk's command chair, with enough buttons to start a war. A flight attendant stepped into the aisle and, lifting a silver lid, offered me hors d'oeuvres on my granite cocktail table, filling first class with aromas of the finest French restaurant, a scent I always envied as I would waddle back to steerage, back to my economy seat 35E, always the middle seat, always the middle when traveling with a child. I was self-conscious as economy passengers tottered by, checking out my digs. More and more flight attendants appeared every other minute, and I kept answering no.

"No, I don't want that expensive wine. I don't drink."

"No, I'm not interested in the *Wall Street Journal* or *Harvard Business Review*. Do you have a *People* magazine?"

Getting my students to leave me alone was easier than making those flight attendants go away.

In Rio, we traveled with an inconspicuous bodyguard dressed in a pressed gray suit, shorn hair, and *Mission Impossible* sunglasses. Inconspicuous as well, Steve donned his Lincoln Memorial T-shirt and Adidas, while I tried to blend into Latin culture by highlighting my hair blonder two days before departure. We screamed American to the point that a group of young locals treated us like Madame Tussaud mannequins and posed next to us for photos without asking permission.

Our marriage challenges took a backseat to Rio's spectacular beauty. El Cristo hovered in incandescent light of wispy clouds over the steamy Brazilian city sprawl, with azure skies mirroring Copacabana and Ipanema beaches, mingling into one vast, sparkling sapphire. And we put ourselves first, from ascending Sugarloaf Mountain to sipping tea among trumpet trees in Serra da Bocaina National Park.

We celebrated Easter inside the baroque São Bento Monastery, erected in 1641, its lavish interior studded with rococo wooden carvings and gold and copper walls, as incense dusted the air and blended with Gregorian chanting. We tried to access the ornate organ loft after the service.

To Steve, the monk responded, "I'm sorry, you are wearing shorts."

To me, the monk responded, "No, you are a woman."

After arriving in São Paulo, we switched our limo service to a bulletproof van. It wasn't uncommon for thieves on motorcycles to pull up at intersections, draw guns, and demand money. We arrived at the São Paulo Hilton looking like Jethro and Elly May Clampett at the registration desk.

"Steve!" said a man's voice behind us.

I turned around to see the reincarnation of a Latin Calvin Klein, the most impeccably dressed man I will ever see in a gray pinstriped suit, pinstripes so crisp that it was humanly impossible to wrinkle them. He stood broadly with his hands clasped in front, extravagant thick gold rings on several fingers, and a posh wristwatch. A textured, checked brown tie accented his dark complexion and coffee eyes. He looked too good to be real. Next to him was a chiseled hulk, aka inconspicuous bodyguard #2.

Steve whirled around and lit up. "Leon! Barb, meet Leon Alvarez, president of Ford, South America. Leon, meet my beautiful wife, Barb."

Beautiful me wore no makeup; Steve and I were slightly underdressed for the introduction, wearing hiking pants and boots and sweaty shirts after hiking in the rain forest during our eight-hour drive. Steve had forgotten about his meeting with Leon. During their impromptu meeting, I stared out our hotel window at a Starbucks across the street from our room like a dog yearning for a fire hydrant, knowing I couldn't safely cross the street alone for a drink. But what a problem I had, in

Brazil on my honeymoon, locked inside my bedroom, without my husband.

But reality returned on our trip back to Denver when I spotted a familiar shaped building from my first-class window: "Look, Steve! It's Kohl's!"

LATER, IN EARLY June, we held our wedding reception at our home. At that time of year, early summer in the Rocky Mountain foothills draws a menagerie of critters to live together on our property, property fringed with buds of black-eyed Susan and Shasta daisy: magpies in the ponderosa boughs, fawns in the plum brush. Bats in the gables, cougar prints in the rain. Wrens scold Honey, honeybees ignore her. Coyotes yip over their kill, and woodpeckers tap on shiny CDs, hung on the cedar siding to scare them away.

The confluence of wildlife outside mirrored the hodge-podge of two hundred guests that we invited inside our home to celebrate our marriage. Worlds collided; basically, no one knew what to do with the other. CEOs from billion-dollar companies stepped aside as screaming children dipped their fingers and occasionally their tongues in chocolate fountains. Cliques formed, neighbors with neighbors, Nebraskans with Midwesterners, former students with former teachers, curious guests with nosy guests who explored the house's crannies. One couple disappeared completely, searching for liquor. Guests glanced away from small talk when conversation dwindled or just loitered near the food tables, grazing.

This all changed, thankfully, when one guest showed up, everybody's best friend: the great equalizer, music. Within the backdrop of Celine Dion's and Andrea Bocelli's "The Prayer,"

Steve grabbed his mandolin, and I grabbed my voice disguised inside my wedding dress. Together we grabbed two hundred guests and corralled them into the great room for a grand performance, first the two of us, and saving the best for last, everyone else in an impromptu sing-along.

Sticky-fingered children heard the music and forgot about the chocolate fountain. Singing voices, like love, mask socioeconomics and age and race. Music united our family and friends together as surely as its presence in my life electrified Steve's interest in me. Together, our guests all celebrated our Declaration of Independence from divorced living. Our marriage took six months, January to June, to take root, mature, and blossom as a couple.

17

The Vow to Family

DAYS WERE PLEASANT AND FUN AGAIN. INTENTIONALLY living our vows aired out our relationship.

So we turned our attention to the fifth vow we promised our family.

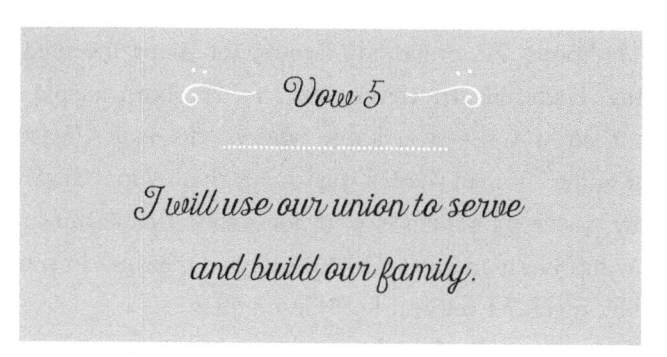

Vow 5

I will use our union to serve and build our family.

Our fifth marriage vow coincided with an important promise we made in the vows to our daughters, promising to be their sanctuary, that soft and safe place to land for the rest of their lives. As we had crafted vows in Tasmania, a quote by Jani Ortlund caught our attention: "I believe that a godly home is a foretaste of heaven. Our homes, imperfect as they are, must be a haven from the chaos outside. They should be a reflection of our eternal home, where troubled souls find peace, weary hearts find rest, hungry bodies find refreshment, lonely pilgrims find communion, and wounded spirits find compassion."

This marriage vow blended well with providing a safe sanctuary for not only our girls but also our mothers, brothers, and extended family. But in order to do all this, Steve and I needed to prioritize *us*, so we added Vow #6 on the refrigerator:

Vow 6

I will renew our love daily.

We found the key to these vows: traditions.

Traditions. As everybody knows, Germans invented traditions. Traditions are clever covers for stubborn people who want their way. Do you know why we decorate Christmas trees? Some German wanted you to copy them. Does the Easter Bunny leave eggs hidden in your house too? That carrot-loving bunny has German roots. When someone sneezes, do you say, "God bless you"? Ever heard of "Gesundheit"?

Being German, I had a tradition of starting traditions. Katie and I had made a habit of accessorizing the Kohl's lingerie mannequins with purses and fluffy stuffed animals, then warming them up with hiking boots, scarves, and wool hats. In church, we would sing hymns off-key to annoy the worshipper in front of us. We plopped a candle on a McDonald's hamburger and sang "Happy Birthday" to Honey every year. On the other hand, Steve, Ali, and Emmy had read bedtime stories to their dog Wister, sang at nursing homes, and played hide-and-get-lost in the countless crannies of his house.

Steve and I started our own traditions. And we kept it easy with simple gestures. When one of us was arriving home, the other would light a candle. If one of us was traveling, we'd toss notes and cards in suitcases. We bought each other quote books and read them to each other. Holding hands as we fell asleep kept us connected. Every night, we'd request, "Name three things that were funny today." I'd sing Steve to sleep, and he'd serve me hot chocolate in bed in the morning. For our daughters, we hung stockings at Christmas for boyfriends and made family calendars and pulled up chairs for all the dogs at the holiday table.

With a full-fledged family at home, I recognized the importance of honoring family by eating dinner together. Trouble was, I needed to learn how to cook, so I informed Steve.

"You want to learn to cook?" he asked, cocking his head sideways like Honey did when she didn't want to miss something important. Now, my husband had basically been ravenous for twenty years, having resorted to living off restaurant leftovers or, worse yet, other people's plates as they dined, another one of his winning quirks. Steve rushed to Barnes and Noble and bought me cookbooks with simple recipes. Knowing my love of picture books, he also ensured the cookbooks had large print and colorful photographs on every page.

It still didn't work. He gave up and became a vegetarian. Then, Ali joined in.

Now I was in real trouble. Their eating choices cut my cooking options by at least fifty percent. But a good wife looks after her family's health. Whole Foods, the Walmart of healthy living, beckoned me.

My college degrees did not have warranties and proved worthless as I navigated the interior of Whole Foods. The outside doors swooshed open, and I immediately felt the obsessive residue of Johnny Appleseed's work. Before I even entered the store, brimful baskets of organic apples tilted sideways, filling the vestibule on both sides.

Of course, the produce section took center stage. I passed vegetables I deemed extinct, since I had read of them but had never seen them before. Green labels represented organic foods. I began pricing the difference between organic choices and Whole Foods' brand names. I was trying to save money. Like that mattered in this store.

Whole Foods was like an interstate during an election year, with billboards high above the groceries, pointing out the value of healthy foods for the uneducated like me. One banner caught my eye: "Did you know that only 2 of every 100 eggs sold are cage-free eggs?" What a sneaky, manipulative advertising attack, drawing on the sympathy of hungry animal lovers. But it worked. I instantly vowed to buy only cage-free eggs in the future. The six in my fridge were already imprisoned. But I had chosen the path of responsibility for my future.

It was like I had just adopted a rescue dog or something.

I tried to decode all the new lingo, new words, new foods. My surroundings were as unfamiliar to me as my 1980 BASIC computer programming class. I walked more slowly through the aisles than my eighty-year-old German great-grandmother did back in the sixties when she accompanied my mom and me to Prairie Market. Grandma was slow because she couldn't comprehend the English labels. I was slow because I couldn't either.

I noticed that the brand Kraft was like a four-letter word here, wiped clean out of existence with a know-it-all attitude.

Whole Foods' offering of macaroni and cheese, labeled Daiya Cheezy Mac Gluten-Free Dairy-Free Pasta, had pictures on the box the color of sepia, the color of my aforementioned great-grandmother's face in photos. I have no idea how they even got macaroni and cheese in that box, because it contained "no cheese, no milk, and no gluten."

There's a reason Kraft had $26 billion in sales last year. It's called common sense: mac and cheese.

But I was determined to provide wellness for my family. I visited the meat section. A grading system of 1 to 5 was prominently displayed and repeated above every glass section. I guessed the manager used to be a teacher and didn't want people looking over the shoulder of the person next to them for help. According to the chart, Level 1 meat represented every piece of meat I had eaten in the last fifty years—animals exposed to earth. Level 2 meat had no pesticide exposure. And you can imagine Level 5 meat. Yes, it was cloned meat from Dolly, the perfected sheep. Perfect DNA, celestial quality, like heaven. Labels marked most of the meat choices as Level 4, which must have meant resurrected animals before their ascension.

In the frozen food section, I found veggie burgers. I put one in my basket, checking the price. It was five dollars. Geez, one burger. Was my husband worth a five-buck fake burger served at home? I put the package back in the freezer.

Even the aisle markers were bizarre: "Milk Alternatives" (no wine, I checked) and "Delectable Desserts." I made a beeline for that aisle but was profoundly disappointed. All I found were frozen gluten-free pancakes. But alas! I did find frozen, completely normal, unimmunized Belgian waffles. I checked the price: $3.69. Was I worth two Belgian waffles? La la la. I put them in my basket. And organic air popcorn! How could air be anything but organic?

I picked up a spinach salad on sale, because I wanted to learn how to make the salad for Steve, and I figured the easiest way to remember the recipe would be to eat it. As I checked out, the guru clerk asked, "Did you find everything you wanted?" *Really? How would I know?*

I loaded the groceries and sat in my car. You'd be amazed what you learn sitting in a parking lot. Whole Foods customers have specific MOs. First, they are serious people. No one left the store carrying balloons or smiling. They appear driven, focused. They drove Audis and jumbo SUVs. They were like those friends that you could be like in two years if you tried hard. They looked informed—all right, smart—too smart to be sidetracked by Del Taco's three taco special for 99 cents on Tuesdays. And they were generally childless, which contributed to the focus factor. I would know. And by sitting in the parking lot, I figured out why people who eat healthy are fit and rich. It's because they leave the store with only one bag of groceries—a recyclable bag, of course. Contrast that to my shopping at Walmart, where I leave with enough plastic bags to choke a whale.

All this thought about food made me hungry. So, being Tuesday, I reached over the passenger seat and grabbed the last of my three Del Taco tacos. I swallowed it down with a swig of Diet Coke, laced with saccharine, crossed myself, and begged forgiveness. I'd return to shop later, because that's what a good wife would do. But not until I reached into the backseat and finished off my cupcake from Granny's Pie Shop.

OUR VOW OF USING OUR UNION TO SERVE OUR FAMILY CAME in handy at Christmas, when Ma visited us for a month. She hadn't flown for thirty years, so Denver International Airport rivaled the International Space Station. She hadn't been to a shopping mall in ten years either. I borrowed a wheelchair and headed to Southwest Plaza Mall for her Christmas shopping.

"Ma, this is different from mail order." I wheeled her into the J.C. Penney store, set the wheelchair brake, and parked the car. In those five minutes, Ma had visually scoped out the Alfred Dunner section.

"I'll take that. And that. Barbie, isn't that pretty?" In ten minutes she charged over $300 of clothing for herself. Imagine the thrill, actually buying clothes that are to scale, as opposed to the two-inch versions of them in catalogs.

I took Ma to the one place that defined shopping in the early twenty-first century. The mall elevator closed as I turned her wheelchair around to face it, and up we went.

"Ma, this is the first place I want to take you, and you are gonna pick out something for you. It'll be for you from me for Christmas."

"Barbie, I don't need anything."

The elevator doors swished open, and heaven opened before Ma's eyes. Straight ahead of us, angel wings fluttered inside windows two stories high, attached to beautiful young women. I wheeled Ma into the center of Victoria's Secret and spun the wheelchair around like a kaleidoscope, enabling her to take in the swirling hues of purples, baby blues, and pinks of a thousand bras, panties, teddies, and unmentionables.

"Oh, my," Ma gasped.

"This is so you, Ma. Pick your favorite."

I recognized a familiar, flushed expression on her face, then realized it was the same shade as Steve's face when he first visited my classroom. Her eyes darted sideways, unwilling to focus on any one thing. Maybe she thought she might have to include this in confession later.

"Ma, you're not Catholic. And my brother, Mike, he's the pastor, he'll absolve you. I've got you covered."

She laughed nervously. She lit up, straightened up, and recognized we had something in common.

"Do you shop here often?" She smiled. Slyly. Intentionally. She was interrogating me. A mother's prerogative.

Oh. I answered honestly. "Ma, I'm as Lutheran as you are."

"In that case," she replied happily, "wheel me over to that wall. I think those panties must be irregulars. They don't have any material in the back."

We left Victoria's Secret with her one unmentionable. Which shall remain unmentioned.

Ma finished her Christmas shopping in two hours but did not enjoy the last fifteen minutes because she couldn't see anything in front of her. Sacks and boxes piled atop her lap; she was a moving Leaning Tower of Pisa. She wore a new red cap and new slippers for her granddaughters since they wouldn't fit anywhere else. Scents of Chanel No. 5 and Gucci Premiere wafted around her wheelchair like Pig-Pen's dust.

On our way back to the car, she gazed sideways at Victoria Secret's storefront windows. She had to, since sacks blocked her view.

"You know, Barbie," she began, craning her head back toward me, "I went to the dance with Virgil Bloomhorst. But I came home with Warren Vannoy." She paused, confessing proudly, "I was a naughty girl."

Asking about my elderly mother-in-law's sex life was too good to be true. "Why'd you do it, Ma?"

"The same reason you wear black panties to school," she replied with a smile. "The same reason we did it later against the barn under the stars," she added wistfully, her face decades away. She looked me square in the eye, with twinkles inside her own. "I did it for you, Barbie. You wouldn't want to be called Barbie Bloomhorst, now would you?"

18

Three Hearts Dancing

AT 7:40 IN THE MORNING, TWENTY MINUTES BEFORE STEVE and I prepared to leave Ma's farm, she dropped the most helpful bombshell a child could receive from an aging parent: "I believe I would like to move into the Legacy Terrace. It's time."

No arm twisting. No pleading. No deals.

What we didn't understand was that she meant now, as in, unpack your suitcases one week before Christmas with a looming blizzard forecast. Who could blame her? Her recent medical issues necessitated that she live half the time at the farm and the other half at Steve's brother's home in Missouri. And at ninety-two, she was worn-out. No more four-hour rides in the country. No more bathroom breaks in truck stops.

We dropped everything. But Steve had the presence of mind to make a suggestion.

"Angel," he began, opening Ma's closet and collecting hangers, "this is going to take a while, and it's going to change Ma, us, and our lives. What vows do we have left?"

One vow immediately popped into my head. I couldn't believe how thankful I was to be married to a man who thought like this. Together, we figured out we had four vows waiting in the wings, and three fit our situation well:

~ *Vow 7* ~

I will step into our moments with gratitude.

~ *Vow 8* ~

I will welcome God as our partner through daily prayer.

~ *Vow 9* ~

I will ask for special requests on essential points.

Ma, Steve, and I shot up prayers every morning for two weeks as we boxed up her possessions, nearly a century of eras—prayers for discernment, prayers for sanity in the midst of piles. Ma's farmhouse was a bona fide twentieth-century time capsule. Sorting through ninety years of life daunted us: What should we keep? LPs of Benny Hill or Frank Sinatra? Ma's baby blanket or Aunt Bertha's quilt, the one she designed sitting in her wheelchair after being stricken with polio at age fourteen? In the kitchen, spices dating from Columbus's unsuccessful run to the West Indies in 1692 lined the cupboard shelf. Steve unlocked Papa's leather books from the office safe, copyrighted from 1852 to 1895.

"Ma? What's the story of this jewelry?" Steve asked as he sorted bracelets on the kitchen table. He leaned over to me and whispered, "Can you write down what she says? She's the last living child who knows."

I jotted her thoughts in shorthand, and the yellow notepad became the Vannoy Book of Life.

Steve suggested we go to Waverly's True Value Hardware and buy some boxes for packing. It was another incongruent moment in our lives. I never bought boxes; they were too expensive. Instead, I relied on liquor store boxes or the appliance boxes in my mom's basement.

"Are you kidding?" I asked. My frugal motto appeared. "Let's get them for free."

"Angel, it's 5 degrees outside. A store's more convenient and our time is worth something."

His time, maybe, at $500/hour for personal coaching. And I still didn't want to figure out how much money I made an hour as a teacher.

I pressed him. "Let's go to the strip mall behind McDonald's and look for boxes behind the grocery store and bar."

"I've never done that before. Won't we look like homeless people?"

"Weren't you a homeless person once, remember?"

"You have a point."

"And who's gonna be scouting out the back alley of Trackside Bar in 5 degree weather? When it's snowing?"

So we bundled up in Papa's oversized farm coats with fur-trimmed hats, scrounged up mismatched gloves, and drove from the farm in the blustery weather, weather that can only be summed up as "Nebraska." Behind the Trackside Bar and Lovegrove's Grocery, Steve nervously scanned the alley. Rusted green dumpsters, paired in twos, formed a pattern behind the storefronts. Cardboard boxes, flattened and soggy, littered the alley.

"There's our booty!" I said emphatically, disguised in an I-told-you-so tone.

Steve looked over his shoulder.

"This isn't *Mission Impossible*," I said, patting his arm. "C'mon."

I taught Steve how to be a commoner again, pilfering through Jack Daniels and Pampers boxes. We stuffed the SUV full of cardboard, barely closing the hatch when we heard a vehicle rounding the corner, plowing the road, approaching us in the alley. His truck's blade sliced through the icy snow.

It was John Tucker, the farm neighbor who looked after Ma, the owner of the Waverly True Value.

John lowered the plow, then his window. Though dressed for the Arctic, his Midwest warmth shined through. He lowered his head to identify us. "Hey there, Steve! Whatcha up to?"

I nodded hello and slinked away, stuffing boxes into our vehicle.

"We're moving Ma to the Legacy," Steve said, trying to hide his green glove on his right hand and his black glove on his left, "and Barb knew just where to get boxes."

"Helen's moving to the Legacy, huh? Good for her!" said John. "We have extra packing boxes back at the store. We'd have given them to her for free!"

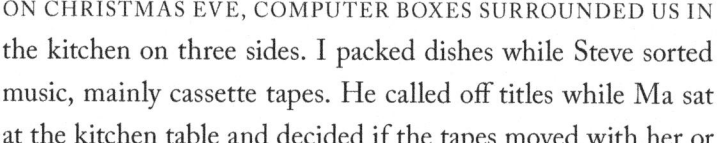

ON CHRISTMAS EVE, COMPUTER BOXES SURROUNDED US IN the kitchen on three sides. I packed dishes while Steve sorted music, mainly cassette tapes. He called off titles while Ma sat at the kitchen table and decided if the tapes moved with her or would be shipped to Goodwill. Steve dug into a box of tapes and pulled one out.

"Ma, what do I do with *Down Memory Trail* by The Sons of the Pioneers?" he asked.

"Oh, let me see that," she replied. "Warren picked that up for me on our way back from Alaska," she added, so excited that she pulled herself from the table and shuffled toward the cassette player.

She insisted on playing the cassette. But her arthritic fingers trembled, fumbling as she tried to set the tape upright and slide it into the player.

"Steven, play this for me," said Ma.

A tinny melody drifted into the air, a ballad full of violins and acoustic guitar and piano, all held together with brushed drums and a steady bass. Ma closed her eyes. Her shoulders and neck dropped, and she melted away, disappearing decades away. A smile she undoubtedly gave to Papa years back appeared before us. She lifted her arms, her right arm high as if Papa's hand were there, the other touching his imaginary shoulder. She swayed, her slippered feet shushing the linoleum in tiny steps.

Steve caught my eye and love filled his; this moment would never come again. This moment represented an essential point in our marriage.

He asked for a special request, a hallmark of one of our vows. "Dance with me?" he asked Ma and me.

He took Ma's uplifted hand and the three of us danced in the boxed-up kitchen, to the music she and Papa had danced to half a century before, on a snowy Christmas Eve, in the home where their life stories mattered.

We leaned together and became one, arms draped over shoulders and waists, turning endlessly, endlessly, like ballerinas in a music box. Ma's head rested on Steve's shoulder, her eyes dancing with mine, our laughter adding a higher chorus. He softly kissed his mom on her cheeks and me on the lips. At the end of the song, when the tape recorder's button snapped off and ended the magic, Ma giggled and added a few hip gyrations. But looking up, she saw Steve's teary eyes.

And her mother's love knew. "Let's dance again," she said.

Steve rewound the cassette, and our musical carousel went round and round one more time.

Ma went to bed shortly afterward. Steve took a shower first while I wrote. In those ten minutes, I wrote lyrics on a Subway napkin to capture the night's magic. I passed the napkin to Steve as I stepped into the shower and he stepped out. And in those twenty minutes, he wrote the music to preserve the words.

The next morning, Ma plucked through an old box of cornflakes, checking for bugs, an old Depression trick. We sang our song for her, "Three Hearts Dancing":

Christmas Eve, on our family farm, packing up Ma's life
Ninety years, her country life just slipped inside this box
She said, "The tapes can go, but can we play this one now?
It reminds me of my only love."

Trembling fingers could not make the old cassette
    work right
So she asked me for some help to listen to her song
The song began, her beauty came alive
And I asked my two great loves to dance

Three hearts dancing to one beat.
And the music of our love goes on
Ma laid her head on my chest
And the sweetness of my wife's breath softly on my neck.

Ma said she used to dance with Papa all the time
Oh, she smiled, as she stepped inside her yesterdays
It brought her back to Papa's warming arms
As she gently swayed inside my own.

I held these two ladies who fill up my world
My heart drifted to the time we'd be apart
Ma looked at me—she seemed to know my every thought
And she asked us for another dance.

A week and a half after Ma had asked for our help to move her—and two days after a Nebraska blizzard snowed us in anyway—I sat on Ma's master bathroom floor, reaching blindly inside a large sink cabinet. Ma sat on the toilet seat, supervising what stayed and what went. I pulled out dozens (I repeat dozens) of wadded rags, remnants of the Depression's signature mindset. I pulled out an enormous tube of K-Y jelly, 12 ounces of fun, its label old from a bygone era. (I just had to investigate its origin. It was introduced in 1904 by VanHorn and Sawtooth Pharmaceutical.)

I held the tube up and silently waited.

Ma's animated version of US history prattled on. "And Millie—that flimsy, little floozy—and George danced all night! They married in—"

But her voice disappeared and her face flushed. When she saw the K-Y jelly, her expression contorted into a little girl's embarrassed face, soft eyes cast downward, a demure pained smile, like her soul had been caught in a cookie jar.

"Ohhhhhhhh!" she exclaimed. "Oh my, oh my, oh…" her voice trailed away, into a corner.

Laughter bumbled against my lips. "Keep or throw away, Ma?"

Finally, she giggled. "I think we can throw that away now."

I pulled out more treasures. An old Comet bottle, crystallized over decades. Papa's old shaving kit. Lipsticks. Old toilet brushes, crushed into shapes of clouds and dog piles.

Then I found it: another enormous tube of K-Y jelly. Still sealed. Unopened.

By the looks of it, it dated back to the fifties when Steve was born. Now I understood why Steve was the last child. I became the Statue of Liberty and held the tube up like a torch.

"Really, Ma?"

She sighed. Lightning does strike in the same place twice, but embarrassment? No. She asked me the mother lode of all questions: "Well, Barbie, could you use it?"

ALL THE LEGACY Terrace needed was a pair of dice to become a living Monopoly board. I picked up my game piece, the shoe, and explored its facility, bouncing over its colored squares and found out that everything anyone needed was just around the corner: beauty shop and bank, ice cream store and pool halls, gardens and post office. Other game pieces like ambulances served as everyday taxis to and from the Legacy. Life was compact here, brimming with men and boatloads of women, on foot, in walkers and wheelchairs. Las Vegas patterned carpets and tall velvety roller chairs filled an elegant dining room, goldened with richly textured, striped wallpaper.

At the dining tables, high schoolers served as the wait staff, their patience and respect for elders a surprising, refreshing sight. The dining room was a germane sea of red and white—red sweatshirts and white hair—as everybody prepared for the Cornhusker football game. Outside its doors, walkers lined up like Harleys in Sturgis. Exquisite derby hats lined the lobby display cases while aging residents who shed their egos long ago greeted us with pure smiles. In the gardens, a blind resident fed the ducklings, somehow, and an owl hunted them in the darkness, his hoots lulling the Legacy residents to sleep.

Upstairs on the third floor, Steve measured out the walls to the nearest inch so Ma's favorite paintings, including those she made herself, would fit into her new one-bedroom apartment.

I added the feminine touches of a pink bath set and handed Ma her antique doll, which she placed upon her twin bed, spreading its skirt evenly. Her apartment eventually became a showroom for future residents. A spinning wheel was the apartment's focal point, a family heirloom checked through Ellis Island, along with other antiques that filled her space, transposing her inner beauty as objects upon her shelves.

We only forgot one thing. Heat.

Our ninety-two-year-old mother enjoyed her first night in her new home with an outside temperature of 15 degrees. That's 15 degrees Nebraska, not 15 degrees Fahrenheit. When it's 15 degrees Nebraska, eyeballs freeze. And that's how she brought in her new year on January 1, the beginning of the best years of her life, as she would say, the anniversaries of Papa's death and our wedding.

By moving Ma, we had relied on three vows. We were thankful on so many levels: grateful that Ma had usurped the typical dilemma of moving a parent into a higher level of care, grateful that her timing was over my Christmas break, grateful that she looked forward to spending time with friends already living at the Legacy, grateful that she could afford its luxury. We honored special requests—to miss Christmas back home, to dance in the kitchen. We prayed for help and found perfection in Ma's new home.

But one remaining vow lined up for duty when we returned to Denver, due to an unforeseen glitch. As we settled Ma in over the two weeks of Christmas, Katie decided she wanted to get to know her father better and moved in with him over holiday break. I arrived home to her empty bedroom. We were suddenly empty nesters one year ahead of schedule.

19

The Unique Unfoldings

THIS SHOULD HAVE BEEN THE HAPPIEST TIME IN OUR MAR-
riage. Our relationship was strong. Ma thrived at the Legacy.
My mom enjoyed traveling to Mexico every year with family.
Our daughters were moving forward in their lives. Our brothers
and their wives were content. Honey slept wherever she wanted.
Our health was excellent. And after being married for three
years, Steve and I would officially retire together the following
summer. He was unwinding his business career of forty years,
finalizing the sale of his business to Craig to escape the grind of
international travel; after twenty-three years of classrooms, my
last group of students was a gem.

But I was lost without Katie.

For fourteen years, she had been the capital letter at the
beginning of my sentence and the exclamation point at its end.
But she had also made the same statement of importance with
two other father figures in her life, Uncle Mike and Uncle Steve,
who helped raise her. And now she had another father figure,
my husband, Steve. This arrangement confused her. She had
Uncle Mike, who gave her leftover communion wafers in the

backseat of his car when snacks were sparse. He drove four hundred miles out of his way to Kansas for her one-hour soccer game. Uncle Steve dressed in drag as Britney Spears for Katie's Halloween party and danced to Lizzie McGuire whenever she was sick to cheer her up.

Enter Steve Vannoy, nationally known parenting guru. Could it all have been too much of a good thing? Like me and my four choices of final resting places, Katie had four options of fathers. Unlike me, she made a choice. She followed her gut and realized she finally needed to make amends with her real dad.

I reached for the gift of gratitude that, after sixteen years, a world with her dad had opened wide. But there was a vast space in my head that used to occupy thoughts of her; my teaching demands tried to fill it, but I wouldn't allow it. Now, all three daughters lived separate lives—Katie with her dad, Ali in Montana, Emmy in Baltimore. We needed new passions. And our tenth vow was poised to challenge us.

Vow 10

*I will celebrate and support
your unique unfolding.*

Like many men whose identities are tied in their professions, Steve ruminated, briefly, about what he was going to do next. Then, he didn't waste any time. He earned his sailing license, first in the San Juan islands on *Raven's Dance*, a forty-three-foot wooden yacht under the command of our friend

Howard Edson. The yacht's owner granted Steve and me use of the captain's quarters on the stern of the ship, framed with cabin windows on three sides. The views would have been stellar if Steve and I hadn't thrown up overboard, coating the windows with vomit for a week.

Next, he chartered a boat with his buddy Dale in the Abaco Islands, followed by our sailing trip to the British Virgin Islands. This was all in preparation for Steve's bucket list item of captaining an Alaskan Nordic Tug up Alaska's Inside Passage with me, Gilligan, his first mate. Navigating rough, converging swells of Pacific tides around Alaska's peninsulas was nothing compared to docking against gravitational currents.

"Look at that guy," Captain Steve said, pointing to a man standing on the edge of a slip as we idled into the Auke Bay marina. "He's so drunk he's peeing off the dock."

"Let's dock on the other side, please," I answered. "I'll jump off and secure us. I see a cleat there." Leaping off, my string line instantly pulled taut and began dragging me toward the dock's end, past the urinating sailor.

"Hang on, sweetie, I'll jump over and help you!" Steve shouted, and after jumping off the tug, he quickly realized that its 170 hp turbocharged diesel engine was still in gear. It was no use. The tug now pulled both of us, our feet slipping over creaky dock boards as the boat bobbed toward a shore jutting with boulders.

"Let me help you," said the drunken sailor, zipping up his pants and zigzagging down the dock toward me. He threw his weight into my line as Steve managed a split leap back on board.

Fortunately, Steve cut the engine before the $225,000 tug reached the boulders.

Unfortunately, I pushed Steve in airport wheelchairs between our flights home.

Steve healed. He amped up his hiking passion and spent months on the Appalachian Trail. The Colorado Trail. Kilimanjaro. Canyonlands National Park. The Kalalau Trail.

Meanwhile, I shopped. I also got certified in Animal Disaster Rescue in Arizona. So I shopped down there too.

And I resumed writing again, resurrecting my truest passion next to travel. I joined Lighthouse Writers, a Denver-based writing community, and made friends with like-minded people who, like me, picked up words off the street and played with them.

I was making up for rushed time, for time spent trying to be two parents at once and conducting orchestras of learners who would ignore my musical score and bring themselves in whenever they wanted, in their own beats of time. I finally had the freedom to dream, time to breathe.

High on my list was transforming Steve's manly mansion. I was tired of walnut wood trim and paintings of retrievers with dead ducks. Feminine feng shui didn't exist in our home.

I had owned a Barbie as a child, but she didn't make the move to Denver. Her leg was amputated while trying to break in Johnny West's horse, Thunderbolt. I had little in common with Barbie, outside of my name; I had pigtails and freckles and played softball with a Goodwill mitt. Also, I owned few toys, since most of the things I played with as a child were outdoors: snowmen, leaf piles, basketball hoops. But I could dream. Barbie was my go-to gal to reclaim my femininity. But my frugality intervened, and I refused to spend $25 on a new Barbie. So I peeked into the nearest thrift store.

Let the hoarding begin.

Beautiful Barbie #1, dressed in an exquisite sequin-speckled brown evening gown, peered from a showcase window.

"Won't you be my neighbor?" she pleaded from behind the glass, her arms forever posed in rounded anticipation. I checked her price: $2.50. Was she worth the cost? I thought about Steve's veggie burger at Whole Foods, a full $2.50 higher in price. I deliberated. Hard.

I rescued Barbie and she became my neighbor, resting on our kitchen counter, next to Papa's antique shaving kit, which inexplicably had ended up in our dining room curio.

"Just wait until Steve sees you," I said to Barbie, fluffing her dress, primping her hair.

"Who's this?" Steve laughed, later, picking up Barbie #1. "She's pretty! I like her."

His fondness of her demonstrated how he supported our tenth vow: I will celebrate and support your unique unfolding. In our long version of our vows, Steve promised: I will honor who you are and do everything I can to help you discover and develop even more of your spirit, joyfulness, goodness, dreams, and greatness. So I returned to the thrift store and lined up behind the seniors, jealous of their discounts.

The next Barbie I found was London Barbie, so I brought her home.

"I like the feather in her hat," Steve responded, stroking her blue felt hat, "and you only pick ones in good shape. I'm proud of your pickiness."

I gave him a kiss-me smile because, roughly translated, he meant, *I want to support Barb's unique unfolding.* His generosity gave me an idea. Since he appreciated the Barbies so much and wanted me to be unique, I would honor him by collecting Barbies from the twenty-six countries the facilitators in his company, Pathways to Leadership, had traveled to. I would lavishly display the Barbies as tributes to Steve's talent, his perseverance. His ingenuity.

I am so thoughtful and resourceful, too, because I remembered where I got my wedding dress—eBay—and discovered eBay sold Barbies too. Mind you, not Amazon. Amazon is not as thrifty.

Swiss and Russian and Australian and Indian and Brazilian and Peruvian and Canadian and Japanese Barbies and a couple dozen more Barbies started in-fighting for shelf space in the dining room curio. I called Steve's office and asked the staff if any of Steve's sessions included a trip to Argentina, because Argentina Barbie's makeup was heart-stopping and I couldn't wait much longer.

More Barbies took root inside dresser drawers and sprouted in sacks until I bought thrift store display cases so they could bloom on all three levels of the house. But I still needed more room; luckily, I remembered the unfinished wine cellar beneath the house. We didn't drink, so the racks were empty—the perfect size for Barbies. Better still, Steve never went down there. *He'd never know.*

Four hundred sixty-two Barbies later, I had single-handedly inflated the cost of gently used Barbies in Denver by 50 percent. How many thrift stores does the Denver Front Range metro area have? Ask me. I expanded my Barbie search and rescued more as we traveled around the country, in Phoenix, along the Mississippi River, Oregon, and the Dakotas, both of them.

The high standards I held for my students transferred to my expectations for my Barbies: evening gowns preferred, mint condition, hairstyle intact, positively no chewed-off hands or feet. And, where space permitted, I took the Barbies out of the box, deflating their values. Why? I wanted to enjoy them. Someone, someday, would do that, eventually. It may as well be me.

At first, family and friends chuckled at the collection. Then Steve began ushering contractors into our dining room—and our loft and rec room and breezeway—where sea to shining sea of Barbie faces lined up like a Miss Universe beauty pageant.

"Which Barbie is your favorite?" Steve would ask them.

Don't laugh. While a few of my women friends disapproved of Barbie's image and refused to pick a favorite, all contractors—no exception—would dart their eyes, study the Barbies, and unfailingly point toward their favorites.

Men. You can't take the Barbie out of the boy.

Then Steve would ask if the contractors had any female relatives. Most did, so Steve had permission to give away the favorites.

Except for the Barbies of the World collection.

Those belonged to Steve.

Barbie dolls began my passion as a collector, all at thrift store prices. I proceeded to amass thousands of hardback picture books and plush storybook characters like Clifford, Spot, Olivia, Biscuit. In our home, Steve helped me create a turn-of-the-century children's library with 4,000 titles, accompanied by a secret tunnel entrance lined with statues and cherubs, the ceiling frescoed with a replica of Florence's Duomo. I created a separate girls and boys reading area with all our hundreds of storybook characters, which admittedly looks creepy at night.

Build it and they will come, and sure enough, kids flocked over, neighborhood kids and grandkids, and former students. Even this house rooted for me. Once, when Steve was gone, our hot water heater broke. I mopped out its oversized storeroom, gleefully. I told Katie, "This room is the perfect size for a quaint display of porcelain Victorian dolls, accented with bridal lace and veils."

Eventually, Boyds Bears and Cherished Teddies and Starbucks Bearista Bears created a flash mob in our home until, finally, finally, I was vindicated; our home was suitably balanced between masculinity and femininity.

Meanwhile, with trepidation, Ali, Emmy, and Katie asked us, "What are we supposed to do with all of this when you guys are gone?"

I smiled. I had no idea.

20

The Band Is Born

AS MY TEACHING CAREER APPROACHED ITS END, I BEGAN marking the passage of time with the beauty of seasons instead of holidays. We returned to Lincoln the following Christmas for Ma's first sing-along at the Legacy Terrace. She had gained noticeable weight since we last saw her. Lifting her pant legs, we couldn't find her ankles; her feet and calves were hard and had ballooned to the size of her thighs. She needed to go to the emergency room. Immediately. Her congestive heart failure medication wasn't working anymore.

We drove to St. Elizabeth's Hospital, taking the side streets through neighborhoods glowing in manger scenes and inflatable Santas on snowy frozen lawns to distract us. We pulled into the emergency entrance, where the Christmas magic disappeared.

The triage nurse barraged ninety-three-year-old Ma about her medical history, beginning with her health record just before the Great Crash of 1929. "How many surgeries have you had? Do you know what year it is? When did you last have a bowel movement?"

"Speaking of bowel movements, let's get Ma to the bathroom," I suggested, excusing her, since she was two questions behind the interrogator anyway. I whispered to Steve as I wheeled her out, "Make up things to stop all these questions. She needs the doctor."

At 10:30 p.m., technicians took X-rays, then wheeled her into a small exam room, donning her in a white hospital gown with pink dots. The only decoration on the wall was a crucifix, fitting for a Catholic hospital.

The nurse wrapped Ma's legs and torso, compressing them to combat the fluid retention. Ma looked like a vanilla ice cream cone with pink strawberry sprinkles, all the fleshy fat spilling over her waist. Finally, the nurse gave her Tylenol PM. She'd been awake over twenty-four hours. She kept chatting with the hospital staff as they came and went, bragging about her son's musical talents and offering her own. A chaplain came by.

"How can I help you?" he asked.

"The Lord's Prayer would be nice to hear," answered Steve.

"Certainly," began the priest. "Our Father, who art in Heaven..."

Ma's alto voice lifted into song. "Hallowed be...Thy name..." she continued and continued, drawing in passing nurses from the hallway until she reached the climax, the part of the song that is so high that only angels dwell there. And because her lower body was so constricted, she had no problem sailing through the high note.

"FOREVER!" the alto sang, hitting the high G, her eyes closed, peaceful, Tylenol PM-induced.

Three nurses, Steve, and I finished the song. "Amen!" we chorused.

The priest looked at Ma, then to Steve and me. "You all sing well," he said, surprised.

The charge nurse brought consent forms for Ma to sign, asking her questions about a living will, her next of kin. Formalities.

"Helen, do you want to be resuscitated?"

What did I just hear?

It was 12:30 in the morning, and this ninety-three-year-old woman hadn't slept in twenty-four hours. Her legs were shaped like those of a Butterball turkey. She'd been poked and X-rayed for two and a half hours. She hadn't eaten in seven hours. And she had taken a Tylenol PM two hours ago.

Ma was confused.

The charge nurse rephrased her question. "Helen, if your heart stops beating, do you want us to start it again?"

Shocked, Ma pulled herself up in her bed and looked sharply at the nurse. "Of course! I'm not done yet!"

AT 2:30 A.M., Steve and Ma slept; I held Ma's hand and cradled my husband's head in my lap. The exam room was quiet, like being tucked inside a locket, save the heart monitor's beep that had began disappearing from my awareness a few hours before. I caressed Ma's fragile fingers and traced her pink fingernails, rubbing her arthritic joints until my touch stopped on her wedding ring, placed there seventy-three years earlier, never once removed. I watched the second hand on the clock tick by, marker by marker, but I didn't feel the passing of time. I was beyond it, inside a holy moment, a soundless, timeless place we land upon only a handful of moments in our lives.

I watched the rise of Ma's chest, in, out, inhale, exhale. The breath of life. Every breath of hers, a gift. The inhale, God's grace dipping into her body. The exhale, my prayer, my hope that He'll give her more grace. Grace, hope, grace, hope, in out, in out, God was present. God was in the room.

And there was an empty chair. The bedside commode.

Oh, no, I couldn't do that.

Steve always said you can't avoid a don't.

An empty chair. You-Know-Who always sits in an empty chair.

No…no! Don't put Him there, Barb! You're a Christian woman! You aren't capable of thinking that, are you?

But wait a minute: I wasn't on Ambien. There was no vortex. No labyrinth. Just my prayer—and my empty chair. And pastors had taught me that Christ could show up anywhere.

I did it.

I saw Him—or did I imagine Him? I straddled two worlds—the sterile emergency room and an ethereal cloudy curl of heaven; either way, it didn't matter anymore.

There He was. Jesus in his dazzling robe, fully clothed, sitting on the potty. Serene. Interested.

I didn't move, but I was amused. It was, after all, 2:30 a.m. So I went with it. I offered, "Do You want to trade seats?"

He smiled, discerning my confluence of emotion. "No, thank you," He replied, "I do believe you have the best seat in the house, though."

"Thanks for being here," I said, or I prayed. I didn't know which.

As He received my gratitude, Jesus's face became more peaceful, if that were even possible. His words to me were as soft as Ma's breathing. "Where else would I be?" Jesus seemed to say.

I glanced over His shoulder to the crucifix hanging on the wall. He turned around and stared at it. Then he conceded.

"Not one of my best days." His eyebrow lifted, and with it, His spirit. "But definitely yours."

Touché.

I stroked my husband's hair. "Thanks for giving me this memory," I whispered. "I'm glad I get to be in it."

"Me too. I'm glad you invited me to share it."

Then Jesus shifted in His chair.

I reacted. "Oh! Do you need to go? Bathroom's just across the hall."

Amusement lit His eyes this time. "Well, I need to go, but not there."

He stood and gazed at Steve and Ma. Between their two lifetimes ticked over 150 years of life. And with mine added in, over two hundred. And the power of each day of those two hundred years pierced His gaze.

Jesus raised His arms. His fullness emptied into us.

"Precious, aren't they?" He asked.

Ma snored.

TWO DAYS LATER, Ma was released from St. Elizabeth's at 11:00 a.m. Her sing-along was set for 1:00. She insisted on stopping at Walgreens and picking up lipstick, her remaining foible in an otherwise comfortable ego of hers.

She made her grand entrance in the Iron Horse Saloon for our annual sing-along right at 1:00. Ma was anything but humble after her ordeal. "I'm back!" she shouted, crossing through the saloon's foyer to greet her punctual seventy guests.

"Helen! We heard! How are you? How are you?" her fans chorused.

Ma blushed. "I'm in pretty good shape for the shape I'm in!"

The three of us led the sing-along for two hours, including a birthday song for Honey, when our ninety-three-year-old mother blew out the candles for our fifteen-year-old dog.

Because the hospital's priest complimented our singing, Ma thought it was a sign from God. As a Christmas gift, she bought us a sound system to play music together—a new keyboard, mics, speakers, mixer, the works—and made us agree to come back to Lincoln and perform at the Legacy. So our sweetly feminine dining room, resplendent with Barbie regalia, transformed into a recording studio with heavy metal equipment.

We named our band We Scream American, aptly suited because, as we traveled, not one person ever incorrectly guessed where we came from. We first performed in our home for several groups of friends, dinner theater-style. The playlist approached one hundred songs, covers from the 1940s: "You Are My Sunshine," Ma's favorite, to James Taylor to Michael Bublé.

With the help of our first manager, Dawn Shepherd, resident guru of Denver's senior centers, we branched out to retirement homes and nursing facilities, graduating into coffee shops, restaurants, country clubs, and nonprofit functions. Our groupie friends followed us and cheered us on, ignoring the sour notes as practice sweetened them. Sometimes we played for a full house; other times, bar managers simply stuck us in a far corner or even inside an empty room. We seeded our tip jar, as musicians commonly do, and we occasionally paid for our friends' meals just to have an audience; consequently, we are the only band in history to earn a negative $3 in tips in one evening.

We turned Ma into a rock star by recording and releasing a music video on YouTube of our "Three Hearts Dancing." We recorded our song at Coupe Studios in Boulder, despite a poor vocal day for me. Our sound engineer, a former piano tuner, climbed the walls as we sang. Even God joined in with an extra Bible verse: "On the eighth day, God said, 'Let there be pitch control.'"

AFTER THE RECORDING, we watched the sound engineer bend our vocal tracks to pitch perfection, rendering our voices, and therefore our band's sound, unrecognizable, so we changed our name to Postcard Note. Our producer, Bryan Boorujy, filmed the video in our home gardens, but also, more importantly, in the city of Elmwood, Nebraska, inside a house listed under the National Register of Historic Places. Steve, Ma, and I danced, sang, and acted. But someone else stole the show: Honey, debuting in her first music video too.

21

The $46,758 Beer

A FEW MONTHS BEFORE WE RETIRED, WE JOINED THE ranks of old people and decided to buy an RV. A perfect solution for free time, it would allow Steve to travel without getting into an airplane and enable me to see the fall colors of Vermont, something impossible to do because of fall conferences in October. Better yet, Katie was headed to Syracuse University in New York, so an RV trip was the perfect excuse to stop by and see her. Steve and I attended our first RV show and grabbed dinner at Bubba Gump, sharing one Coors Light.

We don't drink anymore, because the last beer we split cost us $46,758. Our $46,758 bottle of beer loosened us up just enough to return to our first RV show and confidently offer a lowball price for a Montana 36-foot fifth wheel. Five minutes before the show's closing, with RV fumes clouding our judgment, we offered $10,000 off the sticker price. We smirked as the sales manager excused himself and ran the numbers. He returned and accepted our price. We became instant, clueless owners of an RV, a rig that didn't fit in Yosemite National Park or Death Valley or any provincial Canadian campground.

Buying an RV reminded me of the picture book *If You Give a Mouse a Cookie*. In the story, a boy offers a mouse a cookie and discovers all the strings attached, like the mouse needing a glass of milk to go with it, and then a straw, and then a mirror to check for a milk mustache, and so forth.

In my version, *If You Give Your Husband an RV,* he's going to want a Ford F250 diesel to go with it. It will remind him he needs tinted windows and a $1,500 hitch to pull it, and so on and so on. My husband, Mr. Nebraska Farm Boy, who yearned for his childhood pulling hay stackers and combines, found an irrefutable way to get back to his country roots: He lived in Morrison, a small town. He had his woman and he had his dog. All he needed was a truck.

A handful of hours passed. A diesel Ford F250 joined our family. I learned that men name their vehicles, so "Tall Boy" Vannoy pulled in the garage next to my Subaru, "Backster." Speaking of the garage, Steve deemed it too accessible for burglars, so he promptly installed bars over the garage windows, added padlocks on the garage doors and Fort Knox-sized deadbolts leading into the house.

One night while under the dining room table, Honey said, "Daddy? When Mommy moved in, she only got window security stickers from Home Depot."

I considered not coming home for a couple nights because breaking into my own house was too exhausting. When Steve traveled, I slept in the truck. It was the safest place in our home.

I now own a truck I can't back out of the garage. I own an RV long enough to rival big rigs at rest stops. I have driven my RV a total of 1.5 inches. That's negative 1.5 inches, backing into the chocks.

AFTER THIRTY-THREE YEARS OF TEACHING CHILDREN, twenty-three of them in public education, Steve threw me a surprise retirement party, followed by another reception at my school. Three hundred favorite people showed up. I gave each of my students a note inside a tooth fairy box and displayed each one of my class pictures, certain that the kids and their families would appreciate how children grow up.

But instead, I heard, "Get a load of Ms. Lynn's hair there and there and there!"

My students brought their own children, tiny faces with their parents' familiarity etched inside their smiles. I posed in pictures, stooping low, with my now high school students, forgetting they had grown, perhaps subconsciously wishing for those precious days with them years and years ago. On my last day of school, Katie and I walked out of the building, holding hands. I recall lifting my face toward the sun as I stepped outside, with a single thought: freedom. I wondered if I would ever return to a classroom, to hear twenty-five children burst into laughter at once, to watch a proud child strut away from my desk as if earning an Oscar, to have a chance to make a worldwide difference every single day of my life.

I retired from teaching the same year Katie graduated from high school. My dream came true! I was officially a stay-at-home mom for two months before she would go to college. The only glitch was that Katie lived with her dad.

She boarded a plane and went off to Syracuse University for her freshman year. Steve, Honey, and I followed her in our fifth wheel twenty-four hours later, ensuring that we wouldn't miss parents' weekend sixty days later. And how glad we were—her high school boyfriend chose Syracuse as well (what a surprise), and he also chose to dump her on parents' weekend at 10:00 p.m. after our lovely dinner and Katie's choir concert. I hated social media at that moment, because while Katie sobbed in my arms at 10:26, her blockhead boyfriend posted a Facebook photo of his new girlfriend before the eleventh hour.

"How could he, Mom?" sobbed Katie, clinging to Honey.

Some things don't deserve a response. Some things don't deserve to live either.

My good-riddance memory of her boyfriend was his silhouette, skateboarding across campus with a pillow tucked under his arm toward Bachelorette #2, his glazed eyeballs reminiscent of that elk I had encountered a few years earlier.

That night, Katie, Steve, and I camped out in the last vacancy at Villages RV Park at the intersection of I-90 and hell with no air conditioning, windows wide open. Honey picked up on the drama and commenced her newly acquired nervous tic of licking her behind, trancelike. Unbelievably, I could hear Honey's slurping above Katie's whimpers and the whine of eighteen-wheelers zipping by, above the distracting blare of the *Spider-Man* movie, above Steve's chomping of popcorn.

What's a scorned mother to do? Lose it.

"HONEY! STOP LICKING YOUR BUTT!" I screamed to the population of Syracuse.

I hooked up the RV myself the next day and towed Steve away.

22

Castles and Cathedrals

ON OUR FIVE-YEAR ANNIVERSARY, STEVE SURPRISED ME with a ten-day trip to Europe to renew our vows. He wouldn't tell me where we were going.

Ever since I was fifteen, I dreamed of its castles and cathedrals and Steve knew it, so I packed my bags with the only essentials I knew: Oreos, a journal, Tootsie Rolls.

"You still have our vows in your wallet?" he asked me, thumbing through his at the airport. He leaned in for a kiss. "I get to show you the world. How lucky am I?"

Geneva was our first stop, with a misty train ride to Montreux, its sister town on the lake, entwined together with vineyards stretching up the gentle rise of the Alps, bordered with thousands of blossoming flower boxes dotting Lake Geneva in red and yellow hues.

In the distance, Chillon Castle materialized into view, its turrets clouded in fog against the Dents du Midi summits. Chillon stood upon an island, invisible in the haze, casting the illusion of enchantment that instantly satisfied my lifetime of yearning. Entering its courtyard, I confirmed the belief that everyone has a place they visit for the first time that whispers, "You're home." For me, it was a European castle.

Steve disappeared around a cobbled corner for a few minutes as I feasted on the castle's ambience.

"Angel! Come here!" said Steve. I followed his voice and found him atop a narrow staircase, standing inside a turret overlooking Lake Geneva. He was grinning. "I had to make these castles of yours a reality. Get up here for the view."

THE TURRET REPRESENTED all my childhood and adult fantasies; it was the yellow brick road, the tunnel to heaven, and the Broncos winning the Super Bowl, all rolled into one.

"Yay! A turret!" I exclaimed. Steve's pride drew me immediately upward.

I bolted up the stone staircase, carefully keeping my head down to delay the sight I anticipated. But on my last step, I whacked my forehead on the door's threshold. Both feet flew up, knocking me flat on my back. My first view from the turret was its ceiling, which had stars spinning in its rafters.

A welt pushed against my entire forehead. "Angel!" Steve cried, kneeling beside me.

It was then that I vaguely remembered my high school European history teacher's comment about short doorways, which slowed down invaders.

I covered my forehead with a cap, and we meandered up through the cobbled village of Montreux to a quaint stone church on the hillside. Inside, a few parishioners contemplated, prayed, eyes closed.

"Angel, a special request. Will you sing for me?"

I stepped into our tradition of singing solos in yet another church around the world, first in Melbourne as Steve proposed and, later, in New Zealand, Mexico, Kauai, Vancouver, the British Virgin Islands, Newfoundland, and now Switzerland.

(I can't believe I got to write that sentence.)

I'm glad we had the snacks, because Steve answered every woman's anniversary dream on our next stop: trudging across a glacier on the Top of Europe, near Jungfrau, in -30 degree winds, colder and more awful than snowshoeing in the Keystone Valley. I hoped to be rescued by some St. Bernards, but the only two I encountered in the Alps barked in a sideshow tourist booth. I didn't want a picture of the dogs but instead asked for a picture of me to prove I was still alive and could muster a smile, because I was fuming at my husband's choice of European travel. For the photo, I took off my Michelin Man hats and gloves because I needed to look natural, beautiful, carefree.

(A footnote here: As a point of information, I figured out that Maria von Trapp was a sham. What woman in her right mind would hike in the Alps in a skirt without water? And then sing about it?)

Steve reassured me, "Angel, relax now. You'll love where I'm taking you next."

From Jungfrau, we boarded the infamous Glacier Express train. All Steve shared was that we rode the train until the tracks ran out. We disembarked and found a chauffeur with a sign labeled, "VANNOY."

"Where am I, and what is the name of our hotel?" I asked the man, blankly.

The chauffeur remained professional, though his eyes enlarged. "Ma'am, you are in Pontresina, and the name of your hotel is The Grand Hotel Kronenhof."

Pontresina's quaint village is akin to Aspen in the States. The Grand Hotel Kronenhof had been the setting for a James Bond movie, its location nestled in the valley of snowy mountain ski slopes. Snowflakes began to fall as the chauffeur opened our doors. Pontresina's cobblestone streets were deserted, save the yellow streetlights, speckling with snowflakes.

The hotel's foyer towered three stories high, gilded with marble posts, rich mahogany walls, and velvet red chairs, throne-sized. But my eyes spotted the most superior interior decoration—live bunnies in a large cage in a corner. Easter was the following day.

I darted toward the bunnies, sticking my fingers in their cage and ogling them, as the stiff concierges stood at attention, moving only their eyes, watching me. I returned to the front desk and regressed to my first-grade understanding of the world:

"I love your bunnies! I used to have one living in my dining room. Her name, er...his name was Ellie May!" I bragged breathlessly, "He was housebroken and had the full run of our house. My dog Honey would round him up at night for me and get him back in his cage to sleep!"

I was excited to see that I had something in common with foreigners.

The receptionist glanced at her manager, wondering how to unwind me. The bellhop brought our suitcases up without a word.

The next morning was Easter. We attended the German Easter sunrise service in Pontresina's town square's chapel. And while Steve and I had already attended Easter services in English, Portuguese, Spanish, and now German, the rhythms of the cadences and pauses of the liturgies mirrored each other, regardless of language, a comforting surprise.

European store owners, especially those with bakeries and chocolate shops, embellish their storefronts for Easter with the same vigor as we decorate for Halloween, with chocolates and bunnies, twinkling lights and colored eggs. We entered an elegant chocolate shop for Lindt strawberry truffles. I taste-tested its richness and found it sickeningly sweet, too foreign for me.

I approached the glass counter. "Do you have any other chocolates that aren't as rich?" I asked slowly, loudly, in case the concessionaire didn't understand English.

Politely, she stepped right, indicating an exquisite display of other brands inside the case. "Yah. Toblerone, here." She tapped two other selections. "Teuscher. Ragusa."

The chocolates looked so dressed up in swirls they didn't look real. I preferred letters. "Do you have any M&M's?" I asked.

The concessionaire slammed the showcase door. "Never."

We traveled next to Rome and the Vatican. Steve had bought us two first-class airline tickets, but I rejected the idea. "It's a short flight. I don't want to spend $1,800 on a seat for one hour. I can ride in economy," I insisted.

Steve shrugged his shoulders, understanding my frugality and knowing this was not the mountain he wanted to die on. He took my hand briefly. "It's only a little over an hour. I'll miss you," he said, preboarding ahead of me.

I passed his seat on my way back to steerage as a flight attendant took his meal order. The plane took off and I waited for my drink, and I hoped for cookies. The aroma of seasoned meat wafted into my row until I couldn't stand it any longer. I decided to pass Steve another note. I jotted a note on a napkin and buzzed the flight attendant.

"Excuse me," I said, "could you please pass this note up to my husband in first class?" I had folded the napkin in case she was snoopy. "He's in 3D."

"He's in first class and you're back here?" she asked.

My note read: "Sweetheart, could you please send part of your meal back here in steerage? All I have are peanuts. Unsalted. Love you."

I got a piece of chicken.

ON OUR WAY to the Vatican, we entered a subway train crawling with passengers. I pressed my purse close, zippers closed against my body. I took one step inside and could not take another. A teenaged boy planted his feet squarely in front of me, his face and eyes eerily vacant. I stepped around him, forcing Steve to follow me, thereby giving the boy's accomplice enough bustling distraction to slip his hand inside Steve's pant pocket. What happened next only happens in movies.

I heard a disturbing commotion. By the time I turned around, Steve had morphed into some prehistoric gorilla creature with no semblance of human evolution. His rage was palpable. Steve grabbed the pickpocketing punk and, with one arm, slammed him into the subway floor, choking his neck. Aiming a shaky fist, Steve heroically managed to balance our dinner's doggy bag in the other. His swift and powerful response stunned and paralyzed the pickpocketing punk, as well as all the other subway riders.

For a few seconds, Steve's humanity hung in the balance. I had never, ever observed that unrestrained expression in my husband. In an instant, though, I knew that Steve was not going to hit him, even though his anger spewed. Instead,

Steve got in the punk's face and screamed, "Don't you ever touch my family again!" And with the same rush of adrenaline, he yanked that lanky lowlife by the neck and threw him off the train in one smooth motion. My last memory of the guy? Horizontal in the air.

Then I realized his accomplice was still on board, and that we would be stuck together until the next subway stop. But I guess the angels were circling—on behalf of the accomplice— since Steve grabbed his collar and one-armed him off the train too. And like a movie's timing, the doors swished shut as I saw his legs flailing midair on the platform—but not before an Italian man stepped in and slapped the accomplice's face, a symbolic retribution for the entire population of Italy.

Steve had watched plenty of *Ghost* reruns and had the perfect retort for the hooligan: "Get off my train!"

Even the whiz of the closing door couldn't have been scripted better.

I never dared to stick my hand inside Steve's pocket for Chapstick anymore without permission.

The Vatican, with its 4.5 miles of museum walkways, felt like congested cattle chutes for nearly two hours. Like cattle, we couldn't move any faster than the rear ends in front of us. But when we entered the Sistine Chapel, the heavens opened up: massive, priceless beauty. The stories recounted on the Sistine Chapel's ceiling chronicle mankind's greatest tragedies and triumphs, one masterpiece of art in numberless strokes.

For the first time inside the Vatican walls, the mob's presence melted away from us—it was just Steve, me, and this magnificent creation. An intermittent, prerecorded "Shhh! Shhh!" echoed within the enormous chamber, reminding everyone of the chapel's sacredness. Cameras were absolutely forbidden, their light potentially damaging the newly restored pigments of paint.

I couldn't take my eyes off Michelangelo's painting of Christ behind the altar. As a child, I saw Christ as a four-story tiled Gothic figure inside a stately Lutheran sanctuary; in my adult life, He morphed into a warm, charismatic person, and just before meeting Steve, an invisible presence I could place in a school chair. But visualizing how Michelangelo understood Christ, I understood so much more, Christ in His wholeness: His strength through lifted, rippled shoulders (about to swipe away evil), the piercing command of His eyes, His humanity of soft curls of hair, the aura of His heroic yet peaceful power, as human and angelic figures simultaneously recoil and reach toward Him.

Steve and I sat in two chairs along the wall and observed everyone's awe. Steve reached in his pocket and pulled out his vows.

So this was where he wanted to take me. It was the closest we had ever been to heaven, the perfect place to recite our vows, with hundreds of witnesses around us this time, including the biblical ones preserved on the walls. And angels too.

"Shh! Shh!" said the prerecorded voice inside the chapel, shushing again a handful of tourists.

And so we began—this time, me first—taking Steve's hand and looking into his eyes. I didn't need my vows. I'd memorized them. "I will give my best self to you."

It was Steve's turn. "I will see and trust your sacred goodness." He smiled and looked around the chapel.

"I will forgive myself and you to protect and nurture us back to wholeness," I promised.

"I will—"

"—sir, stop that immediately!" said a security guard, harshly. He came out of nowhere, now standing next to Steve.

The tourist seated in the chair next to Steve immediately stuffed his cell phone back inside his pants pocket, the place he was trying to snap a forbidden photo.

"Photos are forbidden!" said the security guard loudly, a great contradiction to the peacefulness in the room. I wouldn't have been surprised if the security guard had grabbed the phone, thrown it on the floor, and shot it.

We finished reciting our vows, aware that life can interrupt their execution, no matter where you are.

AS WE FLEW back from Rome to Denver, I pulled out my journal and reflected on our ten-day anniversary trip: *Our vows are never about our wishes, because wishes have endings. Vows are about loving, and loving doesn't know how to end.*

23

Life at the
Monarch House

....

"SWEETHEART."

I roused Steve from a late-morning nap. We had traveled to Phoenix for the wedding of my brother Steve and Jillene over Thanksgiving.

"Sweetheart, it's Ma. Tabitha Rehab called and said she's got another bout of congestive heart failure. She's on her way to the ER now." Steve called St. Elizabeth's Hospital in Lincoln and was somehow able to speak to her. I heard her feeble voice through Steve's phone.

"Ma, I'll catch the next plane to Lincoln and see you very soon. Ma? Can I talk to your doctor?"

I embraced him, leaning closer to him, listening. "We have her on a respirator now. Her heartbeat is quite erratic."

"I'll be there as quick as I can," Steve replied, his face ashen, with a look of concern I had never seen before. Because it was Thanksgiving, Steve booked the first flight out early the next morning.

"Katie, Honey, and I will drive the car back to Denver tomorrow, and I'll fly out right away," I promised him.

He arrived in Lincoln on Friday. "It's hard looking at her, angel. She's hooked up to a huge machine," he said, choking back tears.

"Sweetheart, right now, Katie, Honey, and I are in Holbrook, Arizona, driving back to Denver. I'll fly out right away," I assured him.

We drove to Denver from Phoenix in a day, and three hours later, I flew to Lincoln. When I got to St. Elizabeth's, I didn't know who looked worse, Ma or Steve. Now that she was off the respirator, Ma's heartbeat looked like spin art with bursts of irregular static rather than signature high and low peaks. For a week, we took turns staying overnight with her as her spirits and energy improved. She received many visitors—her pastor, family, and friends.

But one night, just before midnight, the attending physician escorted Steve and me into a waiting room to discuss her discharge. She directed us to sit down. We had contacted both the Legacy Terrace and Tabitha Rehab about her upcoming release.

"I've contacted Helen's social worker, who is looking for an available bed in hospice," the doctor advised us.

Heavy silence fell. "Hospice?" Steve asked, "Are you serious?" His voice trailed off. "How can that be? Yesterday everyone told us she'd be going either to rehab or assisted living at the Legacy."

"Her heart can't keep up with all the fluids this time," she answered matter-of-factly. "We can keep her comfortable in hospice. The social worker can explain it to you, give you options."

"But she always bounces back from this," Steve argued, rising to look out the window at Lincoln's streetlights, "and she's in good spirits. She's laughing and eating well and—"

"We can't reverse or sustain the condition of her heart anymore, Steven," the doctor replied gently. "I am truly sorry."

The doctor left the room. Steve and I stared blankly at each other.

"This can't be happening," he said, staring at a house lit for Christmas across the street.

"I'm right here with you, sweetheart," I said softly. "Let's try to get some sleep and deal with this fresh in the morning."

The next day, the social worker confirmed Ma's prognosis and asked us for our preferences for a hospice facility. We didn't have a clue. Ma's mortality was always a year or two away, not a day. We asked our relatives and they suggested a few locations, which we visited that afternoon.

"I have an important request, angel," Steve said to me later that day. "Tell me which hospice is best for my ma."

I held his hand and understood. As a single mom, I knew one of the loneliest places was the place of decision. "The Monarch House," I replied, knowing my affirmation loosened the knot in his heart. The Monarch House was the winner, the unfortunate winner.

Steve asked Pastor Neil to break the news to Ma.

"Helen..." Pastor Neil began, touching her shoulder in bed, "the doctors don't think your heart is going to recover this time. They recommend hospice, and Steve and Barb looked into a few for you and have made arrangements. Have you heard of the Monarch House?"

If Ma had an emotional reaction, her face didn't show it. She nodded. "Yes."

Steve swallowed hard and turned away, still holding Ma's hand. I pounded down the exploding pressure inside me, knowing it was my job to keep it together.

Paramedics arrived shortly afterward to her hospital room, ready to transport her to the Monarch House.

Steve and I carried Ma's personal belongings in the hospital drawstring bags as we followed behind the stretcher, our feet shuffling past numbered rooms with heart monitors beeping, conversations ongoing, until we arrived at an elevator.

Our senses couldn't process any stimuli. The view ahead represented a vacuum of hollowness, our hearts crushed with the reality of Ma's destination. Even the stretcher's wheels were soundless. We could not speak what we could not feel. We neared the end of the corridor, rounded into another, and another—our maze, Ma's journey.

From the rafters above, the fluorescent lights wafted a delicate, music-box melody of harps and flutes, each note landing upon our ears, then connecting into our earliest childhood memories. Sifting and slipping into the cracks of our unresponsive hearts, like snowflakes melting upon a frozen autumn leaf, the notes wove a song: "Brahms' Lullaby."

The familiar lullaby announced the birth of a child, inside hospital corridors, waiting rooms, the cafeteria, the chapel. The lullaby didn't offer hope. It announced it.

And Ma heard it. She broke the deadly silence and began humming along. Steve gave me a can-you-believe-it look and sang softly, halfheartedly, as did I. Finally, the paramedics smiled and joined in.

I HAD NEVER been inside a hospice before. The Monarch House exuded a calm ambience and security. Three Christmas trees, christened Remembrance Trees with ornaments honoring those who had passed, twinkled near a brick hearth of a crackling, double-paned fireplace. I inhaled redolent aromas of comfort foods, potatoes, cinnamon. Pastoral paintings lined two short hallways, with three patient rooms each. At the end of one hallway lay Ma.

We promised her that one of us would be at her side, day and night. And so our vigil began.

I took the first shift; my husband had slept at the hospital for ten days, setting his watch for the doctor's rounds. He checked into a hotel across the street. I had no clothes and no clue as to their whereabouts. I undressed and found an extra patient nightgown in Ma's closet and threw it over my head. Pulling out the sofa couch, I waited for the night-shift nurse so I could monitor her care until it would become routine. Around 1:30 a.m., the nurse left us alone. Plopping on my stomach, I rested my head between my hands and watched Ma sleep, the rise of her chest, the sound of her breath.

I woke before her and washed my face, applying the complimentary face lotion. Grasping the front of my nightgown, I stumbled out of her room, disheveled, because I couldn't find my glasses. A fuzzy woman glanced up from cutting something brown on a plate, and her body froze. She leaned closer for a better look at me, which gave me a chance to see her identification tag. She was Janet, a hospice nurse.

"I'll be done with your breakfast here in just a minute, dear," she said, slowly. "Why don't you go back to bed and I'll be there in just a few minutes."

She thought I was a patient.

I looked down at my nightgown. "I'm Helen Vannoy's daughter-in-law."

The nurse apologized. "Sometimes the patients look better than their family members caring for them."

I found my glasses and realized my face lotion was actually diaper ointment.

Nothing prepared us for our hospice experience. It was December 5. Was Ma even in the right place? At the hospital, Ma's heart monitor had blipped sporadically, but here, without the monitor as a reminder, Ma seemed to return to her normal self, engaging, peaceful. For the first few days, we didn't bring up the fact that we all lived in a hospice. We talked around this obvious fact like some silly superstition—walking around a ladder instead of under it. But after those first few days, Steve finally put reality on the table.

"Ma, you do know where you're at," he said, leaving ample time for her response.

"Yah, I know," she answered, in a neutrality we didn't want to test. "But I'm not going anywhere. The Lord's still got work for me to do."

The Lord's still got work for me to do became her mantra, along with, "And I'm going to be at that sing-along."

That sing-along was December 21, longer than Ma's hospice staff predicted she could survive. Her body would continue to build up fluids until she could no longer breathe. And yet, she had beat the odds numerous times before with congestive heart failure.

Steve couldn't accept Ma's diagnosis. He encouraged her to continue her rehab in hospice. Ma teetered on the edge of her bed as Steve helped her stand, balance, sit, stand, balance, sit. He didn't bother to contact the Legacy Terrace to give notice for her apartment. We didn't expect a miracle; we expected Ma and her sturdy body to once again beat the odds and delight the relatives.

Consequently, in the first few days, we turned to our one friend who provided dependable, transcending comfort and hope: music. Steve's guitar lived in Ma's room, and Ma sang with us for hours. For years, she had promised Steve, "I'll be singin' till the day I die, and then I'll be singin' in heaven." We sang solos and duets and trios, for anyone who wanted to listen.

MA SETTLED INTO a routine, watching her soap operas and Lawrence Welk, reading her large print *Guideposts* magazine. Seeing her read the magazine made me remember some exciting news she needed to know. "Ma!" I jabbed my finger at the title. "Did Steve tell you? Did he tell you anything about *Guideposts?*"

Steve jumped in. "Ma, you remember my days on the park bench, when I was living on the streets, when that man came up and told me, 'You've done good things in the past, and you will again?'"

Ma's eyes crystalized into pure recollection. She nodded. "That man was an angel."

"Well, Ma, I sent my story to my agent, and *Guideposts* said they're going to publish it."

Ma gasped, her mouth opened in delight. Then, her eyes traveled to a faraway place where surprise collides with joy, where emotions suspend words. And there she remained for several seconds. A grin melted into her face. Her glassy eyes widened, full of conviction.

She whispered, "I am going to be so popular."

A BIRDFEEDER HUNG next to a stout lilac bush outside Ma's window. Two dozen sparrows began appearing at sunrise and perched there for the day; oddly, they never chirped or fed. In the bitter December winds of Nebraska, they fluffed themselves, peered inside, watched her. This went on for three days.

"Stupid birds," I said, straightening out Ma's sheets, "it's freezing out there and they don't eat a thing. They just sit in that lilac bush, all puffed up, staring at us. Like Hitchcock's birds."

A long silence followed. "Don't you see, Barb?" She broke out in song, again, filling the room with her shaky vibrato— a hymn, her hymn: "His eye is on the sparrow, and I know he watches me."

Of course. How could I forget? It was the first hymn the three of us sang at her church during the offering after she forgot her lyrics and teeth at home.

Ma's hospice room began losing its pallor: Her room became a reception hall with loud, happy conversations, often standing room only. The hospice staff politely asked us to keep the noise down. Her nieces brought in canned jams and held contests for the tastiest one and filled in each other's gaps on spotty family stories.

In the first four days, thirty-five visitors arrived, showering her with scarves, Avon perfume, Christmas odds and ends. The pile of gifts warranted a Christmas tree. Steve and I decorated her room, stringing lights around her window, the armoire, her door. Guests would enter the room hesitantly, reverently, and leave shaking their heads, saying, "What is she doing here?"

Hospice enabled us not only to see her guests' sacredness, but also the world's. The Monarch House summoned a timelessness. Nightly news didn't matter. Neither did the Dow Jones average. Or weather, as it pertained to time.

When the sing-along was only a week away, I recognized inexplicable instances of favor over us. How was I able to phone Ma while driving in the middle of Nowhere, New Mexico?

I booked the last seat available on a flight to Lincoln. Riffs between two family members disappeared as each individual stood on opposite sides of Ma's bed, holding her hands.

I accepted the possibility that Ma may be right, that God still had work for her to do. So I relaxed. I bid on Barbie dresses on eBay. There wasn't much competition for the dresses in the middle of the night during the Christmas season. I let go and believed and became a trusting observer of days. I started expecting miracles. And after ten days, Ma still looked more rested than Steve or me.

The next morning, Ma asked for a phone. "I want to call my friends at the Legacy and church and invite them to that sing-along," she said.

Steve and I couldn't miss this moment. We gathered up their numbers, dialed them, and put Ma on the phone. Lying prone in her hospice bed, she called her friends and family.

"Hi, Lawrence, this is Helen. I just wanted to invite you to my family's sing-along this Sunday," Ma said cheerfully.

The silence on the other end was palpable. "Helen? Helen? Is that really you?" The question kept repeating itself with each new caller.

Ma contacted all her guests, except one person, Anna. According to Ma's premonition in hospice, Anna had recently died. Everyone else said they would attend. All seventy-four of them. Four days before Christmas.

"Ma, let's call Anna's number and see if she really passed. If she didn't, you can invite her too," Steve suggested delicately.

"She's dead, I'm telling you," Ma warned.

We dialed anyway, and a woman picked up the phone. "Hello?" she answered.

"Anna?" Ma said.

"Yes, this is Anna, who's this?"

"Anna's back," Steve said matter-of-factly.

Ma's eyes dilated to twice their normal size. Panicked, she covered the cell phone on her chest and whispered to us, "You didn't send the memorial, did you?"

Now Ma knew how her voice felt to the other seventy-four.

SINCE STEVE AND I didn't have any other major responsibilities going on besides caring for our mother in hospice, we agreed to oversee an enormous holiday party four days before Christmas. The easiest part would be leading seventy-five people in song; the most challenging part? Getting Ma to the Legacy. Steve finally found a cab company that would willingly accommodate her poor health. In the meantime, the Monarch House called their attorneys about discharging a dying hospice patient from their care.

The Legacy Terrace's hairdresser stopped by the day before the sing-along and styled Ma's hair, fumigating the room with hairspray, indifferent or clueless about Ma's oxygen line.

The night before the sing-along, Emmy took the night shift, enabling Steve and me to sleep together in the same bed for the first time in three weeks. Seconds after we made love, my cell phone dinged.

It was an eBay notification, informing me that I had been outbid by four cents on a Barbie dress.

24

The Last Sing-Along

I HELPED MA DRESS THE NEXT MORNING WITH THE PANTS Katie picked up at Penney's for Ma's ever-widening girth. Emmy painted her nails, and Ali applied her makeup while listening to Ma's stringent guidelines: "Use that lotion in the tall white bottle that takes away my wrinkles." It reminded me of the Phyllis Diller quote, "If you don't have wrinkles, you haven't laughed enough."

She looked beautifully festive, a ninety-six-year-old angel on top of a tree; her green sweater glittered with angel outlines, which matched her green earrings and accented her ivory string of pearls. Warm pink eyeshadow and lips lined in Christmas red made her smile in the mirror before we left hospice. A fleece blanket covered her swollen body, from her waist to her shoeless feet. She once again resembled the old Helen—her signature hairstyle, her sparkling eyes, her smile—except there was more of her.

Steve signed a clipboard full of medical waivers before we loaded Ma into a handicap-accessible cab. Ma arrived at the Legacy Terrace in style, in a shiny, long black van. As we pinned on her corsage, Steve stared at me until our eyes met.

My husband mouthed, *I love you.*

He wheeled her into the Iron Horse Saloon, where her guests waited, just before 2:00. She laughed and announced, "I'm back!" but I heard only a few giggles. From the entry door, I watched everyone's reactions.

Her appearance had changed more than we comprehended in the three weeks since her guests had seen her. As she entered, the silence mingled with reverence and fear, and for a moment, I felt sorry for her. I couldn't judge those around her, because we had the benefit of seeing her change slowly over time; they did not. I read on their faces their own mortality as they gazed at her, some afraid to touch her, others reaching out their hands to graze hers. All kept their distance as if she were some porcelain doll. The somber reaction reminded me of a funeral procession to the altar before its time, and her wheelchair, the casket.

But Ma stayed strong, her gaze focused ahead on a Christmas tree full of ornaments in its boughs, the ornaments she had asked us to prepare for her sing-along guests. Steve wheeled her to the place of honor near it. He turned her wheelchair around and locked it into place.

Once guests recovered from the shock of her appearance, the love of family and friends overpowered the silence. Emmy and Katie, smiles chiseled on their faces, served coffee and cookies. We ran out of chairs.

The spirit of celebration had spilled over. Legacy Terrace employees left their stations and joined the party. A few employees, on their day off, also stopped by to become part of the celebration. Even the mailman showed up.

For an hour we sang Christmas carols, and because of Ma's love of music, many of her guests were skilled singers, so four-part harmonies filled the saloon. After the singing, Ma made her last request. She wanted everyone to know that she was a music video star, so our producers Bryan and Nancy, along with their mom, Loraine, showed our "Three Hearts Dancing" video on the saloon's big screen.

"Play it again," Ma commanded.

When the time came for people to say their goodbyes to Ma, the energy in the room dimmed once again, but this time it was cloaked in gratitude. The awkward silence returned to those standing in line to visit Ma one last time, as if all appropriate words had skipped town like a tumbleweed. But three words stuck around, repeating themselves inside the Iron Horse Saloon and slipping inside many hearts, echoing their presence: *I love you.*

I sat in the van's backseat as Steve and the cab driver wheeled Ma back inside it, strapped her in, and closed the doors. For a few seconds, the best seconds of my life with Ma, we were alone. Our eyes met. Her mouth turned into a grin. Twinkles lit up behind her glasses. Simultaneously, we threw our heads back and burst out laughing.

"We did it!" she said, uncontrollably laughing for the longest time, and me, laughing until my stomach hurt. And we became two young girls, best of friends, proud of ourselves that we had outfoxed everyone—better than sneaking out of bed at night, sweeter than stealing rhubarb from a neighbor's garden on a sticky July afternoon.

What did we do? Everything that's important in life, that's what: We took away the capital letter in Death's name and put it in the no column, because it's common and therefore not important. And we put all those we love, our family and friends, including ourselves, in the yes column, the important column. In the proper noun column. In the "I Will Always Matter with a Capital Letter" column.

25

The Open Window

STEVE KISSED MA GOODNIGHT AND RETURNED TO OUR hotel room. I was on night watch for Christmas Eve. As I tucked in Ma's sheets and adjusted her oxygen mask, I reminded her, "Listen here, missy, Santa still has twelve hours to make up his mind about you." Tucking her blanket snugly around her body, I wagged my index finger and winked at her.

"Behave."

What is the appropriate Christmas gift for a patient in hospice? What do you give a person who doesn't need anything in this lifetime? Steve and I decided the best gift we could give Ma would be laughter and beauty.

I kissed her awake on Christmas morning, her forehead cool and softly wrinkled. "Merry Christmas, beautiful," I whispered. "You behaved. Santa came for you last night." She opened her eyes, aged into purity like polished stones, and within her sleepy smile I saw the innocent child her mother must have seen almost a hundred years ago. For an instant, she became the precious little drowsy girl with rumpled hair. I took her warm hand and kissed it.

Steve came through the door, guitar in hand. "Merry Christmas, dear Ma," he said, approaching her bedside with a mask of joy. I knew him well enough that he must have stood outside her door a few seconds before entering, wiping tears with his handkerchief and sighing away his awful sadness before putting on his game face.

"Merry Christmas, son," she answered, trying to imitate Santa's gruffness.

"Looks like Santa made a pit stop here," Steve said. "Did he stop for me too?"

Ma looked at me. "Santa?"

I eyed Steve suspiciously. "Well, I hear Santa loosened his standards a bit to keep his popularity up in the polls."

Emmy entered the room, her emotional transparency thinner than Steve's. She smiled cautiously. "Merry Christmas, Grandma," she muttered, pecking her cheek with a kiss.

"So let's see what Santa brought all of us," I said, heading toward the new stockings hanging on the armoire. They were all silly animals, a giraffe and a monkey and a hyena, none of which entered God's head as reverent decorations for His son's birthday party.

Ma opened her stocking first. Inside was an orange, her favorite stocking stuffer from ninety years ago, a story we had heard about ninety times. We opened reindeer hats and elf ears and stuffed animals that sang annoying songs, along with tacky bracelets and toe rings. We dressed ourselves up and emailed pictures to the family.

Ma opened her last present from Santa, *The Little Book of Snowflakes*, filled with detailed photos of snowflakes and beautiful quotes. Despite everything, Ma remained curious. I watched her trace the snowflakes' delicate angles and crisscross patterns with her finger, as if memorizing something beyond us.

Just before bedtime, Steve and I tidied up her room. Ma said softly, "This is going to be my last Christmas." It was the first time in one month she had commented on fragility, the end of her life. Steve choked up and reached for her hand as I reached for the other. Ma was, at last, beautifully transparent, whole.

"Ma, it might very well be your last Christmas..." I said, "here. But I imagine that the best of Christmas is celebrated every day, every second, in heaven."

She nodded thoughtfully but did not reply.

THE TIME CAME for Emmy to say goodbye. "I'm memorizing your hand, Grandma," Emmy said, just above a whisper.

"Emmy, you were so wonderful back here with me..." Ma said slowly, winded. "I just loved every second. I want to thank you over and over for that."

"Grandma, if anyone gets to heaven, it's you."

Steve and I sat quietly in the background, watching their love story unfold. I grabbed paper. I remembered how my own mom and aunt wrote down the last words of my grandma in shorthand, so I discreetly decided to do the same, for Emmy someday.

"My favorite thing was watching how much Grandpa loved you. He just couldn't wait for your meals," Emmy began.

Ma squeezed Emmy's hand and passed down the generational stories from nearly a century ago. "Well, you know, we worked together on the farm the first year when we got married. We had to be close to hitch up the horses, so we rented an old house. It used to be a grain bin...and it was so cold my mother had given me three wool comforters with head protectors at the top...and we'd have all three of those on top of us—Kippy our cocker too—and we'd be warm, but our tops would be frozen. And the room had two heaters, one beside the doors where you could dress. But the skunks lived there too."

"Tell me about your mom," Emmy said.

"My mother's hands were always so warm. She never wore gloves. She'd put my hands in hers inside her muff. We'd go places in those old carriages and we'd have bricks that we heated to put our feet on, and my dad had a fur overcoat so he could stay warm." She sighed and shook her head. "I guess you just had to live those days to explain them to everyone else. I wrote all this down in my memoirs. Never got them published though."

I spoke up. "Ma, I can help tell your story. What would you call it?"

There was a thoughtful pause. "Honest Helen." Ma looked at me. She knew my offer was sincere. "My memoirs are in my dresser."

Emmy's voice finally broke. "Grandma, we'll be together forever."

Ma remained solidly soft, patting Emmy's hand. "Emmy... we already are. Love is always the answer. The only answer you'll ever need."

Two days later, Ma wouldn't eat anymore. Steve tried coaxing her with her favorite foods, but she made up her mind. The hospice staff shared that it was common for patients to refuse food near the end. In the meantime, we had to call a jeweler to cut off Ma's wedding ring, on her finger for seventy-four years. Her congestive heart failure was turning her ring finger purple. He soldered it back up for her so she could wear it as a necklace the very same day.

On December 30, our friend Melanie came to see Ma. She

was brave enough to ask Ma the question, braver than Steve and me: "Helen, are you ready to meet your Lord?"

"Yes."

ON NEW YEAR'S Day, Ma proclaimed, "Today I'm going to meet my Lord." Her vitals pointed toward heaven too. Then we realized why—her husband had passed on New Year's Day. All Ma wanted us to do was to sing with her, all day long. After two hours of morning singing, Steve's fingers grew tender from strumming his guitar.

"Ma, do you want to keep singing or do you want to take a break and watch *The Bold and the Beautiful* in five minutes?"

Her eyes popped open. Ma took a break.

When family members called to wish her a Happy New Year, she informed them, "Today is the day that I am seeing my Lord." Finally, at seven that night, my mom phoned Ma, and she acquiesced that the likelihood of passing in the next five hours was slim.

"Ma, you can't decide when it's going to happen, that's God's job," Steve said.

She slept unusually well that night. The next morning, Steve and I stood on either side of her bed and woke her gently.

"How are you, Ma?" Steve asked.

Ma opened her eyes and stared straight ahead. Her eyes were instantly bright and carried within them a fullness I had never seen before on her face—let alone on any other face.

"I'm in heaven," said Ma, mesmerized. Then a giddy smile spread across her face. "And everything looks like home." It's beautiful! There's even a clock. I love it here!"

Ma had obviously prayed to pass in the night and expected

to wake up in heaven. It wasn't until she turned to the left, and then to the right, that she saw our haggard faces.

"Oh, it's you," she said flatly.

"I hate to disappoint you, Ma," said Steve.

Over the next days in the new year, Ma's breathing became more labored and she rested almost constantly, but still sang every day. Fluid continued filling the spaces where air belonged. On January 6, six weeks after being admitted to hospice, her breathing shallowed. At dinnertime, her legs became restless, reflecting her agitation. We dimmed the lights to relax her. The nurse and I called Steve, who for the first time in two days left hospice for a twenty-minute hotel shower. The nurse shared the news and put Steve on speakerphone.

"I'll be right there, Ma. I love you."

"I love you too," she mumbled, breathing lightly.

"Helen, this will help you relax," said her nurse. She injected the morphine into Ma's IV.

Ma nodded and squeezed my hand. The nurse left.

Her hand warmed mine. Would this be the last time? The saddest words in our language: *the last time*. The last time she laughed. The last time her eyes sparkled. The words we cling to, the thoughts that slip beyond our voices and disappear somewhere in our heart's back pocket, the safest of places.

In the five minutes it took Steve to bolt across the street, I shared time with Ma that still haunts me. She tried talking, but I couldn't understand her words. Stroking her hand, I leaned in closer to her lips.

"Say it again, Ma, I don't understand."

She murmured again, her voice silky, intentional but unintelligible. It was as if she were whispering someone a secret. She spoke in cadenced phrases, conversational pauses between. Was she trying to tell me something? Was she praying? Was it the morphine?

I spoke over her, over a dying person. How could I? Her voice trailed off, and I didn't want to stop loving her with silence. "Here comes music, Ma. Just listen to my voice. You can't get lost in music, Ma."

I leaned closely to her ear and sang just above a whisper, in a half voice, half my heart in my throat. And I lullabied her, with Katie's cradle song, a new song for Ma, the song she'd take with her, willing myself to sing through its last line: *For love takes us all of our lifetimes to tell.*

STEVE ARRIVED AND laid his hand on my shoulder. "I'm here now," he said to me. "Go get some sleep."

Instead of sleep, I sobbed. For Steve, for regret, for relief. I'd read somewhere that tears are prayers too. They travel to God when we can't speak. I finally kissed his cheek, damp, and Ma's forehead, warm. I left mother and son alone.

I wanted to stay close. I stepped into the hallway and needed silent strength, the behind-the-scenes sort.

So I called my mom, thankful that I could hear her voice. The only constant voice throughout my entire lifetime, from cradle to now, the voice that death and divorce and all the horrible things that life coughs up cannot pull me away from, the voice whose words I have woven inside every significant memory I have, to make sense of it all.

I took a pillow and blanket into the den, where the fireplace still glowed, where the hospice Remembrance Tree drew me near. I touched several ornaments. A beaded angel with lace wings. An unpainted airplane. Hearts with yellow bells that I jingled.

It was Epiphany, January 6, the day the Wise Men found the Christ Child, also known as the manifestation of Christ. The Christmas celebration was over. Tomorrow, the trees would most likely be removed, the ornaments, these jewels of hope, tucked carefully away in boxes until next Christmas. And Ma's ornament, a red snowflake tagged, "Love, Helen," would be among the jewels.

After the sing-along, I had tucked it away inside my purse, and I pulled it out now and hung it on the tree. I wanted Ma to shine in her own light tonight, not in her memory. She was uniquely created, a snowflake that would never melt.

At four o'clock in the morning, Steve knelt beside me.

His words barely made it out of his mouth. "She's gone."

And we held each other.

Steve had sung Ma to heaven, strumming his guitar, lullabying her smile, her last words. A hospice nurse, on the advice of a Catholic chaplain decades ago, left the window slightly open to make it easier for one's spirit to travel. Ma had sung with her son twenty-one hours before she passed by him toward that window; indeed, she sang until the day she died, just as she said she would, and I believe it was her harmony, not her spirit, that first arrived at heaven's door.

MA'S SERVICE WAS dignified and traditional. Ushers presented each guest with a single long-stemmed silk red rose, Ma's last gift, her thank you. Pastor Neil and Steve shared eulogies, and Ma's friend Judy sang "How Great Thou Art" with a voice that surprised even her. I sang "The Lord's Prayer," as I had done at my dad's service.

There was no time to rehearse the song properly. I approached the choir loft. Wilma Sundeen, Lincoln's premier prodigy for eighty years and dear friend of Ma's, sat at the piano, without any music in front of her. She whispered, "What key would you like to sing it in, Barb?" and all I had to do was float my voice atop the gift of her.

We brought two red roses to Waverly's Rose Hill Cemetery for Steve's parents. Surrounding us were all the Vannoy family plots, including mine. And we laid Ma to rest next to Papa, on his right side, where the frozen Nebraska soil offered no Kentucky bluegrass, where dandelions and sprigs of clover grew no more.

AT MA'S RECEPTION, Wilma asked me, "How can you possibly sing at a family member's service? I couldn't do it."

It's because I'm not there.

I imagine myself on an ocean beach, where I am alone, save one person in a sailboat, in this case, Ma, on the horizon. I close my eyes and inhale the might of the waves approaching me and taste God's life inside the salty air. And before I exhale, I consider the depth and certainty of the waves beyond the sailboat that I cannot see. And I breathe and sing one note of that conviction, then offer the rest as thanks to God, who completes in me my song.

above: Our first family portrait. From left, Ali, Katie, and Emmy,
Morrison, Colorado, January 1, 2008. *below:* Performing music
at our wedding reception, Morrison, Colorado, June 2007.

above: Barbie's Barbies, among the 250 displayed in my
writing studio, including Britney Spears Barbie. Over
six hundred more await their turn, ladies in waiting.

above: Steve and me filming our first music video, "Three Hearts Dancing," at our home in Morrison, July 2014. *below:* Our first overnight RV campout. Walmart parking lot, Littleton, Colorado.

above: Emmy, Ma, and Steve on Christmas Day 2014 in the Monarch House.

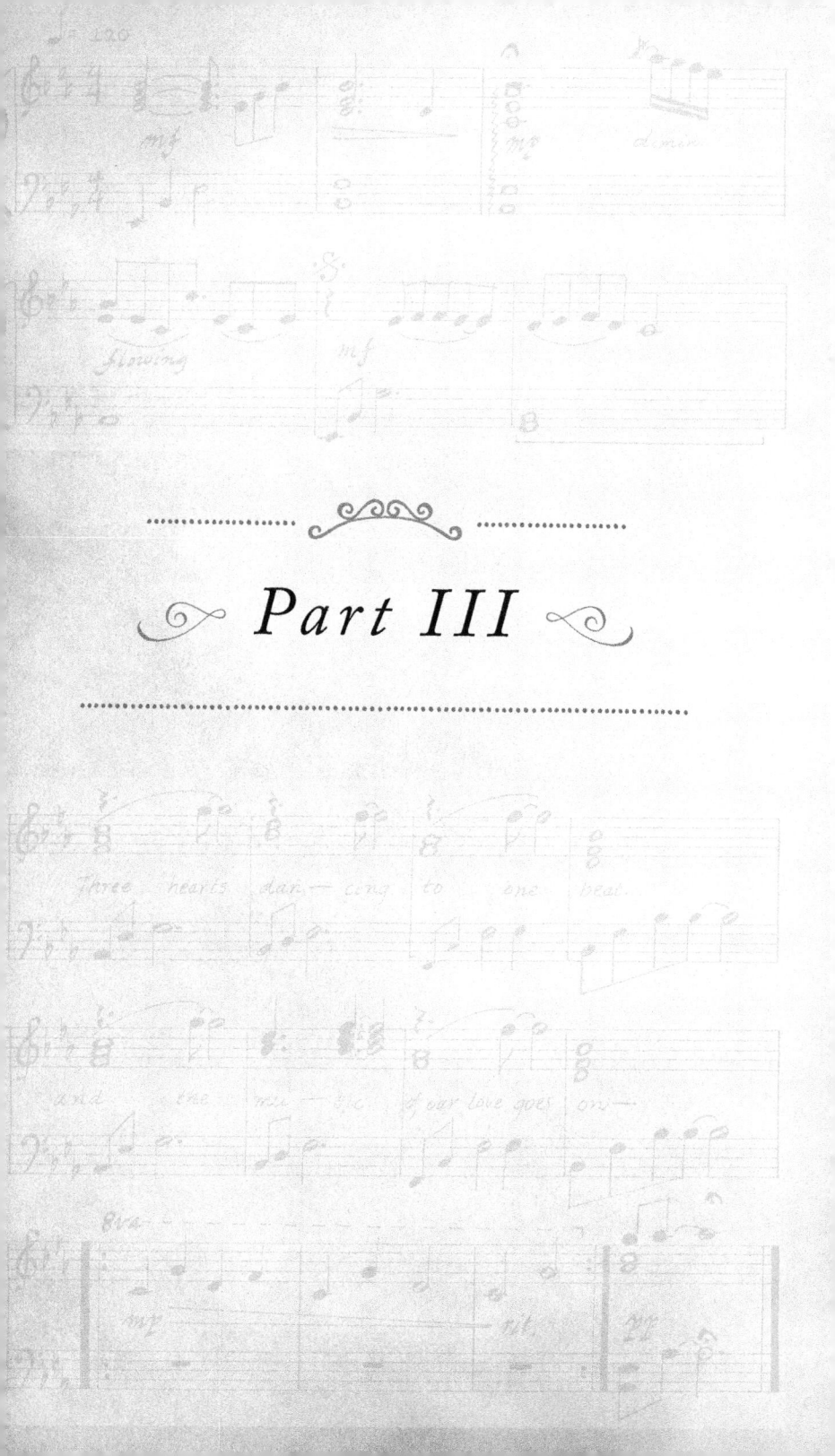

Part III

Three hearts danc — cing to one beat,

and the mu — sic of our love goes on —

26

Honest Helen

WE BURIED STEVE'S MA ON THAT COLD JANUARY DAY. FIVE months earlier, we had stood with her next to Papa's grave, upon Kentucky bluegrass, browning in the low light of autumn. Upon the double headstone were the names *John Warren Vannoy* and *Helen Elizabeth Vannoy*, etched inches apart, separated by a heart's inscription: Married 63 years. That August, our eyes had glazed over the engraving of Ma's name in favor of Papa's. We laid a red rose on the left side, under his name. With her son's help, Ma pulled up dandelion roots and a few sprigs of clover near the rose, dusting away clumps of fertile Nebraska soil from the headstone's base.

"Steven, can you say a prayer?" Ma had whispered.

The three of us held hands, and Steve obliged. He spoke of family love, of protection, of gratitude. After our amen, one western meadowlark's trill interrupted our silence in the crown of the elm above us. It alighted on a willowy branch, then lifted off again, carrying the prayer's echo elsewhere.

And the bird did not return, but now, in Ma's apartment, the silence did, its stillness reverberating inside the walls that were no longer her home. Steve had left the Legacy Terrace in search of packing boxes, so I walked into Ma's bedroom and sat upon her quilted bedspread, the bed she had meticulously made seven weeks ago, fluffed with matching calico shams. Her antique porcelain doll, gifted from her mother in 1921, sat precisely centered inside her twin-sized iron headboard, the doll's laced skirt smoothed carefully into a perfect circle by Ma. Just as always.

Ma's bedroom walls encapsulated her ninety-six years. Above her dresser, colored photos of her grandchildren lined the wall evenly, fading into a row of black-and-white high school graduation pictures of her three boys. Their portraits formed a mantle above a cherrywood desk stuffed with greeting cards for every occasion. Snapshots of her lab Marshall and cocker spaniel Kippy took center stage on the dresser, the photos' pigment aged inside simple oak frames hand-carved by Papa.

Her room still smelled of her ointments and lotions and makeup but not her perfume, because she always tried new scents from mail-order catalogs and never did find one that matched her beauty. Or so she said. On top of her rocking chair lay her new Christmas outfits, never worn, tags attached. A worn black leather purse was draped over the rocker's arm. Just as always.

I soaked in her essence for a few minutes and rose, deciding to clean out her pine dresser first. Family history taught me the antique bedroom set belonged to her parents, gifted to her and Warren on their wedding day. Ma swore everything could be preserved with teak oil, and the dresser's grains attested to her belief, their lines shiny and smooth, save one water ring, perhaps where one of her boys placed a glass on a humid Nebraska day. She had covered the blemish with an ivory doily and seemingly forgave the stain by placing angels of all sorts atop it, wooden, china, glazed glass.

I opened the top right drawer of her dresser, the unmentionable drawer, as women her age would call its contents, a drawer like my mother had. Drawers like that contained more than just undergarments, slips, and lingerie; I knew this drawer was a woman's treasure chest, a dainty trove of cherished items—dare I say the enshrined items—slipped silently away in mothers' memories and pushed wordlessly into safekeeping. Ma had proudly told me that no one had opened that top drawer, except her, in sixty years.

The drawer slid open, smooth friction against the wood, and a musty fragrance greeted me. I first discovered mundane items, things she must have quickly shoved in as she rushed around as a farm wife: instruction leaflets on how to tie scarves, plastic shower caps, bras that survived the Depression, old shoelaces. There were also common things you would expect to find in an old dresser, like whisper-thin embroidered hankies, a silver Timex watch, and knit scarves, carefully folded.

But digging deeper I found the precious remnants of Ma's heart, unlocked inside the drawer but entwined in her soul for decades: a locket of chestnut hair from her son Eddie, who died of cancer at age twenty-eight; ivory wedding gloves from 1941, lightly soiled; two of Papa's John Deere belt buckles; and a six-by-eight-inch box. Inside the box, I found yellowed handwritten memoirs, detailing her life as a young farm wife and mother.

"Here they are," I said aloud. *I'll help you tell your story, Ma.* I tucked them inside my shoulder bag for later.

I decided to leave everything in the drawer and allow Steve the gift of packing it up.

The contents of the remaining dresser drawers rewound memories in my own heart. Next to $150 cash, I collected six identical plastic squeeze coin holders from the 1950s and 1960s, the ones where you'd squeeze the corners and the top of the case would pop open. Inside were silver coins minted before 1965, like my grandmother used to collect for me and my cousins when she worked as a Sunshine Foods cashier in Sioux Falls. Coin holders like Ma's littered our house, too, freebies from local Sioux Falls businesses like State Farm and Western Bank. Pressing one open made me remember how I slipped nickels and pennies inside it after collecting pop bottles near the railroad track, then traded in the coins for penny candy at the Red Owl.

Rummaging deeper through two bottom drawers, I uncovered Ma's mail-order Christmas presents, unwrapped but labeled with names on Post-it Notes; my job would have been to wrap them. Assorted key rings from different decades, scattered between sweaters and aprons, puzzled me. What did they open? Did it matter anymore?

Steve still hadn't returned with the boxes, so I began folding Ma's Christmas clothes hanging over the rocking chair. I'd make a quilt using clothes inside her closet for Steve, because he would remember her wearing those garments. After I folded her unworn clothes, I reached for her purse and sighed.

Another breach of privacy.

Opening a woman's purse and going through its contents is like entering the holy land with sacred relics strewn everywhere, begging delicacy. Every item mattered now—but also back then. A lady shuffled through her purse and pulled out solutions to answer the day. Many of Ma's quirky trademarks I held in my hand: crumpled tissues, multiple Chapsticks, lipsticks. A folded

Lutheran church bulletin jutted from an outside pocket, her checkbook tucked inside a zippered compartment. I felt a tiny perfume bottle inside and uncapped it. Its scent was sweetly rose, yet I was grateful its scent didn't remind me of her.

Unfolding her wallet, I noticed her driver's license with the face of a much younger woman with gray hair—not white—before Ma gave up driving. A flip through her plastic wallet insert revealed a well-loved photo of her three sons (Steve was perhaps age two) and a Hy-Vee grocery card and her frayed Medicare card, lettered on an old Corona typewriter.

Ma was a card-carrying member of every registered US nonprofit agency since World War I. I pulled out her membership cards and dealt them on top of her bed. Since I had been a first-grade teacher, I alphabetized them out of compulsion: Children International, Covenant House, Defender of Wildlife, Habitat for Humanity, Humane Society, Nature Conservancy, National Geographic, People's City Mission, Salvation Army, Shriners Hospitals, Smile Train, and the VFW.

She was also a card-carrying member of Omaha Steaks, which made plenty of profit off her generous personality. You can't take it with you, she would say.

I shook the rest of the wallet, and a few quarters and pennies spilled out. Swiping the inside of a narrow inner pocket, I felt a small photograph. Its edges tattered, Ma had scotch-taped all four sides. She had trimmed it to wallet size, a faded black-and-white photo of Ma and Papa. I turned the picture over to check for a date, but instead recognized Papa's rigid handwriting inside his scribbled note.

It was the clue we'd been seeking for eight years.

27

Harness the
Power of We

I TURNED OVER THE PHOTO OF MA AND PAPA. MA WAS deliriously happy, joyful beyond description, mouth wide open. Papa, his smile wide, was in the middle of an uncharacteristic chortle. I wondered what they knew that I didn't. Tracing their faces, a smile appeared on mine, whisked from somewhere beyond my days. I flipped the photograph over and reread Papa's cursive message to Ma: *Harness the power of we.*

I laid the fragile picture next to me on Ma's bed, contemplating a dawning epiphany. I noticed the happiness of the photograph first. The joy on Ma's face was downright ethereal, a look I knew I had never quite mastered in my lifetime, but one whose echo I had seen on her face for the last nine years.

As I looked back on her life, it made sense that Ma had tucked this photo inside her wallet: The first words I ever heard her speak? She yelled across a room through a phone: "We are fun people!" Clearly, Steve picked up on her optimism, which drew me to him. And she had run toward joy, in every variation of its expression, since I met her: running into Steve's arms on her surprise birthday party, running toward the microphone to own it, chiming in to sing harmony with us during a church offering, running toward dinner at the Legacy, always an hour early.

And Papa's handwritten words ignited something in me, stirring the question of why he would write that phrase on the back of the photograph. I could understand why he used the word *harness*. He was a Nebraska farmer. But the power of we? The power of two? Given that he'd written it on the back of a photo of the two of them, he must have been referring to them as a married couple. They understood how the two of them harnessed power together.

Papa and Ma worked their fields, picking two hundred acres of corn by hand with a horse named Bucko and a narrow wagon. They paid for new parcels of land in cash the following spring, all the while surviving the bite of Nebraska winds living in a grain bin, cold as a barn, with their cocker spaniel Kippy as their heating blanket at night.

With all the silk and husks they shelled in the barnyard, they returned the shucks to fallow fields and fed the cobs to the hogs. They dug posts for new barbed wire fences to lay claim to their new property every spring until three hundred acres grew to almost eight hundred and their cash grew to millions.

Papa served on the bank's board of trustees while Ma's hospitality knit the burgeoning town of Waverly into a tight community. Because they knew the people and the land so well, they became trustees of the Rose Hill Cemetery in Waverly, where my headstone now stands, seventy years later. They created trusts for their own grandchildren, tithed to their church, and gifted parcels of land to neighbors, creating a masterpiece of legacy.

The two of them could not have accomplished this individually.

The two of them—together—could harness the power. The power of joy. The power of hope, goodness, purpose. The power of marriage.

Steve and I knew this in theory: A by-product of marriage is power. But there are so many things we must remember about marriage to make it work. Unless we intentionally focused on any one of those aspects, life would water them down.

Looking back, Steve and I had an inkling of it during our wedding preparation and service itself. I recalled the scriptures we selected: *Oh magnify, oh magnify the Lord with me, and let us exalt His name together* was one. Our other verse was *Father, make them one, as we are one.* Surely these passages hinted at the power of two lives joined together, and, sure, even Pastor Del prayed for it during the service.

But we forgot about it. We had used the passages as customary tokens for the service, like wedding mints and flower petals.

And the power of we wasn't intentional.

Just me and my vows.

Steve and I had spent an entire year crafting individual vows to hold ourselves accountable to the gift of marriage. I promised him: I will give you my best self. I will see and trust your sacred goodness. And so on.

But what about *us*? What did we—together—promise to our marriage?

Nothing.

That's what was missing. One vow unifying both of us. Our ten vows were egocentric. I. I. I. No room for the power of we. No room for the intentional power of us. No room for the intentional power of joy. Robert Louis Stevenson seemed to grasp joy's power when he wrote, "Find out where joy resides and give it a voice far beyond singing. For to miss the joy is to miss it all."

And I smoothed the photograph of Ma and Papa, thinking of examples of famous public proclamations, versed in the plural. "The Star-Spangled Banner": What so proudly *we* hailed, at the twilight's last gleaming? The creeds at church: *We* believe in the Holy Spirit, the holy catholic church. The Declaration of Independence: *We*, the people. And Queen's crazed sports anthem that fans scream: *We* will, *we* will rock you.

The word *we* packs a lot of punch. A lot of infectious power. And even though Steve and I had a notion about it, we weren't bright enough to do anything about it; we were, however, bright enough to include extra space in our promises, both emotional and physical, for that eleventh vow.

And Ma and Papa's photo and words brought it all to light.

Although Steve and I created intention in our vows, we'd glazed over two obvious omissions: first, the power of *us*, our individual quirks and experiences, strengths and passions, mistakes and talents that mingled together to cement our bond together; and second, the power of joy that puts marriage into the starting gate and propels it beyond the finish line.

Being around children all my life, I thought joy just happened. But like children, marriage grows up. How could we harness this joy—and us?

By kindling an eleventh vow, starting with the word *we*. And empowering that eleventh vow with the intentional pursuit of joy in our marriage, like when I ran home and left Katie tangled up in dog leashes to run toward Steve's joy.

Steve banged at Ma's apartment door, presumably with his arms full of packing boxes. I ran to open it.

28

Writing Our Eleventh Vow

OUR SIX-WEEK HOSPICE STAY CREATED ANOTHER LOSS when we returned home. Our seventeen-year-old Honey could no long climb stairs, her leg muscles atrophied after staying in my mom's ranch home for nearly two months. Her hearing had noticeably deteriorated as well, so she no longer greeted us at the door.

We'd find her in our closet, either crying in loneliness or sleeping on our dirty clothes. She heard us when we clapped, but that was all; her ears would perk up and tail beat as she rummaged through the house, searching for us. But once we loved on her, her limitations seemed to disappear. She continued to blitz and to offer her toys to guests and to help me retrieve the mail, a half-mile away.

We prayed we wouldn't lose Honey and Ma in the same year.

Unpacking Ma's belongings for display inside our home brought her spirit back to us—like the 1873 spinning wheel, her antique bedroom set, and my favorite, her handwritten notes. Handwritten notes are for refrigerators, keepsake boxes, and dusty attics. They are the treasures time cannot steal, memories cannot erase, people's personalities dancing upon the tip of their pens. Finally, we took our dusty, framed wedding vows off the bathroom wall and got to work.

Steve came up with the first suggestion of our eleventh vow: "We will leverage our experiences and marriage to add goodness and joy to the world." I think he was proud of himself. Granted, he did have a natural way with words.

"That sounds like a mission statement you'd see in your office," I countered. "How about we will have fun being ourselves so others enjoy life?" I asked hopefully.

"That sounds like a first-grade classroom rule."

After a vote, I grabbed my calligraphy pen and added our eleventh vow next to the empty bullet point at the bottom of our ten vows.

> ## Vow 11
>
> We will serve the world
> and add joy to it by harnessing
> who we are.

Ma had left me plenty of room to write that bonus vow so I wouldn't ruin her embellished flower border.

"Let the fun begin," Steve said, clapping his hands. We committed to the vow, prayed for direction, and prayed for our marriage like it was a new person. But mostly, we prayed for more fun.

We displayed the new vow on the refrigerator.

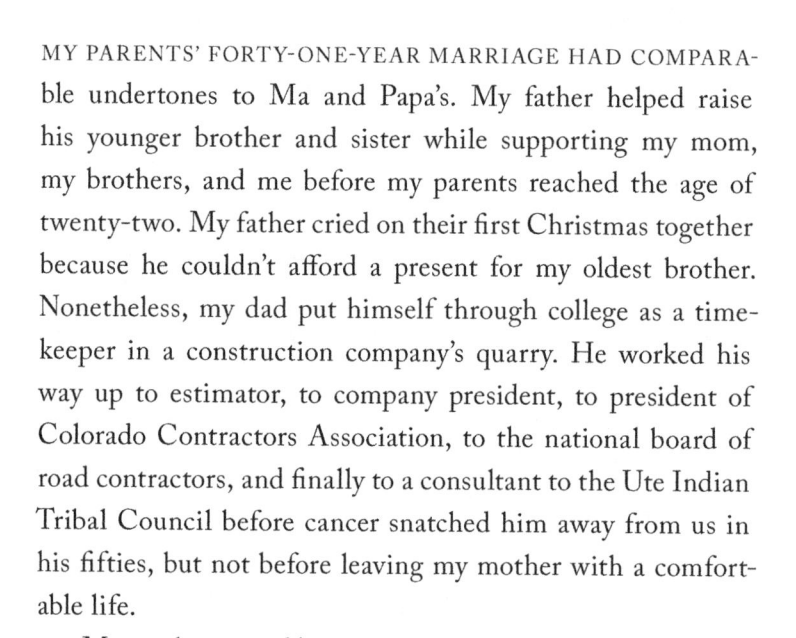

MY PARENTS' FORTY-ONE-YEAR MARRIAGE HAD COMPARA-ble undertones to Ma and Papa's. My father helped raise his younger brother and sister while supporting my mom, my brothers, and me before my parents reached the age of twenty-two. My father cried on their first Christmas together because he couldn't afford a present for my oldest brother. Nonetheless, my dad put himself through college as a time-keeper in a construction company's quarry. He worked his way up to estimator, to company president, to president of Colorado Contractors Association, to the national board of road contractors, and finally to a consultant to the Ute Indian Tribal Council before cancer snatched him away from us in his fifties, but not before leaving my mother with a comfort-able life.

My mother stayed busier than my dad at home, turning us kids into athletes, academics, Christians, Boy Scouts and Girl Scouts, cheerleaders, teachers, pastors, musicians, and busi-ness geniuses. Yes, she was the proverbial wind beneath our wings, and she finally wised up to that gift of hers and became an administrator in churches for over forty years, making pas-tors look good and congregants look even better in God's eyes. In their spare time, the most significant time for me, my par-ents helped raise Katie when I divorced.

Steve and I had big shoes to fill: our parents'. We took an inventory of what strengths we offered and considered the synergy of harnessing our energies together. Where we already worked in tandem, we wondered how we could up-level our efforts.

"What am I good at, sweetheart?" I asked Steve.

"Shopping," he answered easily.

"Seriously," I said.

"Seriously, shopping."

"I find great values."

"Yes, you do. At thrift stores, you find value in junk."

"I see possibilities, second chances." *Like in my students. And shelter dogs.*

Steve pulled out a pen and a three-by-five-inch card from his shirt pocket, his most beneficial quirk that explained his business success.

"Let's see, angel," he began, jotting his thoughts. "You are the world's greatest first-grade teacher. You get kids. You sing like an angel. You play piano. You love dogs. You're good at designing gardens and hiking and travel planning. You're a writer and you love it—"

I sat down and let the worship continue.

"—and you love animal rescue and are a collector of, oh my God, everything. Let's see, Barbies, children's books, storybook animals, glass animals, fairy gardens, Cherished Teddies, those china dolls—"

"And Christmas ornaments!" I added. I counted on my fingers like my first graders did. "We have our Barbie tree, Disney tree, my first-grade teaching tree, Ma's bird tree, your Pathways tree, Honey's tree, oh! Our family tree, the—"

"I get it."

"What else, sweetheart?"

He studied me. "Your faith. In God, in me. You are always there for our family."

That meant the most. So I kissed him. "Okay, your turn!"

"What are my strengths?" he asked coyly.

"Easy. Leadership, leadership, leadership. You're a quintessential musician and singer. You know wildflowers like a forest ranger. You design beautiful gardens. You write music and screenplays and best sellers. You're a mentor at church. You're more disciplined than anyone I will ever meet. Let's see, what else. Business savvy, an entrepreneur, a sailor, an outdoorsman, a good dad to Honey, a dog lover. And you know how to serve people and make money and save it."

"So you can spend it," he finished.

"Whatever."

"What else, angel?"

I studied him. "You make people feel on fire after they've been with you. You always find a way. No one would know how wicked your humor is. And I especially like you in bed."

"Shall we?"

29

Heartbreak and Honey

KATIE AND I RETURNED FROM A EUROPEAN TRIP FIVE
months later in June, picking up Honey late at night from my
mom's. When Honey saw us, she didn't run toward us; instead,
she walked gingerly, her back hunched, tail wagging slowly.

Steve and I took Honey to an emergency vet the following
day, where he diagnosed her with hip dysplasia and put her on
steroids and laser treatments. She bounced back after a few
days, enabling me to take her outdoors on a walk down the
driveway and back, sniffing the latest neighborhood news. But
the hump reappeared.

The vet offered little comfort, placating our concern, dodg-
ing our fears. "This prednisone will keep her hip pain at bay," he
would say during each appointment, "and time will tell."

We bought Honey a strap to support her body so we could
help lower her to relieve herself. She would then waddle off
happily on a bone-burying mission in the middle of my Barbie stacks.

One morning, she couldn't lift her hind legs to stand, choosing instead to pull herself around using her front legs. We made

another trip to our vet. As Dr. Crawford examined her, Honey pressed her body against me, eyes wide, panting, a sign of pain.

While performing a rectal exam, the doctor paused and pressed against Honey's stomach. Honey whimpered.

"Barb, I feel a mass inside her rectum here." Her voice remained steady, but my comprehension of her words lulled into slow motion. "For dogs this age, it's almost always malignant. It probably also explains her bad breath."

Honey's tumor was my first reality check that my dog could actually die and leave me.

"How much longer?" I asked, barely.

"It's totally up to you, Barb, and what her quality of life is like."

"Will she let me know?" I hoped the vet would say yes, because I didn't want to make that decision.

"It's totally up to you, Barb," she repeated.

For days afterward, I couldn't stop touching Honey, holding her, stroking her, memorizing the feel of her body, staying connected to her. She continued to eat well but panted with greater intensity.

On a quick backpacking trip with his buddies, Steve checked in when he could. One night, he heard the grief in my voice and returned home the next morning and found me sobbing in Honey's fur. He wanted to wait a few days for improvement, but I couldn't put Honey through any more.

It was time. I begged Steve to call a mobile vet who euthanized animals at home. I couldn't verbalize permission to end her life.

He struggled on the phone and made the appointment for the following day, August 7, at 4:00.

The night before, we tucked Honey into her bed at the bottom of ours. Her breathing was shallow, but at least she wasn't panting. I turned on music from the picture book *Guess How Much I Love You*, a lullaby I wanted to remember her by. Its simplicity—piano and violin—reflected her purity and truth in my life for eighteen years. I played it over and over, letting my memory of her melt into the lullaby's melody so I could retrieve her life inside the music later. I watched her sleep, closed my eyes, and smoothed my hand against her, memorizing every curve of her body, fingering her paws, kissing her forehead.

She was my most long-standing friend I'd ever had, my heartbeat at my feet. She slept with me and ate with me and explored the world with me. Steve and I told her a bedtime story like we had a hundred times before, laughing through our tears. We prayed mercy from God for her, that we would see her again in heaven. I almost prayed for God to take her in her sleep, but I couldn't. I couldn't let go yet. I lived to kiss her head the next morning.

A text from my brother Steve woke me up. I looked at Honey, thankfully sleeping peacefully, not panting. I read my brother's text: "Barb, Mom told me about Honey, and I'm so sorry. I'm in Calgary but am flying down to Denver to see her before the vet comes to the house tomorrow afternoon. See you around noon. Hang in there. Love, Steve."

I took Honey out to relieve herself in her garden, and she wagged her tail for the opportunity to go. It would be the last time I saw her tail wag. *Only a dog would wag its tail for something like that.* My brother Steve arrived at noon, tears seeping in his eyes. He held her and baby talked her and reminded her what a good girl she was. We reminisced about Honey's life. How she was the mascot for Katie's soccer team. How she chased FedEx trucks. How she ate Peanut Jesus Christmas ornaments off the tree. How she buffered our marriage struggles with her innocent voice. How she loved us.

Later, my mom and Katie joined us as my husband picked four beautiful wildflower bouquets for Honey from our gardens.

My brother, his face red, eyes swollen, said his goodbyes and left.

Katie invited Honey and me outside on our porch swing. My beautiful child had anticipated Honey's passing sooner than I and had brought back a Murano glass heart pendant from Venice on our European trip.

"Mom, it's to remember that Honey is always here with you, just like she is now," Katie said, placing the necklace around my neck.

Steve stepped outside next to the swing, offering his arms to take Honey inside. "Angel, I'm going to take Honey upstairs and let her rest a bit."

I knew Steve wanted to spend time with Honey before the vet arrived, so I handed her off. He said Honey collapsed against the baseboard, exhausted. That was my sign that she was ready, that I was ready too. He brought up the black-eyed Susan and Shasta daisy bouquets and placed them around her.

Steve, Katie, my mom, and I lay on the floor around Honey when the doorbell rang at 4:00. Its sound lanced my heart, hollowing it into blackness. I didn't want to hear it chime again, so I rushed down to greet a respectful veterinarian who had paperwork for me to complete. Steve didn't want to sign the authorization. So I did.

The vet came upstairs to our bedroom. Honey lay in the middle of the room with Steve, my mom and Katie on their bellies stroking her, flowers on all sides.

"I'll give Honey a sedative first," the doctor explained

quietly. "Then I'll administer the final shot to slow her heart." She paused, adding, "Sometimes it requires two doses." She suggested that we distract Honey from the shot by giving her a treat. I took it and offered it to Honey as the doctor injected the sedative behind her neck. Honey whimpered but ate her treat.

I will never trick a dog with a treat again.

We passed Honey around the circle as she began to get groggy, each of us not wanting to let her go. Tears flowed as we assured her that we loved her and thanked her. When Honey lay between Steve and me, the vet injected the shot that would stop her heart.

"I don't want this to end," Steve said, throwing his head into the air.

I wanted it to end. I couldn't take it any longer. But Honey kept hanging on, breathing slower but steady.

"I think she needs another shot," the vet said, quietly. "Sometimes that's what happens." She injected Honey again.

I realized why Honey was still with us. The same reason my dad stayed with us. He needed permission to go, assurance that we'd all be okay. As sure as I knew I loved my dog, I knew my dog needed to know that.

I had read somewhere that dogs understand our thoughts through picture images, so I imagined myself holding Honey in a full hug so snug that we were one. I lifted her wooly, white ear and whispered so no one else could hear, and sent myself to her through the image in my head, then added, "Mommy loves Honey," a promise I had told her thousands of times over thousands of days. "Mommy be back."

My hand had been underneath her chest, and her heartbeat gradually became fainter. I disappeared in my grief for a moment, then returned to feel my hand underneath her body. My world ended.

"I don't feel anything anymore," I choked.

The vet reached over me and touched my dog. "She's gone," she said quietly.

Something within me imploded, like the universe had instantly folded inside itself into a mere dot, then exploded again; I wailed, startling the vet, who left the room. Katie comforted me because Steve was a mess too. My mom remained alone in her grief, until we all held each other for several minutes. After twenty minutes, Steve gave the vet permission to pick up Honey. I kissed her one more time and pulled my pink robe around her and closed my eyes; I did not want the memory of seeing her limp body being lifted in front of me.

Honey died seven months to the day after Ma passed. The same day my first dog, Ginger, was born.

Upon Honey's death, my world was a plateau of grief with gentle rises of misery. I looked at the illustrations of *Dog Heaven* by Cynthia Rylant, a picture book I'd lent out dozens of times for my students whose dogs had passed. When I had spurts of energy, I'd return to Honey's secret garden and deadhead her Shasta daisies, her black-eyed Susans, her dotted horsemint, then scatter her seeds throughout our property on cool fall evenings, and patiently remember I'd have to wait two years for the seeds to re-clothe themselves back to their previous joy.

About a month after she passed, Honey appeared in my dream. She stood in a doorway. My dream lifted into semiconsciousness, so I called her name. She looked at me and leaped out of my dream and into my arms, her body perfect in detail to my memory—her ears, the girth of her body, her soft curls atop her head. And there she stayed as long as I willed her, until I knew I could wake up and keep her joy with me.

Steve bought me a cremation ring made from her hair and ashes, something I wear to figure out the point of all the pain. In her memory, I planted a white bleeding heart in her garden, and later in the springtime, when it bloomed, I split the hearts open to understand why they bled beauty at the bottom.

30

The Eleventh Vow
Reaches Out

THE NEXT TWO YEARS INTRODUCED THE ELEVENTH VOW
to our lives.

After Ma and Honey died, we harnessed our phrase, the
power of we, in an unexpected direction. Instead of uniting
our lives for the good of others, we turned inward, melding
our shared experience and grief, soothing each other's heart-
break. We always thought we'd launch our eleventh vow with
our individual strengths and positive energies. Instead, we
could only find direction through our mourning, the process of
acclimating meaning into losing both Ma and Honey. Through
time, our grief for Ma turned to precious gratitude. It was hard
for me to admit, though, that grieving Honey was harder than
grieving Ma.

For several months, our energy drained, a slow leak in a
tire. I flickered our eleventh vow into sluggish action, easing
my spirits by walking dogs at a nearby animal shelter. While on

an RV trip, our first without Honey, we stopped at Mountain Home Humane Society in Northern Arkansas. There, a volunteer showed us around, my favorite volunteer ever, a kindred spirit. As we toured the shelter, she ignored every person there. Instead, she was the shelter's storyteller and shared every single dog's story, having memorized their worth. And like Steve and me, she spoke for the dog.

She stepped in front of a cage with an Australian cattle dog named Gus. "Hello! My name is Gus," the volunteer began, her voice dark and low. "I'm a laid-back senior boy who needs time to get used to you. I'll obey you but can't stand little kids. They just cut my balls off so pardon my mood."

Later on the tour, she showed us the dirt entrance, where fundraising efforts had begun for a remembrance path of bricks. Honey's brick leads to the shelter now.

I found myself cleaning out our house whenever I missed Honey, a way of untangling my heart. I'd drop off our goods at different thrift stores until one became my favorite. It belonged to Soul Dog Rescue, an organization that transports over 3,000 dogs to Denver each year, primarily from the Navajo reservation in New Mexico. They estimated that over 20,000 homeless dogs roam the reservation. I shopped at that thrift store, of course, and we began writing checks, eyeing their need for additional transport vans.

Steve's and my shared sadness had leaked into our newest vow, where we could actually do something about it.

And, like the power of words in our vows, I saw the power of words on a shelter's bulletin board, changing everything:

A Dog's Last Will and Testament

Before humans die, they write their last will and
testament, give their home and all they have to those
they leave behind. If, with my paws, I could do the
same, this is what I would ask.

To a poor and lonely stray, I'd give:

* *my happy home*
* *my bowl and cozy bed, soft pillows and all my toys*
* *the lap which I loved so much and the tender loving touch*
* *the hand that stroked my fur and the sweet voice which*
  called my name

I'd will to the sad, scared shelter dog the place I had
in my human's loving heart, of which there seemed
no bounds. So, when I die, please do not say, "I will
never have a pet again, for the loss and the pain are
more than I can stand." Instead, go find an unloved
animal, one whose life holds no hope or joy, and give
my place to him.

This is the only thing that I can give...
the love I left behind.
—Author Unknown

These were the words that unlocked my heart so it could love another dog.

We mourned Honey through every season and a few more. I could only consider adopting another dog who lived in the direst of conditions, so I prayed for a dog who desperately needed us. Katie spotted a dog's face on Petfinder that looked pitiful, so the next day, I traveled eighty miles to check her out.

She definitely fit the prayer request.

Via Soul Dog Rescue, Button, a Yorkie mix from the Navajo Nation in New Mexico, became our newest daughter. Her adoption fee of $125 was a bargain, because the bargain served as the loss leader of the $2,115 vet bill we paid two days later. Button was emaciated and had fleas, ticks, worms, kennel cough, and a digestive infection that required a hospital stay with IVs. I made a special request of Steve when he saw Button for the first time, as he tromped through heavy snow up our driveway returning from a trip at 12:40 a.m.

"Daddy?" said Button, who had just revealed her human voice. "Will you forgive Mommy?"

Button's photos soon vied for space next to our newest vow on the fridge. Our love for Honey had spread to our mangy little dog. We realized we brought Honey and our marriage into our lives to cherish; we brought Button into our lives to do the same.

Over the next months, Steve and I leveraged everything we knew our marriage to be, our quirks, passions, strengths, family and friends, love, and failures, and put them to the test to raise the measure of our marriage through our new vow. And when we made it that intentional, we played right into its hand.

The thousands of seeds we had scattered from Honey's secret garden—Shasta daisies, black-eyed Susans, horsemint, blanket flowers, phlox, coneflowers—bloomed. We are now our own floral outlet. Our acre of property, lined with 7.5 tons of paver stone paths, provides steady bouquets for bridal showers, weddings, funerals, neighbors, hundreds of church friends, and nursing homes. I have to wipe out the vase sections at the thrift stores every Saturday to keep up.

Honey's secret garden is now a pet memorial garden for families who lose their precious pets; the blooms of their memorials add brilliant tributes in our bouquets.

Our vow then catapulted us onto a cruise ship floating down the Mississippi River, playing a gig on American Cruise Lines, playing keyboards and singing James Taylor melodies with my husband as he strummed his guitar. Old folks with stiff drinks listened to us and lip-synced my words. A year earlier, we had recorded a demo tape with the help of fifty friends and landed a contract to perform. We're not getting rich; we had to fly one of our daughters down to babysit Button in our RV while we played. The cruise line paid handsomely, but between Emmy's airfare, car rental, and Uber, our first big music break netted us -$349.

Nonprofit opportunities sprouted on three different continents. With his Nebraska background, Steve traveled to the Dominican Republic for Plant With Purpose to leverage his farming roots and plant cocoa trees to make chocolate. The local bank there is nothing more than a box buried in the ground, but its presence now enables families to send their children to college.

Nonprofit work also has a perk of making new friends—who network with other new friends—in high places, like our friends who own Dairy Queens. They bribe us with enormous custom-made Blizzards, making us deliriously happy enough to support Night Lights, an organization that provides qualified babysitters for their special needs children once a month so the parents can hit the town. Our Dairy Queen friends introduced us to Project Angel Heart, so our church kids can decorate food sacks to brighten deliveries to patients with life-threatening illnesses.

The following fall, I posted a Facebook selfie of me standing between two Sherpas who together summited Everest seven times. Steve had just performed a guitar concert for their nonprofit, Namlo International, which was rebuilding a school decimated by the Nepali earthquake. The two Sherpas had assisted Steve when he reached Everest base camp on November 8, 2016. My husband was astounded when, after no cell service for a week, he had three bars on his phone at base camp. Delighted, he called me as I was watching television that evening.

"Angel! I made it! I made it! I'm at base camp and am talking to you!" he said.

And he proceeded to share his expedition details.

Finally, he finished and took a big breath. "There! Now, what's new there, angel?"

"Well, I think Trump is going to be our new president."

Silence.

More silence.

"Hello?" I asked.

"What am I supposed to do with that information up here?"

OVER THE WINTER, Civil War broke out in our home as 800 Barbies, 250 plush storybook characters, and Steve battled for territory. My solutions? The Barbie collection is used for nonprofit fundraisers. Storybook characters pose in Metro Denver libraries to hype their summer reading programs. I still have to pay my library fines.

Steve's an eternal entrepreneur, so he started his own nonprofit, 10GreatestGifts.org, an organization that supports parents and grandparents in developing and nurturing joyful and healthy children and grandchildren with qualities and values like responsibility, self-reliance, and honesty. He's conducting research for his new book, *The 10 Greatest Gifts I Give My Grandchildren*. The fact that he doesn't have any grandchildren yet doesn't seem to stop him.

Sometimes, all this is overwhelming. One of Steve's greatest gifts to me in our marriage is that he teaches me to see the world in abundance, as opposed to seeing it in scarcity, an understandable view from being a single parent. I now accept and expect that the world opens her hands every morning with more goodness and gifts than I can handle. Family. Friends. Beauty. Laughter. Meaning. Hope.

There's lots to do in this world. We want our daughters to enjoy magic like this. Our wills stipulate that 10 percent of any income our daughters might receive be designated to a charity of their choice. It's irrevocable, since we don't want them to miss the fun.

Steve and I like making our marriage vows work for us, in addition to our working for them. With the addition of our eleventh vow, to open our relationship beyond ourselves and our family, our marriage started taking care of us—our love, our happiness—by magnifying it, fortifying the other ten vows.

The two of us could never have accomplished these things individually. Our eleventh vow is as permanent on our refrigerator as the Frigidaire label. Or Button's picture. *We will serve the world and add joy to it by harnessing who we are.*

31

An American Stumbles into an Irish Pub

OUR TEN-YEAR ANNIVERSARY STARTED DOWNHILL WHEN I broke my kneecap walking into an Irish pub. In Ireland.

I seemed to stumble forever, flailing my arms, wobbling my legs as if I had no brain at all, the Wizard of Oz scarecrow. Steve did an impressive rendition of my fall over that cobblestone curb in Ennis, a village in County Clare. He told me later, "I was thinking, why don't you just fall and be done with it?"

And if a trip to Ireland began as our anniversary gift to each other, we never would have dreamed that our parting gift from the island would be marriage counseling, wrapped up in a booby prize box back in the States.

Now, I acknowledge that most people never get to see Ireland. I was lucky to have been in the verdant country a solid eight hours before my stumble. We chose to celebrate the luck of the Irish because it took us a scant 117 collective years of living to accomplish ten years of matrimony.

Ironically, our marriage implosion had its roots intertwined in the hearts of the Irish, the best people on the planet. The Irish are good-hearted. Period. When they were wee bairns, their parents must have knocked them all out with sacks of potatoes, then awakened them with Mr. and Mrs. Potato Head in plain view, and by the power of suggestion whispered in their wee ears, "You were born on this island for two reasons only: smiles and kindness."

Steve collected me off the sidewalk and assumed the pose I can only describe as "leading a five-year-old on roller skates for the first time" and hobbled me into the packed pub. He and other patrons rushed off to search for a cane or crutches because, of course, I wouldn't accept that my kickboxing body could fail me.

Three Irish drinkers handed me their tablets to distract me with photos of their beautiful countryside. The musicians asked my favorite Irish song and played "Danny Boy." The waitress brought me a Guinness, and a grandmother with an auburn umbrella held my hand, overwhelming me, and I began to cry, so she wiped my tears because I balanced an ice pack on my puffy knee and a quart of Guinness on the other for pain. Two blokes, James West and Artemus Gordon, draped me over their shoulders and dragged me out of the saloon and pushed me into the rental car's backseat. My leg wouldn't bend.

On the upside, I enjoyed the Irish music for forty-five minutes and drank while Steve scoped out pharmacies, trying to understand new friends with strange accents.

The oddest, most comforting thing happened 4,327 miles from home. After stuffing me in the back of the car, one of the blokes headed back toward the pub. He stopped, as if he were tapped on his shoulder, hesitated, and looked at a paper in his hands. Turning back to me, he leaned inside the car window.

"And remember this," he began reading, his eyes squinting, "you know what happens when you get in a fight with a pig?"

Where did he come up with that?

I had heard that phrase only once in my life, forty years ago. I grinned.

"I do know," I replied, grimacing. "You both—"

"—get dirty," the bloke and I chorused.

Bewildered yet excited, I asked, "Where did you get that?"

"Your husband asked me for my name and address, so I grabbed this piece of paper to write it down in the pub. Something told me to read it to you." He handed the paper to Steve.

The Irish know how to care for people because, I swear, they're wired for heaven's miracles. "That's a saying my dad said to me once, back in the seventies," I explained. "He's looking out for me."

The Irishman only nodded in agreement; he seemed to expect providence here.

Back at the Hotel Woodstock, four employees wheeled me to our room in a rolling chair because wheelchairs must be against the law there, or disabilities were illegal, I'm not sure. The cook whipped up dinner at 10:30 and delivered a hot breakfast at 6:00 a.m., and the housekeeping staff provided fresh ice every two hours after midnight. Oh, and they provided clean trash cans. Because guess who couldn't bend down to sit on a toilet?

Irish hospitality continued the following morning at the 1940s hospital emergency room. Adjoining the waiting room and up a few stairs, a boxlike, quaint Catholic chapel stood ready for comfort, with three short wooden pews and a painting of the Virgin Mary and Jesus behind a marble altar. The Virgin Mary appeared everywhere in Ireland, a holy Big Brother, and she beckoned me for relief, for peace, because the waiting room's assorted folding chairs and discarded school plastic chairs afforded my knee little comfort. The altar looked like the perfect spot for me to recline. I felt so much pain that being a human sacrifice looked appealing. My problem was the stairs.

"I wanna go in there," I said to Steve.

"Kenna help you?" a local patient offered. "We kenna lift you over the steps." He grimaced, rising from his chair, holding his side.

"Oh, no, sir, you're in no shape to get me in there," I replied, studying him. "They think I broke my kneecap. Why are you here?"

"Three broken ribs, lass. But your man and I, we kenna still lift you to Jesus."

The entire country of Ireland stood up for me: My entire hospital visit cost $45—admissions, X-rays, doctor, cast, and crutches. I felt like a thief. Casted up, I laid low for a day, then chose joy, because it was easier than peeing in a trash can. Steve and I toured the Ring of Kerry. I hobbled two miles to the Muckross Abbey ruins, witnessed the elaborate ornamentation of the Book of Kells, laughed at the furtive glances of border collies herding sheep, and sang at the Temple Bar in Dublin.

But vacations are not reality, my friend.

Back home, Steve continued to encourage my independence he had witnessed in Ireland.

"Let me know what you need help with, angel," he said. And he went about his projects, his writing, his friends, his house repairs, his laundry.

I sat and wondered how I would get a fresh pair of underwear, three floors up. Or how to step inside a shower with no safety bars. Or retrieve an orange popsicle from the fridge while on crutches.

The problem was that I had proved that I was all woman in Ireland, and Steve was proud of it.

Steve grocery shopped and hauled all the sacks in from the car.

"I'm going to the bathroom," he said.

"The groceries need to be put away," I reminded him.

The 124 plants in the sunroom needed to be watered and fertilized, somehow still my job after all these years. And what about all the geraniums' spent blooms and fallen leaves? And that new hive of honeybees swarming inside the porch light? And Button's poop in the bathroom? And the recycling bins? What about dinner?

Who's Barb again?

The next morning, my normally peaceful husband huffed upstairs as I sat in bed watching *Star Trek* reruns, icing my knee.

Steve blew his nose. "I seriously think we need to consider downsizing. I just can't keep up with everything," my cantankerous husband complained.

After one day? Welcome to my life.

I grinned. Temporarily.

Two days later, I checked myself out of our house and into my mom's because Steve became so sick he couldn't take care of himself, let alone me.

I came home five days later, but returned to my mom's again for a week, because Steve had plantar fasciitis and wasn't a woman who could multitask happily.

Our relationship struggled. How did it happen so fast? I didn't know any other couple who made their vows more intentional than we did. We spent a year drafting them. I handcrafted them in calligraphy. We displayed them in prominent places in our lives—in our bathroom, on our fridge, in our wallets. We recited them to each other in the Sistine Chapel. We memorized them. We let the eleventh vow age to perfection. What were we missing?

I used the phone-a-friend option. "Diane," I said sadly, then rambled, "I'm worried! What's going to happen to Steve and me when we're old and both sick and I'm supposed to walk the dog and I can't water the greenhouse for him and he can't change mouse traps for me or help me unload groceries?"

"Barb, that's why women have children," she explained. "Insurance."

But my mature husband, who doesn't run to his guy friends, invoked Vow #9 again: On essential points, I will ask for special requests.

For the first time, he suggested marriage counseling for a tune-up.

"We want to get way ahead of this and not wait until there's damage that could start to hurt our love and the regard and the respect," he said. "Remember when we drove around Tasmania and explored the dream for our marriage, wrote our vows? One of the first things we agreed to was that we had burned the ships. No going back."

Later that day, I pulled out my old eHarmony profile from 2005, the year I put my relationship interest and intention out to the universe. I never met anyone on eHarmony though, I'm guessing because I didn't drink and because I became so impatient about not getting a match that I thought I'd beat the system and changed my sex from female to male and still came up empty-handed. But I did save the list of my must-haves in a man. I paged through my 2005 must-haves requirements for a husband and realized intention really did work in the world; Steve matched my hopes, spot-on:

I must have someone...

who shares my understanding of the world,
who can see the humorous side of life,
who shares my beliefs,
who is committed to marriage, home, and family,
who is willing to explore our sexual desires,
who is good at talking and listening,
who is financially responsible,
who is gentle and kind,
whose educational achievements match my own,
who will accept my child as his own.

We thought garnering marriage advice from all over the world would serve as adequate premarital counseling. We learned there's a difference between international advice and therapeutic solution.

A therapist soon sat across from us. "What brings you here, Steve and Barb?"

Steve, the planner, spoke up, looking straight ahead. "We refuse to have an average marriage," he began, "and right now, I feel like I'm walking on eggshells at home." He shifted on the couch and continued, "Our vows are very important to us. But right now—and I think Barb will agree—we aren't giving each other our best selves or seeing each other's sacredness."

There were no eggshell problems anymore because I was a certified hard-boiled egg.

The therapist shifted in her seat and looked at my left leg, encumbered in a heavy metal brace reminiscent of the Terminator. Then she looked me in the eye.

Women get it. She smiled, her eyes validating me.

"I am wearing dirty underwear," I began. "Definitely not my best self." I looked at Steve and grinned. He laughed.

"Sounds like Barb needs validation," the therapist said, wisely.

She exonerated me, but then took no prisoners. "And, Barb, your marriage and your husband require and *deserve* assertiveness from you," she continued. "Now, you said you brought your vows in. Let me see them."

Thankfully, our marriage tune-up required only a few sessions. By memorizing our vows, we knew when to call them up. And when one or two vows got pushed down by life, we were able to rely on the others. And they rallied. They had practiced. They knew what to do. The power of the words in our vows brought us back to the joy.

After our sessions, though, our therapist led us out through an inconspicuous door into the hallway, presumably because protecting the health of our lives, love, or marriage weren't valid enough reasons to hold our heads high in front of a waiting room full of like-minded people.

What's wrong with this world?

32

The Power of Words

I WAS AFRAID I'D BE TOLD I WASN'T WELCOME.

The year after I left Bear Creek, having taught there for twenty-two years, my former husband became its assistant principal. Like first-grade printing on the wall, serendipity pulled up a chair in front of me again, and said, "Barb, relax. In case you were wondering, this is the ideal time for you to retire."

I don't know who was more relieved, me or Katie's dad. Our district, Jefferson County Public Schools, had 86,000 students in 155 schools, delivering unimaginable odds that Katie's divorced parents would end up back together under the same roof. I had been loved on by my Bear Creek community for two decades. I decided Katie's dad deserved the same chance. So, for over seven years, I stayed away. I didn't substitute teach or volunteer in my friends' classrooms, despite their frequent, sometimes desperate, requests for help.

After avoiding my beloved school, unable to connect with a cherished space that occupied almost half my life, I finally came to peace that I had done enough honoring. I accepted my friend Diane's request to teach a writing lesson.

I carried my lesson materials inside an oversized brown sack to Bear Creek's front door and, for the first time, had to wait for another school employee to swipe her security badge so I could enter into the remodeled school office. No one looked familiar behind the counter. I drifted toward a woman whom I guessed was the enrollment secretary.

"I'm Barb, here to teach with Mrs. Belter this morning," I explained to her.

"Yes, she told me," she replied, looking up from the computer monitor. "Diane said you were coming. Sign in on the visitor sheet at the end of the counter."

I was now a visitor at a school that I helped transform from a 1950s school building into a $20 million campus.

"Ms. Lynn?" asked a woman behind the counter. Our eyes met and studied each other. "Ms. Lynn?" She rose slowly. "Is that really you?" It was Tracy, one of my former parents, now a school paraprofessional.

My old school instantly became my school again. People make a school, not the building.

She threw her arms around me. "How's Danielle?" I asked her, laughing, my nerves no longer an issue.

Tracy retrieved her phone and, like every parent should, flipped through her photos, pushed its screen in front of my face, eagerly sharing the significant faces in her life, knowing I was one who could magnify them. She gushed and babbled until I saw another former parent, also a paraprofessional, Grace, enter behind her.

I focused on my friends so much that I didn't waste any time scoping the office for anyone else in particular. It was girlfriend time.

Tracy escorted me down my old hallway, crisp bulletin

boards with familiar first-grade peculiarities, stickers, large print, clean margins. I entered Diane's room, hauling my bag of materials. Her students were seated on the floor, ready for my lesson.

Once a teacher, always a teacher.

Inside the first-grade classroom, my seven-year absence disappeared, and I picked up exactly where I left off. Frozen in time were picture books, a hundred number chart, alphabet cards, and rainbows of colorful walls. Another paraprofessional friend of twenty years, Laird, waved at me from the reading table. If teachers are the heartbeat of a school, their paraprofessionals are the school's lifeblood inside.

"Boys and girls, this is Ms. Lynn," announced their teacher, Mrs. Diane Belter, standing up and offering her teacher's chair to me. She winked. "Welcome home."

"Hi, everybody!" I said cheerfully, wading through the aisle. Curious, quiet children peered at me, bobbing their heads above and around desks to see the new kid in town. "I can't wait to meet all of you!"

One boy, who I noticed was already standing—and probably would be for the duration of my lesson—pointed at my bag, squealing, "Did you bring Olive Garden for us to eat?"

Maybe that boy couldn't sit still, and my guess, he probably couldn't read much yet, but he obviously had practiced eating out.

I sat in the teacher's chair. Seven-year-old vibes hit me like waves. I could sense their power again, children's innocent strength, wrapped inside that first-grade magic. I was back in my element, ready to learn from children.

Leaning toward them, I held eye contact with certain groups, first with the squirmy children to calm them, then the reserved children to connect with them, and finally the unpredictable group seated in the back, to remind them who was boss. "I do believe I am the luckiest woman in the world today. I get to be with all of you."

They liked that.

All teachers begin a lesson with an anticipatory set. "Today, we're going to explore the power of words. The most important word for me right now is your name. When I wink at you, please tell me your first name." A garden of children's names blossomed.

"Charlotte."

"Noah."

"Madison."

A boy pointed at himself. "Who, me? Are you winking at me? I'm Daniel."

I stopped winking and lowered my head toward a boy, hiding under a desk. "And who are you?" No answer. There was always one little guy like that. I smiled. "I'm glad you're here too."

I stood up, commanding attention. "All your names are powerful words. To your parents, your names are the most powerful words in their lives. Raise your hand if you think you know where words come from."

One student raised his hand. "The library."

Then, another girl near my teacher's chair said, "Paper."

"Books," answered a girl with baby blue glasses, like Catwoman's.

In the back, a boy, confident he had reached nirvana, waved his hand. "Heaven!"

I brought him back to earth with a nod, then returned to the girl near my chair. "How do the words land on the paper?"

The classmate next to her spoke up. "From inside your head."

I encouraged more backward reasoning. "Where do the words come from inside your head?"

A long pause followed. The risk takers raised their hands, halfway.

"Letters."

"Your mouth."

I had reached their cognitive limit. Sometimes, teachers need to fill in the gaps. "Thoughts," I said. "Inside your heads are thoughts, invisible ideas. Words are thoughts that have come alive and live outside of us," I said. "How many of you have thoughts?" Those children who were using their ears raised their hands. "Are your thoughts important?"

"Yeah—"

"Can I show you some of my thoughts out loud, through my words, my poetry?"

"Yes!"

Children are addicted to rhyme.

"All right! But before I start, I have a question. Does anybody know how many words there are in the English language?"

I saw twenty-four blank faces, twenty-four fawns in the headlights.

"Let me give you an idea," I said, quickly. I held up seventeen towers, each with ten interlinking cubes, juggling them in my palms. "These stand for all the words in our language. A hundred seventy thousand! I can't even hold them all, there are so many. I'd like to show you how many of these words adults use."

"I bet there's a lot!" shouted one student.

I threw twelve towers of cubes back into a box and held up only five towers in one hand. "Of all the words out there, this is how many adults use: fifty thousand." The children's faces dropped, their eyes shifting between my hand and the box. We adults had just lost our superhero standing.

"Now, do you want to see how many words seven-year-olds use?"

"Sure! Yeah!" Children love to try and beat adults. I removed three towers of ten from my hand and threw them back into the box. The children stared at the two towers I held.

Silence.

Humbleness provides the perfect starting line.

I leaned into the class, closer to their eye level, and held up the disorganized box of towers. "How many of you would like to learn the secret of knowing all these words?"

Hands shot up, grins returned. Placing the box on a desk, I said, "Let's start by turning your ears up. Do this. Cup your hands behind your ears and pull them forward." The students imitated me. "Now, let's test your hearing. Repeat after me," I instructed. "I ..."

"I..." the children said in unison.

"State your name," I continued.

"State your name," the children repeated.

"No, say your own names, you knuckleheads."

Giggles spread, followed by a cacophony of names and the excitement that their hearing had drastically improved, upping the likelihood for the lesson's mastery. "Listen!" I said. "Listen for words inside my poems that dance in the air," I said, "words that tickle your brain, sparkling words that make you laugh. Listen for powerful words."

I performed my poems about things I wondered about, like why the Big Dipper's ladle is always empty, why teachers don't have first names, what principals do at night while teachers grade and students do homework. Afterward, I asked the class to name the powerful words they heard. Their choices sprouted like a fireworks fountain.

"*Starry Spoony Highness!*" said one.

"*Meteor!*" said one.

"*Complicated!*" said another.

"*Snitchin!*" said the boy under the desk.

"Why, then," I continued, "do first graders use weakling words, like *nice?*"

"And *cool,*" Mrs. Belter said, flatly.

Holding up the box of cubes again, I said, "Why do you use *nice* and *cool* in your writing when all these other words are free and waiting to be used? They won't come to you. Help me understand. Tell me why you don't use words like these."

The girl with the Catwoman glasses raised her hand. "Because I don't know how to spell them."

She was *afraid*, just like I felt when I walked into my old school after seven years. I could relate.

"Sweetheart," I said, "what would happen if scientists were afraid to make mistakes in their experiments?"

She thought for a moment. "Um, there wouldn't be science?"

This student had some brain power. The world needs more of that. I pressed her.

"So what happens when people are afraid to take chances with words?"

The girl pointed at the leftover cubes tossed recklessly in the box. "That's what happens. What a waste."

I instructed the students to buddy up and go on a treasure hunt for powerful words in their books, then send me a post-card with their top three choices. A week later, I received their responses and sat down to read them.

33

The Power of My Words

....

IN WOBBLY LETTERS, I READ: *COLLISION. KINDNESS. GRANDMA. Broncos. Lizard. Polite. Explore. Water. Dad. Friend. Earth.*

Three words showed up repeatedly on several postcards: *Love. Family. Balls.*

I went to teach students why words are important and left with a renewed understanding of the role that words have played in my life. When people used to ask me why I loved teaching first grade, I thought of its magic but knew not where it came from. Children arrived as innocent as fairy dust and left as tiny beacons of knowledge, and while I lived every day inside their world, I could never explain what happened. Until now.

The magic is in the words. And a first-grade classroom is the place where words are born, and reborn, year after year, cradles of letters and sounds. Here, words linger longer in the air than in any other space on earth, inviting us to capture them, revel in them, then walk away with them into the world, hand in hand. Words, like children, wait to be noticed, then known, then ennobled. Words are the scaffolding upon which we build our lives.

Words have pursued me, and I have pursued them, all my life. From listening to my mother's voice to touching print inside the folds of books to singing along with a car radio, words followed me, to the altar where promises were made, in whispers next to my dying father, inside prayers over my slumbering child.

And finally, the words captured me and became my playground. They breathe life into my choices, unlock stories, people. Words tie my world together, their ribbons guiding me toward the important expressions of my life: the alphabet in my classroom, my vows with my husband, also a writer, the lyrics inside my voice. They have allowed me to understand the world, then travel and explore it. My words became a treasure box, a place to gather beautiful things: people to love, dogs, Barbies, European snapshots, more words.

We would be wise to accumulate things for the sole purpose of sharing their joys with others.

I owe my life and those I love to the power of the word. Words tie our lives together, ribboned as the greatest gifts we give each other, entwining us, the threads by which we accomplish loving. When you knit your words together and throw your heart into it, it's called a promise. When you knit someone else's words inside your own tapestry, it's a vow.

One fall morning, before sunrise in Northern Ontario, Steve and I had bundled up and canoed down a narrow river teeming with thick, willowy grasses. As the sun began tickling the river's edge, hundreds of exquisite spider webs emerged among the reeds, capturing slivers of thin rays, shimmering the pearls of dewdrops like a crystal road as we paddled by. Slowly, the sun's warmth melted the dangling pearls until daylight erased the webs from our sight. Such is the essence of vows. Delicately created. Easily torn, with strands intended for repair. Beauty revealed in the goodness of light, yet even in darkness, they remain.

Since neither Steve nor I had a camera, we returned the following morning, hopeful. The vision was gone. But the certainty of its presence remained. Some things can only be captured in words.

Words matter, because they cling to us, and we matter. Even words cannot contain their own power. They spill over and seep into every dimension of our days, coating them with despair and confusion, yes, but also with humor, laughter, love. Love is life in search of words, and words are wings that lift us, break us, join us, melt us, like rain.

34

Locked in the Library

MY FINGER TRACED THOSE LAST FEW LINES I WROTE: "LOVE is life in search of words, and words are wings that lift us, break us, join us, melt us, like rain." I exhaled ten years of married life, then closed my book's cover. And I pressed my hand atop it, preserving the memories inside.

Button's bold brown eyes fixated upon me, and for a moment I saw Honey's eyes inside them too. "Mommy loves Button," I promised, so she lowered her head back upon my lap.

Together we sat in a child-sized recliner in the library, our children's library, embraced by walnut bookshelves on three sides, with 4,000 handpicked picture books as company.

The Tiffany lamps' golden light cast warm shadows across the book spines, and a delicate Victorian lamp's glow highlighted rosettes lining the shelves. A vintage auburn globe leaned into an early twentieth-century mantle clock, ticking against Roman numerals.

More of my favorite things surrounded me: Katie's photo of Austria's National Library, Hermione's wand, hundreds of my favorite classroom books, among them, *All the Places to*

Love and *Leo the Late Bloomer* and *Dog Heaven*. The secret passageway, the child's entrance, discreetly opened into the library's corner. There is no Dewey decimal system to sort these books, instead, only delineations deemed necessary within the constructs of my heart: vintage collectibles, Christian titles, Little Golden Books, bedtime stories, author series, Disney favorites, nonfiction, poetry, pop-ups, board books, holiday, science, history, foreign language, ABCs, Caldecott winners, and, finally, the shelf that holds titles I call my North Star Collection, children's books that shaped my past and influence my future, the books that set me free.

I rise and pull one of them out, then settle back into my velvet recliner, where Button obliges me.

In my lap is *The Three Questions*, a Tolstoy short story retold by Caldecott winner Jon J. Muth. With familiarity, I thumb through the book until I spot a red kite over a cloudy blue sky, with the three questions floating across the page:

Tolstoy's first question is *When is the best time to do each thing?* The answer is now.

The second question is *Who are the most important people to work with?* The answer is the ones you're with.

That's you, my dear readers.

The third question is *What is the most important thing to do at all times?* The answer is do good for those people.

So I penned this book, seven years in the making, and wrapped up—in words—the very best goodness I could offer you from my life. You trusted and invested your time with me, so I've shared with you all the goodness I could find.

I HEAR STEVE'S muffled voice upstairs. "Angel, in five minutes, I'll be working on the secret room if you want to join me. Angel, where are you?" I place *The Three Questions* on the end table next to my chair. After two years of marriage, Steve finally revealed the secret room adjacent to his library, and now he's turning it into a grandchildren's library—mind you, we have no semblance of any such child. To enter, the child will unlock a latch inside a musty dictionary nailed to the wall. Inside, the grandchildren's library will offer shelves to be filled, along with family heirlooms, weathered like tattered books. An old hundred number chart. Photos of grandparents. Steve's red fire truck. Argentina Barbie from eBay (I couldn't resist her look).

I have five minutes before my library could close, just like my Sioux Falls library did as a child. I look around for a place to hide, praying Steve will give up and overlook me. I eye the secret passageway and my library's crystal doorknob, its brass skeleton key in the keyhole. I turn the key, locking me inside my library, setting me free to explore my universe of books.

But this time, with Button at my feet, I reach only for one large book and tuck it under my arm as I wedge myself inside the secret passageway crowned in Italian cerulean frescoes, inside the ethereal tunnel draped in golden linens and arrayed with cherubs. I am content, for within this one book I have discovered a universe far grander than the one I imagined as a child. I finger the book's title: *The Knot Ultimate Wedding Planner and Organizer*. I wonder: Am I a good mom? I open the cover and try.

Katie got engaged a week ago.

above: Helen "Ma" and John "Warren" Vannoy at the Vannoy farm, Waverly, Nebraska, circa 1980s, inscribed with Papa's note, "Harness the power of we."
below left: Honey running free in the Vermont mountains, September 2011.
below right: Button Vannoy, before she was baptized on April Fools' Day 2017.

above: Steve in Nepal on his way to Everest base camp, November 2016. Since none of his Sherpas spoke English, he could only visit with the yaks to process the 2016 presidential election results. *below:* Our children's library, where the power of words begins, 2019. Photo courtesy of Lynne Farris.

Our 11 Vows

I will give my best self to you.

I WILL GIVE my physical, emotional, mental, spiritual, and social best to you every day. I will stop before rejoining you and ask God to help me in giving you my best. I will give my joyful, loving best to you...my A game! I will continue to develop my unique healthy, growing alive self, and recreate who I am so I can be my best self. I will take responsibility for creating a home, a sanctuary, where it's impossible to not be on a roll. We will create a home and a life where we can cry for joy. We are raising the bar for life!

I will see and trust your sacred goodness.

I KNOW WHO you are. I know your integrity, values, and goodness. I know how much you want to serve me. I will see your sacredness and godliness. I will respect, honor, believe, and protect you. I will always assume the best about you.

I will forgive myself and you to protect and nurture us back to wholeness.

I WILL ACCEPT all sides of me, forgive myself for real and perceived mistakes, take responsibility for my thoughts and actions. I will choose healthy behaviors and use each opportunity to heal, get stronger, and serve you even better. I will love you even more for your quirks and humanity, accept and love exactly who you are and fully forgive you as I have been forgiven.

I will put you and us first.

NO MATTER WHAT happens, I will fight for us. We have burned the ships! I take 100 percent responsibility for myself and our relationship. I will live with courage and transparency and do whatever it takes to tear down any and all walls and replace them with strong bridges. We will always create a safe place to share our full, authentic selves. I will love you fearlessly and endlessly. I will consciously choose to love you even more during our tough moments.

> *I will use our union to serve
> and build our family.*

THE QUALITY OF our love dictates the quality of our family. We love each other, knowing it secures the future of those who count on us. We will sacrifice and defend whatever it takes to strengthen unbreakable family ties.

> *I will renew our love daily.*

I WILL HELP you fall in love with me again, and I will fall in love with you every day. I will do everything I can to fill your love tank and build your security and real love. I will consciously focus on the endless things I love about you and give thanks to you. I will wake up every morning and consciously stop, build our love, and refill our beautiful, empty box.

I will step into our moments with gratitude.

IN THIS SACRED moment, I will treasure every sigh, kiss, touch, thought, and feeling we share. I will greet you with awe, gratitude, and excitement as we come together. I will forever be grateful for the angel in the room next to me. I will be intensely grateful for all the blessings in my life. I will step into this pure moment, rest in your arms, and treasure our simple, peaceful adventure.

I will welcome God as our partner through daily prayer.

ON A DAILY basis, we will join hands and pray, giving thanks for God's love, our love, and our endless blessings. We will consciously turn to Him, build our family and relationships with God. We will faithfully expect His perfect answers.

*I will ask you for special requests
on essential points.*

WITH EVERYTHING ELSE, I will love exactly who you are and
accept you with grace, mirroring Christ.

*I will celebrate and support
your unique unfolding.*

I WILL HONOR who you are and do everything I can to help
you discover and develop even more of your spirit, joyfulness,
goodness, dreams, and greatness. I will take great interest in
your passions, friends, growth, and the significance of your life.

*We will serve the world and add joy
to it by harnessing who we are.*

IT IS OUR mission to serve our marriage, thereby adding value,
hope, and joy to the world.

11 Vows for Our Daughters

- take care of ourselves
- make our marriage and family our priority
- pray for you
- be your champions
- accept who you are, fight for you
- encourage your unique expression
- provide and celebrate opportunity for family
- honor the bond you have with your mom and dad
- make family decisions with you in mind
- model a loving, mature, supportive, forgiving relationship
- be your sanctuary—a soft and safe place to land for the rest of your lives

Acknowledgments

A QUIET, KNOWING SMILE PRECEDES GENUINE THANK yous. I've been quietly smiling for months, knowing I am privileged to acknowledge so many.

To my husband, Steve: You say I make up heaven as I go along; I say I see more of it every day by living with you. Thank you for your constancy, your protection, your example of uncovering goodness inside me, inside everyone, each day, everywhere.

To Helen Vannoy, Ma: I promised you I'd finish your memoir. Here it is.

To Katie: Thank you for believing in me all my life. You shall always be my best creation. Life. Soul. Dreams. If I can do this, you can do anything. Follow your joy, pursue it, share it.

To Ali and Emmy: You graciously allow yet another book to be written about you. I love my bonus daughters!

For my family, Mom, Dad, Mike, Steve, Barb, Jillene: For always being there for Katie and me, no matter what—more words need to be invented to express how much I love, love you. As Dad wrote, "We stand tall, look life right in the eye, and be there for one another."

To my editor, Sandra Wendel: Here's to the Nebraska truck stop where this all began. Your precision, wisdom, and patient eye appear on every page. All editors have ways with words. Only you have ways with thoughts in search of words.

To Domini Dragoone, for giving my book its shape, breath and design. You built a beautiful home for my words.

To Elizabeth Sheridan, for precision in proofreading and clarity.

To my teaching friends, my collateral treasures while educating little people: Diane Belter, Dixie Whittaker, Stacy Stutzman, Marilyn Leimbach, Terry Groeneman, Fran Hoffman, Arlene Thompson, Molly Doll, Karen Wagner, Liz Costello, Victoria Kaye, Renee Otero, Patti McHugh, Debby Johnson, Sue Wendling, and Todd Johnson.

To my paraprofessional friends, who take children's hearts home with them: Tracy Ramer, Grace McCullough, Laird Bohn, Linda Fox, Kathy Miller, and Camille Wood.

To every single student of mine who charmed my life with your magic: Remember who you are. I do.

To my Atonement Lutheran Church kids: You made me believe in your spirit. I pursued a teaching career to be around people like you. I love you.

To my beta readers whose honesty and encouragement made me pull up my bootstraps and try harder: Kathy Torres, Laura Deardoff, Carolyn Lee, Lori Vidlak, Kori Reed, Cathy Beck, Vicki DeCoster, Linda Wright, Annette Langan, Lisa Quaites, and Joette Deitering

To my critique group, who treated my words as their own: Sharon Messinger, Deb Ossi, Jason Gruhl.

To my Lighthouse Writers writing group, whose handwriting in the margins of my first twenty-five pages lit my passion for this project: Andrea Enright, Dana Alshouse, Josie Bouchier, Mary Hanewall, Julie Nolan, Martha Johns, and especially my instructors, John Cotter and Denise Vega, for making my voice feel important and for bringing food to class.

To Pastor Del: It's all about grace. Yep, I listened during confirmation. I love you like a father, Gidge.

To the Pathways to Leadership employees and their clients around the world who believed in my husband's mission to serve children and families through their parents' wellness: Thank you for the hours and years of work on his behalf. I know I could not have experienced all these amazing stories without your hard work. Yoh, friends, baby! Your work paved the way for goodness to shine, worldwide.

For Steve LuKanic: When I was eighteen, you told me my writing was my strongest gift. I never forgot your encouraging words.

For Gail Gerlisits: My eternal thanks for your wisdom in seeing the same spark inside Steve and me.

For Barbara Dalberg: You turned my mourning into dancing. I wish you were here.

For Honey and Button: My heartbeats at my feet, sitting next to me and my computer for years, waiting, waiting.

Above all, for God, His glory: I thought about You on every page and I hope it shows. I followed Your calling and You never left me. This one's for You.

About the Author

BARB VANNOY IS AN AWARD-WINNING EDUCATOR OF twenty-three years, nominated for Colorado Teacher Award, Disney American Teacher Award, and the recipient of "Who's Who Among American Teachers" and Colorado KCNC "Teacher Who Makes a Difference."

She paid her way through college by writing inspirational verse for Blue Mountain Arts and by singing and playing keyboard in a band and summer stock theater. She's a former worship leader and longtime single parent of Katie before meeting her two bonus daughters, Emmy and Ali, and husband, Steve, entrepreneur, corporate coach, and a *New York Times* best-selling author on parenting. She and Steve perform on cruise ships with their band, Postcard Note. Their music video, "Three Hearts Dancing," is available on YouTube.

Barb's passions include European travel, dog rescue, avoiding library fines, and piling books on her nightstand. She lives in Morrison, Colorado, with Steve, their Morkie named Button, and 842 Barbie dolls. Visit her website at BarbVannoy.com.

Made in the USA
Monee, IL
19 January 2021